A Social History of Swimming in England, 1800–1918

Covering a time of great social and technological change, this history traces the development of the four classic aquatic disciplines of competitive swimming, diving, synchronized swimming and water polo, with its main focus on racing. Working from the beginnings of municipal recreational swimming, the book fully explores the links between swimming and other aspects of English life and society including class, education, gender, municipal governance, sexuality and the Victorian invention of the amateur–professional divide in the sporting world.

Uniquely focused on swimming—relatively neglected in the history of sport—this is the first study of its kind and will be an important landmark in the establishment of swimming history as a topic of scholarly investigation.

This book was previously published as a special issue of *The International Journal of the History of Sport*.

Christopher Love is an independent Scholar.

Sport in the Global Society

General Editors: J.A. Mangan and Boria Majumdar

A Social History of Swimming in England, 1800–1918
Splashing in the Serpentine

Sport in the Global Society
General Editors: J.A. Mangan and Boria Majumdar

The interest in sports studies around the world is growing and will continue to do so. This unique series combines aspects of the expanding study of *Sport in the Global Society*, providing comprehensiveness and comparison under one editorial umbrella. It is particularly timely, with studies in the aesthetic elements of sport proliferating in institutions of higher education.

Eric Hobsbawm once called sport one of the most significant practices of the late nineteenth century. Its significance was even more marked in the late twentieth century and will continue to grow in importance into the new millennium as the world develops into a 'global village' sharing the English language, technology and sport.

Other Titles in the Series

Disreputable Pleasures
Less Virtuous Victorians at Play
Edited by Mike Huggins and J.A. Mangan

Flat Racing and British Society, 1790–1914
A Social and Economic History
Mike Huggins

The Global Politics of Sport
The Role of Global Institutions in Sport
Edited by Lincoln Allison

British Football & Social Exclusion
Stephen Wagg

Muscular Christianity and the Colonial and Post-Colonial World
Edited by John J. MacAloon

The Games Ethic and Imperialism
Aspects of the Diffusion of an Ideal
J.A. Mangan

Doping in Sport
Global Ethical Issues
Edited by Angela Schneider and Fan Hong

Scoring for Britain
International Football and International Politics, 1900–1939
Peter J. Beck

Lost Histories of Indian Cricket
Battles Off the Pitch
Boria Majumdar

Amateurism in Sport
An Analysis and Defence
Lincoln Alison

The Magic of Indian Cricket, Revised Edition
Cricket and Society in India
Mihir Bose

Rain Stops Play
Cricketing Climates
Andrew Hignell

The Cultural Bond
Sport, Empire, Society
Edited by J.A. Mangan

A Sport-Loving Society
Victorian and Edwardian Middle Class England at Play
Edited by J.A. Mangan

The Evolution of English Sport
Neil Wigglesworth

Barbarians, Gentlemen and Players
A Sociological Study of the Development of Rugby Football
Kenneth Sheard and Eric Dunning

Cricket and England
A Cultural and Social History of Cricket in England between the Wars
Jack Williams

Athleticism in the Victorian and Edwardian Public School
The Emergence and Consolidation of an Educational Ideology
J.A. Mangan

Pleasure, Profit, Proselytism
British Culture and Sport at Home and Abroad 1700–1914
Edited by J.A. Mangan

This Great Symbol
Pierre de Coubertin and the Origins of the Modern Olympic Games
John J. MacAloon

Leisure and Recreation in a Victorian Mining Community
The Social Economy of Leisure in North-East England, 1820–1914
Alan Metcalfe

A Social History of Swimming in England, 1800–1918

Splashing in the Serpentine

Christopher Love

LONDON AND NEW YORK

First published 2008 by Routledge
2 Park Square, Milton Park, Abingdon, Oxfordshire OX14 4RN

Simultaneously published in the USA and Canada
by Routledge
711 Third Avenue, New York, NY 10017

Routledge is an imprint of the Taylor & Francis Group, an informa business

© 2008 Christopher Love

Typeset in Minion by KnowledgeWorks Global Limited, Southampton, Hampshire, UK

All rights reserved. No part of this book may be reprinted or reproduced or utilised in any form or by any electronic, mechanical, or other means, now known or hereafter invented, including photocopying and recording, or in any information storage or retrieval system, without permission in writing from the publishers.

British Library Cataloguing in Publication Data
A catalogue record for this book is available from the British Library

Library of Congress Cataloging in Publication Data
A catalog record has been requested

ISBN 978-0-415-39076-7 (hbk)
ISBN 978-1-138-88040-5 (pbk)

Contents

	Series Editors' Foreword	ix
	Introduction	xi
1	An Overview of the Development of Swimming in England, c.1750–1918	1
2	Swimming and Gender in the Victorian World	19
3	Social Class and the Swimming World: Amateurs and Professionals	36
4	Local Aquatic Empires: The Municipal Provision of Swimming Pools in England, 1828–1918	53
5	Holborn, Lambeth and Manchester: Three Case Studies in Municipal Swimming Pool Provision	63
6	Swimming at the Clarendon Schools	76
7	State Schools, Swimming and Physical Training	87
8	'Whomsoever You See in Distress': Swimming, Saving Life and the Rise of the Royal Life Saving Society	100
9	Swimming, Service to the Empire and Baden-Powell's Youth Movements	115
10	Taking a Refreshing Dip: Health, Cleanliness and the Empire	126
11	A Chronology of English Swimming, 1747–1918	140
	Index	147

Series Editors' Foreword

SPORT IN THE GLOBAL SOCIETY was launched in the late nineties. It now has over one hundred volumes. Until recently an odd myopia characterised academia with regard to sport. The global *groves of academe* remained essentially Cartesian in inclination. They favoured a mind/body dichotomy: thus the study of ideas was acceptable; the study of sport was not. All that has now changed. Sport is now incorporated, intelligently, within debate about *inter alia* ideologies, power, stratification, mobility and inequality. The reason is simple. In the modern world sport is everywhere: it is as ubiquitous as war. E.J. Hobsbawm, the Marxist historian, once called it the one of the most significant of the new manifestations of late nineteenth century Europe. Today it is one of the most significant manifestations of the twenty-first century world. Such is its power, politically, culturally, economically, spiritually and aesthetically, that sport beckons the academic more persuasively than ever to borrow, and refocus, an expression of the radical historian Peter Gay 'to explore its familiar terrain and to wrest new interpretations from its inexhaustible materials'. As a subject for inquiry, it is replete, as he remarked of history, with profound 'questions unanswered and for that matter questions unasked'.

Sport seduces the teeming 'global village'; it is the new opiate of the masses; it is one of the great modern experiences; its attraction astonishes only the recluse; its appeal spans the globe. Without exaggeration, sport is a mirror in which nations, communities, men and women now see themselves. That reflection is sometimes bright, sometimes dark, sometimes distorted, sometimes magnified. This metaphorical mirror is a source of mass exhilaration and depression, security and insecurity, pride and humiliation, bonding and alienation. Sport, for many, has replaced religion as a source of emotional catharsis and spiritual passion, and for many, since it is among the earliest of memorable childhood experiences, it infiltrates memory, shapes enthusiasms, serves fantasies. To co-opt Gay again: it blends memory and desire.

Sport, in addition, can be a lens through which to scrutinise major themes in the political and social sciences: democracy and despotism and the great associated movements of socialism, fascism, communism and capitalism as well as political cohesion and confrontation, social reform and social stability.

The story of modern sport is the story of the modern world—in microcosm; a modern global tapestry permanently being woven. Furthermore, nationalist and imperialist, philosopher and politician, radical and conservative have all sought in sport a manifestation of national identity, status and superiority.

Finally, for countless millions sport is the personal pursuit of ambition, assertion, well-being and enjoyment.

For all the above reasons, sport demands the attention of the academic. *Sport in the Global Society* is a response.

J.A. Mangan
Boria Majumdar

Series Editors
Sport in the Global Society

Introduction

Swimming is a ubiquitous activity in England today. Thousands of people go swimming daily in the numerous municipal and private facilities across the country. Many people think nothing of going down to the local swimming pool or water park for enjoyment. Gone are the days when only a small segment of the population would willingly venture near the water, and an even smaller segment of the population could actually swim. For such a ubiquitous activity, however, swimming has been poorly served when it comes to academic research on its history.

This monograph has been prepared to help rectify the previous lack of attention swimming has received by exploring the development of swimming as a sport and recreational activity in England between 1800 and 1918. It also seeks to explain the deeper social origins of the emergence of swimming in England, in addition to seeking an explanation of the consequences of the new leisure form on English society at large. Finally, the collection is intended to contribute to (and refine) the broader historiographical debate about the emergence of popular leisure in these years. To retain focus and coherence the studies in this collection all focus on activities that are related to swimming, as opposed to other aquatic activities such as rowing and sailing. This involves coverage of the competitive and recreational forms of swimming, diving, synchronized swimming, water polo and aquatic lifesaving, along with their closely related sub-fields. [1]

Despite the massive expansion of the study of sport and leisure in England since the 1970s, very little has been written about swimming. Attention has focused notably on sports such as cricket, football, horse racing, and rugby, which have large popular followings. These are, primarily, team games, which are seen as inherently more *social*, because of the complex bonding rituals that take place between players and spectators. Swimming has, however (and despite its popularity), been largely ignored. Tony Mason in the introduction to *Sport in Britain: A Social History*, published in 1989, reported that

> As late as 1960 the National Council for School Sports was only concerned with athletics, cricket, football, rugby and swimming and all are covered in this book save the latter. Swimming's absence is unfortunate. We would have liked to have found a place for it, in part because in excess of 6 per cent of the population were swimming by 1980 – more if you include the under-sixteens – and also because of its long-standing role in many communities as a competitive sport from the third quarter of the nineteenth century. Unfortunately not enough work has been done on the subject. [2]

Eleven years later, when Mason and Richard Holt collaborated to produce *Sport in Britain 1945–2000*, they could still find very little on the history of swimming, which consequently received scant mention in the text (and no specialist works on the topic were listed in the bibliography). [3]

And yet, as Mason has indicated, swimming was, and remains, an important recreation and competitive activity in England. Nicholas Orme – one of the few historians of swimming – has written: 'Social history throws light upon swimming, and in turn the history of swimming, once constructed, illuminates the societies which have practised it.' [4] Unlike other physical activities such as cricket, gymnastics and football, which were appropriated by different social classes to reinforce class identity or status, swimming was never indulged in simply by one class or social group. Swimming was enjoyed by diverse elements of society and came to reflect English society *at large*, with all of the cultural prejudices, preconceptions, contradictions and ideals of that culture. At one level, swimming was a part of the great recreational explosion of the 1870s and 1880s. But the progression of swimming also reflected changes in English society at large, notably gender relations and class relations, and did so down to the present.

Of course, modern swimming did not develop in isolation in England alone. Throughout the eighteenth century, in both Europe and North America, swimming began to develop as a leisure activity. It is not the purpose of this collection to recount the history of swimming in Europe and North America, but it is important to remember that indigenous swimming traditions emerged there independently. As with English swimming, however, very little has been written about the history of swimming in other countries.

The aim of this collection is quite straightforward; to explore the history of swimming in England between 1800 and 1918. But it also seeks to explore how swimming reflected different aspects of English culture during this period. The collection is organized along thematic lines, with a total of ten studies, prefaced by this introduction. At the conclusion of the collection a short chronology of English swimming between 1747 and 1918 has been provided for the reader's reference.

The first study, '"An Overview of the Development of Swimming in England, c.1750–1918", presents a historical overview of the development of swimming in England between roughly 1750 and 1918. It serves as a reference frame for the rest of the collection while also providing an overview of some of the main issues to be examined in the remaining studies. The second study, 'Swimming and Gender in the Victorian World', examines gender issues in the swimming world, in terms of how gender affected swimming practices, and how both men and women set about swimming along gendered lines during the period under review. This is followed by 'Social Class and the Swimming World: Amateurs and Professionals', which examines the role played by class and by the related issue of the amateur/professional debate in swimming.

'Local Aquatic Empires: The Municipal Provision of Swimming Pools in England, 1828–1918' studies how municipal bodies eventually came to provide almost all the swimming facilities in England by 1918, and how they promoted swimming in general. This is followed by a series of case studies highlighting three specific municipal areas in 'Holborn, Lambeth and Manchester: Three Case Studies in Municipal Swimming Pool Provision'. The role played by the great public schools surveyed by the Clarendon Commission in the promotion of swimming are examined in the sixth study, 'Swimming at the Clarendon Schools'. Paired with the previous study is 'State Schools, Swimming and Physical Training', which looks at the very enthusiastic attachment to swimming in state schools and the important role state schools played in promoting the activity. The eighth and ninth studies both survey the connection between the swimming world and Victorian humanitarianism. '"Whomsoever You See in Distress": Swimming, Saving Life and the Rise of the Royal Life Saving Society' focuses on the creation and expansion of the Royal Life Saving Society, the first organization to explicitly link swimming skills and humanitarian values into one method of saving life in response to the terrible toll of drownings in late Victorian England. The ninth study, 'Swimming, Service to the Empire and Baden-Powell's Youth Movements' looks at the humanitarian service component of the Scouting and Guiding movements. While different from the methods employed by the Royal Life Saving Society, Baden-Powell's movements helped spread many of the same messages as the Royal Life Saving Society. Finally, the tenth survey, 'Health, Cleanliness and Empire', looks at the inherent connection between swimming and concepts of health and cleanliness, especially at the end of the nineteenth century at the time of the great expansion of the British Empire.

The research for the present work began seven years ago and has since gone through several revisions. I certainly hope that this collection lays the foundations for further research on a neglected but important topic; the history of swimming in Victorian and Edwardian England. Although the collection is my own work, it could not have been completed without the assistance of others. I can in no way adequately thank all of those who aided me in my research, so a simple listing will have to suffice. I extend a sincere thanks and acknowledgement to everyone who has provided me with various help and assistance. Specific thanks go out to the staff of the British Library, at the St Pancras Reading Rooms, especially the Rare Books and Manuscript Room, the Colindale Newspaper Library and the Document Supply Centre at Boston Spa; the staff of the Public Record Office; the staff of the Wellcome Library; the staff of the Camden Local Studies Library; the staff of the Lambeth Archives; the staff of the City of Westminster Archives; the staff of the West Yorkshire Archives Service repository at Sheepscar, Leeds; the staff of the York City Archives; the staff of the Manchester Central Library Local Studies and Archives Service, especially Katharine Taylor and Debbie Cannon; Emma Langham at the Amateur Swimming Association; Brenda Sullivan, secretary of the London Schools Swimming Association; Lt. Col. (retd) A.A. Forbes, curator of the Army Physical Training Corps Museum; Mrs Pat Styles of the Scout Association archives; Mrs Margaret Courtney, archivist of the

Guide Association; Ms Diana Coke, archivist historian for the Royal Humane Society; the staff of the Museum and Library of the Order of St. John, especially Ms Caroline Mulryne; Mr N Bramwell, honorary general secretary of the English Schools Swimming Association; Mr John Long, Commonwealth secretary-general of the Royal Life Saving Society; the staff of the Royal Life Saving Society UK offices, especially Ms Val Sumner; Fr Anselm Cramer OSB, librarian and archivist for Ampleforth Abbey and College; Ms Margaret Ainscough, archivist of Bootham School; Mrs S. Cole, archives assistant at Chaterhouse; Mr Nick Baker, collections administrator, and Mrs Penny Hatfield, college archivist, at Eton College; Mrs Rita Gibbs, archivist of Harrow School; Mr J.G. Brown, archivist of Merchant Taylors' School; Ms Barbara Wilson and Mrs Liz Trevethick, archivists of The Mount School; Mr R. MacLean, librarian and archivist of Rugby School; Mr Simon May, archivist of St. Paul's School; the late Mr John V. Mitchell, archivist, and Ms Avril Pedley, librarian and archivist, at St Peter's School; Mr James Lawson, archivist of Shrewsbury School; Mr H. Eveleigh and Mr E. Smith at Westminster School; Mr R. Custance, archivist of Winchester College; and the staff of the J.B. Morrell Library at the University of York, especially Dr David Griffiths, subject librarian for history. Special thanks go out to the members of my thesis advisory panel during my time at York, Dr Allen Warren, Dr Bill Sheils and Dr Geoff Cubitt; they provided me with a great deal of excellent advice and guidance. Special thanks also go to my external examiner for my Ph.D. defence, Dr Jeff Hill of De Montfort University. Extra special thanks go to my supervisor, Professor Jim Walvin; his oversight has added immensely to my growth as a historian. Without his constant advice and questioning of what I was doing, I doubt I would have finished my Ph.D. and been able to go on to produce this work. Thanks also to all of the staff at Taylor and Francis for shepherding this manuscript through the various stages of publication. Special thanks to Professor J.A. Mangan and Projit Mukharji, my editors and taskmasters who kept me on track and on deadline. I appreciated all of your messages, gentlemen. Finally, I must thank my family, especially my parents, for their support. Without them this collection would never have become a reality. As always, any errors or omissions in this work are my responsibility alone.

Christopher Love
Winnipeg, Manitoba, Canada
August 2006

Notes

[1] The activity referred to as either 'competitive swimming' or 'speed swimming' by the layman is actually simply referred to as 'swimming' by the *Federation Internationale de Natation Amateur* (FINA), the world governing body of swimming, diving, water polo, long-distance/marathon swimming and synchronized swimming. For purposes of this collection, reference to the sporting discipline of swimming will always be explicitly pointed out, while the generic term 'swimming' will be used to describe all areas of aquatic sport, leisure and recreation collectively when required.

[2] Mason, 'Introduction', 5.
[3] Holt and Mason, *Sport in Britain*.
[4] Orme, *Early British Swimming*, x.

References

Holt, Richard and Tony Mason. *Sport in Britain 1945–2000*. Oxford: Blackwell Publishers Ltd., 2000.

Mason, Tony. 'Introduction'. In *Sport in Britain: A Social History*. edited by Tony Mason. Cambridge: Cambridge University Press, 1989: 1–11.

Orme, Nicholas. *Early British Swimming 55 BC–AD 1719, with the First Swimming Treatise in English, 1595*. Exeter: Exeter University Press, 1983.

An Overview of the Development of Swimming in England, c.1750–1918

It is doubtful that it will ever be possible to establish an exact date for when the first human went swimming, but it seems certain that people have engaged in the activity for several thousand years at a minimum. The development of swimming was probably an early feature in many different cultures around the world, and one which evolved independently of any early contact between cultures. It seems likely that breaststroke, the oldest of the 'classical' strokes now used in competitive swimming was the stroke of choice for early swimmers, but all of this is speculation as swimming is an activity that does not require any equipment and which, of course, need not leave behind any physical artefacts.

It is the Romans who provide the first written records related to swimming in England, as Nicholas Orme has pointed out. During the later Roman Republic and the early Roman Empire period various Roman writers, including Cicero, Horace, Ovid, Pliny the Younger, Plutarch, Seneca the Younger and Suetonius, mention swimming in their works. The ability to swim was highly praised and valued in Roman society, at least among men, and the skill was promoted as a necessary military discipline by Vegetius in the later 380s CE. The first swimming records related to England fall in the same mould, being recorded in conjunction with military actions. No records of civilian swimming, or swimming by the native British inhabitants, survive, if they ever existed. According to Orme, Roman baths large enough to be used as swimming pools were built at Bath, Burton and Wells. It is not, however, known if they were ever used in this manner. Evidently there was a limited amount of swimming from the first arrival of Julius Caesar in England until the beginning of bathing culture in the 1700s. It is also important to note that throughout his work Orme stresses that his sources only ever refer to male swimmers. While it cannot be argued that women never swam in these early periods, there is little to no evidence to suggest that female swimming existed in any significant form prior to the 1800s. Even well into the nineteenth century, swimming was viewed for the most part as a male preserve. [1]

By the late 1700s, however, swimming began to be recognized as a sport and pastime in England. The best, although far from totally reliable, evidence for this comes from Joseph Strutt's 1801 book, *Glig-Gamena Angel Ðeod, or, The Sports and Pastimes of the People of England*. In this work Strutt argued that swimming was a natural English pastime, and that it had been part of English culture since before the Romans arrived on the islands. Indeed, he went so far as to state that the native Britons used swimming as a means to remain fit for the constant warfare they engaged in. Although he believed that no records about swimming existed from between the end of the Roman period and the early 1700s, Strutt was convinced that the activity had been continuously practised in England throughout the intervening years. It is clear today that much of what Strutt wrote about swimming consisted of fanciful invention and wild speculation, especially his views on the swimming exploits of the ancient Britons and the Romans. His examination of swimming in England remains quite long on theory and short on documented historical proof. *The Sports and Pastimes of the People of England* is important, however, because it confirms that by the late eighteenth century – the period Strutt knew personally – people in England were swimming. Furthermore, swimming was clearly not a major pastime in contemporary England, for Strutt was concerned to promote the activity among his countrymen; indeed, although his word must be accepted with caution, Strutt claimed that swimming was not as prevalent among the English as it previously had been. [2]

Scattered references to pre-nineteenth-century swimming pools in England, especially London, appear in swimming literature throughout the period under review, although seldom as more than passing comment. The first verifiable swimming pool in England about which records still survive was an open-air bath known as the 'Pearless Pool, North London' or 'Pearless Head Pool', which was purportedly opened in 1743 and which was purpose-built for swimming. [3] The pool was located in Baldwin Street, City Road, and was in use for over a century, finally being built over for other purposes in 1869–70. [4] Thus even before the start of the nineteenth century the idea of a place specifically constructed for swimming existed in the public consciousness. Despite uncertainties about how it operated, it would appear that the Pearless Pool was one of the few swimming places in London open to the public, or at least that portion that could afford to pay, from the 1740s until the 1860s.

Parallel to the provision of swimming pools for the public was the construction of pools at various public schools across England. Harrow was the first public school to build its own bathing place, with the construction of the 'Duck Puddle' in 1810 or 1811. [5] While the 'Duck Puddle' may have been little more than a water-filled muddy hole, it was a sign of things to come. Although it was the middle of the nineteenth century before another school followed Harrow's example, the fact that one of the great English public schools possessed a purpose-built place for bathing that was not in a river, the sea or other natural water site was an advance over previous practice. By the end of the nineteenth century swimming pools would be seen as *the* way to provide swimming at public schools, state schools and in the wider world. Indeed, eventually the possession of a pool almost became a requisite for recognition as a top public school. There were exceptions, of course. Only those public schools with enough land on which to build a swimming pool could do so. Schools not well enough funded to purchase land, or located in confined locations, had to make other arrangements. Both Merchant Taylors' School and Westminster School, located in central London, could not build their own pools during the nineteenth century. Merchant Taylors' eventually did build a pool, but only after relocating to the outskirts of London. To this day Westminster School does not have its own swimming pool, utilizing local municipal pools instead.

Although it is not possible to say if Harrow's 'Duck Puddle' was the first water-filled pit purposely dug for swimming purposes in England in the nineteenth century, it was perhaps the most influential, for Harrow's reputation ensured that its facilities became well known. Whether or not the 'Duck Puddle' was the first purpose-built swimming place constructed since the Pearless Head Pool in 1743, at roughly 500 yards in length it was certainly one of the largest. [6] It is likely that other similar pools had preceded it, but they must have been few and far between and almost certainly for private use.

In this early period the most common form of bathing was, of course, in the sea. Seaside bathing had developed in the eighteenth century and increased in popularity by the end of the century. With the rise of material prosperity and the creation of a professional class, more and more people were able to afford visits to the inland spa towns and the resorts that had grown up on the coast. While mass usage of the spa towns and beaches would have to wait for the expansion of the national railway network later in the century, the trend was established, notably at Brighton, of taking a dip in the waters. It is also clear that by 1800 men and women were bathing together in the sea in some cases. Although there were already trends towards segregation of the sexes in bathing, there was also an acceptance of mixed bathing in some areas and social circles. It is important to note, however, that bathing in the sea was often just that – bathing, not true swimming. Some people entered the water looking to cure their ailments or as a preventative against future illness, the time spent soaking in the water being seen as beneficial. Sometimes, however, it would have been inadvisable to use the term bathing for what went on at the seaside; dunking or submersion might be better terms to describe the experience for many. [7]

The seaside towns and resorts grew as never before during the nineteenth century, but it was not in these locations that important developments were made in swimming. Indeed, swimming appears to have been most assisted in its development by the creation of municipal swimming pools. In 1828 the civic corporation of Liverpool was the first to open an indoor municipal swimming pool in England. The St George's Baths, as they became known, were supplied with water directly from the River Mersey, most likely producing a swimming environment that was only marginally cleaner and safer than swimming in the river itself. Putting aside the question of cleanliness, however, the entrance of municipal bodies into the construction and management of swimming pools was to become a much more common trend in the future, especially after the permissive legislation of the Baths and Washhouses Act, 1846, came into effect.

In order for swimming to develop as an activity, not only did there need to be places for people to swim but also there needed to be organizations to support the activity. Early in the nineteenth century small bathing clubs began to be formed by gentlemen who enjoyed going into the water. Two of the earliest examples of swimming clubs were the Philolutic and Psychrolutic societies at Eton College that existed between 1828 and 1857. The Philolutes were dedicated to general bathing, while the Psychrolutes were specifically dedicated to cold water and/or out-of-doors winter bathing. The Psychrolutes were an elite subset of the Philolutes, and between 1828 and 1857 the club enrolled a total of 26 men, with the last member being admitted in 1843. The Philolutes enrolled over 200 members between 1832 and 1849, counting three members of the royal family among their number. [8] No records of the Philolutes' general activities survive, but the Psychrolutic Society kept detailed records of where its members bathed. Places as diverse as the Serpentine in London, various Scottish lochs, many major English rivers and the Hellespont were included in the list. [9] Although limited to Eton and Cambridge students and masters, and excluding women, the formation of clubs such as the Eton Philolutic and Psychrolutic societies was the start of a movement towards more widespread swimming within English public schools, and perhaps a sign of increased interest in swimming within England in general.

At the same time that swimming was becoming of interest in Eton there were also attempts to encourage more people to become involved in swimming in London. In the late 1830s and early 1840s several organizations were founded in London to promote swimming among the people. Of all these societies, most of which appeared and disappeared in a single swimming season, the most important was the National Swimming Society (NSS). The NSS seems to have been the originator of the idea of a national body governing swimming in England, although it did not achieve that objective. In 1836 or 1837 a man by the name of John Strachan, a wine merchant in Dean Street, Westminster, founded the NSS. [10] This society immediately set about its purpose of promoting swimming by organizing a race in the Serpentine in early August 1837. [11] Initially the members of the society were quite active in promoting swimming. Indeed, the NSS provided some form of swimming instruction in and around London from 1837 to 1838; *The Times*, for example, reported in September 1838 a race, swum by a mixture of NSS students and other entrants, across the Thames from Cremorne House in Chelsea to Battersea and back. Silver cups and silver snuffboxes were being offered as prizes for this race. It was further stated in *The Times* article that NSS instructors (here dubbed 'professors') using the Surrey Canal, the Serpentine and the Thames, had taught over 2000 students to swim since 1837. [12] Over time the NSS also attempted to expand its influence beyond London. In August 1840, for example, the society provided at least one silver medal to the Glasgow Swimming Society for use as a prize. Later in the same month the society provided three silver medals to be used as prizes by the newly formed Oxford Swimming Society. Indeed, it was the policy of the NSS to provide three silver medals a year to any local or regional swimming society in Britain that applied to the London committee. Interestingly, the NSS made no stipulation on the distance to be covered to win the silver medals that it provided to local bodies. The Glasgow race in 1840 was over a distance of roughly 960 yards, while the Oxford race was only over a distance of 400 yards. [13]

In 1841 and 1843 three articles appeared in the press about a British Swimming Society (BSS). It was said to have been founded in 1841, 'to promote health, cleanliness, and the preservation of life by the practice of bathing and by teaching and encouraging the art of swimming'. [14] It is quite likely that these stories may simply be inaccurate references to the National Swimming Society, although there is the possibility that they refer to another society that was also trying to promote swimming in London and England at the same time. [15] Whatever the actual case may be, *The Times* article covering the annual dinner of the BSS in 1843 provides an interesting overview of the society's activities. It was reported that since its previous dinner the organization had run a series of four competitions; a race for youths under 16 years of age, held at the Holborn Baths, for the prize of a single silver medal; a race for the adult members of the society, for three silver medals; the society's annual races; and a fancy swimming competition. The dinner itself was attended by 40 gentlemen, a large number of whom were thought to be under the age of 21, according to the report. The society's programme of providing free swimming instruction was reported during the course of the dinner, and it was hoped to continue on a larger scale in future years.

Whether or not there were one or two organizations purporting to be national bodies promoting swimming across England in the 1840s – and it seems likely that there was only one – the end result was the same. The society or societies were London-based and ultimately had little success in their purpose of making swimming more popular in society at large. The NSS was certainly founded by gentlemen of means, and would seem to have been administered by a governing committee of men. As no records survive on the membership of these organizations we will never know for certain if they catered for female swimmers, but it seems highly unlikely. By the later 1840s all mention of the NSS had disappeared from the press and the organization appears to have dissolved around 1845 or 1846.

Although the NSS was short-lived, the fact that it had existed is important. Years later its activities were looked back on by swimming administrators, for the most part with admiration. The society even held two essay competitions, in 1839 and 1840, for which medals were awarded for the best writing on the art of swimming. The prizewinning essays for the two years in which the competition was run were still referred to in the writings of authors on swimming in the 1890s. [16] Along with the Philolutic and Psychrolutic societies at Eton, the NSS represents the first real attempt to organize swimming at any level. In addition, the society's efforts in promoting swimming by providing lessons was an attempt to broaden the number of people able to swim in England. As has been seen, however, these efforts took place only in the capital, and seem to have been restricted to males only. It would be at least another two decades before swimming began to become a truly widespread activity.

At the same time that the National Swimming Society was attracting attention in the media, there was other activity among swimmers in London. In 1836, only one year before the formation of the NSS, it is certain that privately owned and operated swimming baths were being constructed in parts of London. One such establishment, the National Tepid and Cold Swimming Baths, was located on the Westminster Road in Lambeth. [17] At some later point this facility seems to have fallen out of use, because in 1852 the Lambeth Baths and Wash Houses Company had to convert the 'National Baths' of Westminster Road into baths, swimming pool and washhouse. [18] Swimming in the Serpentine was obviously commonplace in the 1840s, for by then the Royal Humane Society had taken responsibility for providing boatmen on the Serpentine in order to save those who got into difficulty while swimming there. Just how popular the Serpentine was as a location to go swimming was demonstrated during the summer of 1842 (considered to be a warm one), when the RHS estimated that there were crowds of over 8,000 people using the lake on some days. The same was said of one very warm period of the summer of 1843. [19] The construction of private baths facilities, with swimming pools, and the provision of boatmen for safety purposes on the Serpentine is likely to have helped broaden the appeal of swimming slightly. For all these examples, however, swimming remained a marginal, minority pleasure, and it was only after municipal authorities began to provide swimming pools that swimming really became popular.

While there was a clear interest in swimming in the capital, the first opening of a municipal swimming pool was not in London but in Liverpool, in 1828. [20] Thereafter, the St George's Baths in Liverpool seems to have been the only municipal swimming pool in England until the enactment of the Baths and Washhouses Act, 1846 (9 & 10 Vict., c. 74). Passed by Parliament in August 1846, this piece of permissive legislation allowed English local authorities to establish indoor baths and washhouses, laundries and open bathing places. Through the baths constructed by authorities operating under the powers given by the act, cleanliness would be promoted. There seems to have been general agreement about the usefulness of the act, as it passed through Parliament with almost no debate. [21]

Although indoor swimming pools were not specifically allowed under the act, local authorities often built what they termed 'plunge baths' which were used for swimming. Open bathing places, as we have already seen, were traditionally used for both bathing and swimming, and the act simply led to the regulation of bathing activity at such sites. An amendment to the Baths and Washhouses Act, 1846, in 1878, allowed for the construction of indoor swimming pools. Once local authorities began to build swimming facilities and provided access to them at reasonable prices, swimming could become much more widespread within English society.

From the later 1840s to the 1870s swimming was on the cusp of exploding into a popular recreational and sporting activity. Pockets of organized activity existed in London, and ongoing media reports from the 1820s highlighted the strength of northern swimmers, especially in Lancashire. [22] It was during the 1850s and into the 1860s that a large number of swimming clubs, many of them quite long-lived, came to be established across England. Initially these clubs were formed in London and seaside towns, but eventually others were founded in almost every English city or town of significant size. In London, for example, the London Swimming Club was founded in 1859. Members of the club published a handbook in 1861 that recorded the existence of at least three, possibly four, swimming clubs in the metropolis, these being the Bloomsbury Amateur Swimming Club, the London Swimming Club and the London Unity Rowing Club. The possible fourth club, the Albion Club, Kingsland, was thought to be defunct. In addition, prior to 1861 there had existed a Westminster Swimming Society, which seems to have been made up, for the most part, of professional swimmers. This society had a great rivalry with a group of swimmers who used the Holborn Baths, and one F.E. Beckwith – Frederick Beckwith – was named as the society's fastest swimmer. [23] After the absence of any major form of organized swimming, following the collapse of the NSS in the late 1840s, the revival of clubs in the late 1850s and the 1860s is important. Although none of these specific clubs survived for long, they appear to have re-established organized swimming on some sort of footing in London.

The London Swimming Club was followed by other, longer-lasting clubs. One of the earliest was the Ilex Swimming Club, founded in 1861. [24] Two other clubs from the 1860s that still survive today are the Serpentine Swimming Club, founded in 1864 and best known for organizing the annual Christmas Day handicap race in the Serpentine, and the Otter Swimming Club, founded in 1869 as a male-only gentlemen's club as well as a swimming club. The Otter SC became one of the most important swimming clubs of the late nineteenth and early twentieth centuries. The 'Otters' engaged in regular competitions with public school and university teams, in diving, swimming and water polo, through the entire period under review, and they also apparently either donated prizes to various youth organizations for use in those organizations' own competitions or hosted such competitions themselves. [25] The development of swimming clubs that remained in existence for several years at a time was important, for they provided a stable base of clubs from which to form the foundation for a national swimming body.

The year 1869 was important not only for the foundation of the Otter Swimming Club, but also for an even more significant organization. In January of that year a 'swimming congress' was held at the German Gymnasium in London in order to constitute an association of swimming clubs for the promotion of swimming as a sport and leisure activity. Initially this body called itself the Associated Metropolitan Swimming Clubs (AMSC), but the name was changed to the London Swimming Association (LSA) in June 1869. Sometime early in 1870 the LSA became the Metropolitan Swimming Association (MSA) and then, on 8 December 1873, the Swimming Association of Great Britain (SAGB). Eventually, in 1886, the organization became the Amateur Swimming Association (ASA), the present governing body of swimming in England. [26] The development of a national governing body for swimming in the late 1860s and early 1870s was an important event. As in other sports of the period, such as football, formal regulation of traditional activities was beginning to take place. As part of the games explosion in the period, swimming was being brought into the new sporting world and given a standardized, formal structure.

At first, however, the new governing body, whatever its name, does not seem to have had a great deal of impact on the sports scene, or on public views about swimming in general. Unlike the executives of the Amateur Athletic Association (AAA) or the Football Association (FA), for example, the committees of the predecessors of the ASA struggled, for a long time, to expand beyond London. It was not until 1879, a full decade after its formation, that the SAGB expanded beyond six clubs, and it was only after the SAGB became the ASA that membership levels really began to increase rapidly and become representative of the entire country. Indeed, until the ASA was constituted in 1886, the effectiveness of the various predecessor bodies of the ASA was often limited to London and very small areas of the provinces, mainly in the south. Perhaps most importantly, the LSA and its successors established the English Men's Mile Amateur Championship race which has been swum from 1869 to the present. [27]

It would be wrong to assume, however, that because there was no effective national governing body that swimming was moribund. In fact, during the period from 1850 to 1880 the opposite was the case. Swimming was becoming more popular, especially within the expanding middle classes. In 1873 a total of 356,813 persons were estimated to have swum in the Serpentine during the periods when Royal Humane Society boatmen were in attendance to provide supervision. [28] The Baths and Washhouses Act allowed for the construction of wash baths by municipal authorities under permissive legislation. Increasingly through this period various town and borough councils began to make use of these powers, and some even erected swimming pools within their baths, even though these were not explicitly allowed by the legislation. [29] At the same time various private companies and individuals also began to construct swimming baths as a form of investment from which they expected a profitable return. Board of Trade records cover the dissolution of no fewer than 40 such private swimming bath companies between 1866 and 1935. [30] In terms of the large number of swimming pools now scattered around England, these numbers are small, but they simply represent those companies that were liquidated during the period under review. Other private bath companies, such as the one created in York to build and operate the Marygate, or Manor Shore, swimming bath, were often later bought by private individuals, larger corporations or municipal bodies. Such pools would not necessarily appear in any form of record kept by the Board of Trade. We can safely assume that the 40 bath companies mentioned in the Board of Trade records indicate that there was a healthy interest in providing swimming baths on a commercial basis. This clearly suggests that there was a public interest in swimming, and that private investors were confident enough to invest in such schemes in the hope of a return on their investment.

The government during this period generally avoided all involvement in the promotion of swimming, other than to introduce and amend the Baths and Washhouses Act, whose general purpose, as we have seen, was a sanitary one. It was not originally intended to promote recreational swimming. This is not to say, however, that all departments of the government were against the promotion of swimming. In 1868 the Army introduced, for the first time, regulations related to swimming, gymnastics and other physical exercise. Exactly why these regulations were introduced at this time is not clear, although a concern for the prevention of drowning among the troops is evident. Foremost, however, in the regulations is the statement

> The art of swimming is to be taught as a military duty at all stations where facilities for it exist. During the proper season regular bathing parades are to be formed for the purpose of instruction in swimming. The skilled swimmers in each troop or company are to be ascertained, and so distributed that there may be a sufficient number in each squad to teach the rest. [31]

Obvious concern for the costs involved with training are evident here, and the training was limited to those sites with access to rivers, lakes or the sea, but it was definitely a precedent for other government bodies, and a policy which over time would introduce many new recruits to swimming.

Through all this, we need also to consider other developments in Victorian society, notably the impact of the rise in literacy and the expansion of the printed press, on swimming. The last quarter of the nineteenth century was an era when speciality papers and journals dedicated to almost every topic under the sun appeared (and some disappeared with great rapidity). Some of these journals, such as *Punch*, attracted large readerships and survived for long periods of time. Many other publications, however, were short-lived. This extraordinary explosion in printed material was at least partially attributable to the introduction of state elementary education in 1870. Like almost every other sport and leisure activity, swimming received coverage in the largest sporting publications of the day, such as *Sporting Life*, but a specialist press dedicated to the activity also developed. Newspapers and journals with such titles as *The Athletic Field and Swimming World*; *Bicycle, Swimming and Athletic Journal*; *Swimming and Lacrosse*; *The Swimming Magazine*;

Swimming Notes; and the *Swimming Record and Chronicle of Sporting Events* appeared between 1873 and 1918. These numerous titles dedicated to swimming indicate the popularity of the activity. The short life of most of these journals, however, suggests not everyone wanted to *read* about swimming. It was not until the 1920s that a journal dedicated solely to aquatic sports, *The Swimming Times*, was able to survive for more than four years. Clearly swimming was an activity with a growing level of support, but on nothing like the level of the major national sports, namely cricket and football.

It was also in the 1870s that we can see an increase in both patronage and commercial support of swimming. Throughout the nineteenth century it was common for aristocrats or other wealthy individuals to provide prizes for swimming competitions. Local public houses or inns might also be involved in such activities. Increasingly by the late nineteenth century, however, commercial businesses were becoming involved in such patronage as well. With the rise of commercial and especially professional sport and recreation, a range of commercial companies was naturally attracted to sport. Various consumer goods were manufactured to cater for this new leisure activity. Whether it was swimming costumes, soap or Bovril, all were advertised to swimmers over the last quarter of the nineteenth century. This trend towards commercialization increased especially in the 1890s. [32]

The 1870s and 1880s saw the organized swimming world, as distinct from the world of casual recreational swimmers, fixated on organizational issues and especially ones related to growth and status. Up to 1886, for example, there were constant battles over the meaning of professional and amateur status, and which swimmers belonged in which category. The number of affiliated clubs during the period only slowly increased, with just six affiliated clubs in 1873. The SAGB was clearly a struggling local organization at this time, with a membership confined to the area immediately around London. Moreover, not even all the metropolitan London clubs were members. Despite its claim to a national jurisdiction, the MSA/SAGB was obviously unable to act nationally. [33]

One man, however, could do what a committee of gentlemen could not, and the swimming world was transformed in 1875 by his achievement. On 24 and 25 August 1875, on his second attempt, Captain Matthew Webb swam the Channel. *Bell's Life in London*, wrote of Webb's accomplishment:

> Among the many feats of human strength and endurance that have been recorded in the columns of *Bell's Life in London* that performed on Tuesday last – with which all of England is ringing, and of which the whole Anglo-Saxon race should be proud – stands as one of the greatest, Captain Matthew Webb, a brave seaman, having, beyond the possibility of a doubt, accomplished the superhuman task of swimming from Dover Pier to the French shore, unaided by buoyant dress or assistance of any kind except occasional refreshment. [34]

Webb's successful crossing of the Channel was an event which captured the attention and the imagination of the entire nation. Webb's achievement was dramatic – and it had dramatic effects. Boxes of matches with a portrait representing him during his swim were sold, and his image was used for other products. Webb was even the credited author of several books about swimming. [35]

In the same edition of *Bell's Life* (28 August 1875) that reported Webb's swim, there was also a report on the recent Mile Amateur Championship held by the SAGB, which emphasized the attention now devoted to swimming by the English populace at large. Captain Webb had made much of the nation sit up and take notice of swimming as an activity. Further articles in the same issue of *Bell's Life in London* bear witness to more prominent nature of swimming with the wider society. One article mentions that a Miss Agnes Beckwith was to swim in the near future from London Bridge to Greenwich. According to the article, several people had bet against her being able to accomplish this feat. A Miss Emily Parker was also listed as planning to attempt this feat in the future. [36] The summer of 1875 was important for swimming: the amateur mile championship was held by the SAGB; Webb made his dramatic and historic Channel crossing and he was celebrated across the country, indeed around the world; and several professional women swimmers were planning long-distance swims in the Thames for wagers. Perhaps even more importantly, it was *female* professional swimmers, not men, attempting these long-distance swims. They would not have been classified as 'ladies', nor, indeed, amateurs, but Agnes Beckwith and Emily Parker were certainly pushing forward female swimming.

It was in the 1870s, then, and especially after Webb's famous crossing, that swimming began to gain popularity in England. It is impossible, of course, to give exact numbers for the number of people who were swimming during this period. One indication that swimming was becoming more popular, however, was the fact that swimming activities became more varied. Some swimmers were looking beyond simple racing and sought to amuse themselves in the water by other means. Various water sports were developed in the 1870s, eventually resulting in what we know today as water polo. Sinclair and Henry date the origins of the sport to the later 1870s, when versions of the game appeared independently in Aberdeen, Bournemouth and Glasgow. The Bournemouth Premier Rowing Club appears to have been the first group to organize games, with its 'aquatic hand-ball matches' begun on 13 July 1876. The game appears to have spread quite quickly, although many regional variations were developed in those early years. The game seems to have been popular in the Midlands, with teams formed in Birmingham (1877) and Burton upon Trent (1878). Standardization of the game began as early as 1879, when English clubs agreed to equal teams of nine men a side, and in 1880 or 1881 when association football rules were translated to the pool to help govern the new game. [37]

The period after Webb's famous Channel swim saw an explosion in interest and growth in the sport in the 1880s and 1890s that mirrored the expansion of other sports – athletics, cycling, football, rowing, skating and many other sporting activities expanded greatly during the same period. But while there was steady development of swimming in England, the last quarter of the nineteenth century was also marked by dispute and argument. Growth in the sport brought pain and headaches to sport administrators and aquatic professionals. The number of clubs affiliated to the SAGB/ASA continued to grow at a respectable rate year on year, as did the number of amateur championship races run by that body. In 1879 the Royal Navy finally followed the Army's lead and made swimming a requirement for all incoming officer cadets, boys and seamen. [38]

Despite the increase in the number of swimming baths available across London, thousands still swam in the Serpentine during the summer months. In 1881 the Royal Humane Society estimated the number at 250,000. [39] Professional swimmers banded together in 1881 to form the Professional Swimming Association (PSA), which was mainly a group composed of self-styled swimming 'professors', aquatic showmen and racers; the association does not appear to have been very successful, and it folded after only a decade. [40] Its existence parallels the rise of professional sportsmen in other sports, notably cricket and football. All these developments reflected the rapid and widespread emergence of popular leisure among the British people. One man who seemed *not* to have benefited by this boom in professional sports was Captain Webb himself. Driven to ever more foolhardy feats (to earn money), Webb endeavoured in 1883 to swim through the rapids and whirlpools of the Niagara River below Niagara Falls, but he died during the attempt. His death was widely reported, and subscriptions were taken up for his widow and young children. Most commentators chose to ignore Webb's final swim, and instead focused on his great Channel achievement, emphasizing the great swimming involved there. [41]

As with other sports, the contentious issue of amateur versus professional began to trouble swimming, leading to the great amateur split in swimming in the middle of the 1880s. It was to have long-lasting repercussions on the development of swimming. Between 1884 and 1886 there were actually two governing bodies for amateur swimming in England, when eight clubs broke away from the SAGB to form the Amateur Swimming Union (ASU) in protest against the SAGB's handling of the amateur laws. Although only the SAGB's records survive, it is clear that the debate was heated and personal for the two years it lasted, with each organization declaring that all those in the opposing camp were professionals. At the same time, however, the SAGB, now influential outside London, took control of swimmers in Scotland in 1885. The healing of the rift between the SAGB and the ASU in 1886 was produced by the formulation of a new set of amateur laws, and a new national governing body for swimming, the Amateur Swimming Association (ASA). This ensured the almost complete dominance of that one body in the governance of competitive swimming and water polo in England, and in 1887 the ASA was recognized by the patronage of Queen Victoria.

The later 1880s saw a rapid refinement and growth in the formal organization of British swimming. By 1888 a national water polo championship had been established, and Scottish swimmers had elected to govern themselves through a Scottish Amateur Swimming Association (SASA) with the full support of the ASA. [42] In 1889–90, in response to the threat of secession by a large number of clubs in the north of England, the ASA adopted a three-district system of operation to provide better local governance for regional swimmers. [43] This was changed to a five-district system in 1900–01, after a four-year period in which the swimming clubs of Durham, Northumberland and Yorkshire had created their own body outside the ASA as a protest against what they saw as a lack of local representation. [44]

Swimming was changing on all fronts in the last years of the century. Not surprisingly perhaps, as more and more people swam, the need arose to safeguard life. In 1891 the Life Saving Society (LSS) was founded to promote aquatic life-saving and provide training in life-saving techniques among the people at large. And at much the same time, prompted by ASA lobbying of the Education Department, swimming was finally allowed among pupils in London's elementary schools. [45] Most pupils seem to have taken their lessons in the baths recently built by London's various vestries, though later some schools even built their own swimming pools for their pupils. To promote swimming among school pupils, the London Schools Swimming Association (LSSA) was formed in 1893; its annual competitions continue to this day. Finally, with the formation of the Amateur Diving Association (ADA) in 1901 in London, a third aquatic sport was organized in England.

By the new century, it was clear enough that swimming was a thriving activity in England, and the evidence is available on all fronts. The Amateur Swimming Association had secured its claim as the organization governing swimming in England and was now struggling not with simple economic survival, as in 1873, but with the problem of how to ensure adequate local representation and control in its various districts. The ASA had also taken control and begun to promote two of the four modern aquatic Olympic sports, competitive swimming and water polo, while the ADA was promoting the third, diving. Swimming was actively promoted within schools, most notably in London. While the state was still not fully behind the promotion of swimming as a matter of official policy, there was growing recognition of the value of swimming, notably in the Army, Royal Navy and parts of the Board of Education. The promotion of the humanitarian side of swimming, life-saving, was now being undertaken by the LSS, and while it had its growing pains, this new society was accepted by the swimming world more rapidly, and with less fuss, than the ASA had seen. The LSS received royal patronage in 1904, becoming the Royal Life Saving Society (RLSS), and under this name it has promoted life-saving throughout the world ever since.

This dramatic story of swimming in England also had an international dimension. From the 1890s onwards, English competitive swimmers began to involve themselves in competitions against foreign competitors, both at home and abroad. International events, whatever their predecessors, were organized for the purpose of attracting competitors from many countries. In 1890 the first 'international' water polo match had been played between England and Scotland, with the Scots coming out on top. [46] This series of games was continued for several years, with the English eventually becoming dominant. But the most important innovation was the formation of the modern Olympic Games in Athens in 1896. There were four swimming events in these first games, but no official British team or competitors. At the 1900 Olympic Games in Paris the first ever Olympic men's water polo tournament was held, and the

British sent both a swimming and a water polo team. Prior to the First World War, British participation in the aquatic sports of the Olympic Games was enthusiastic and fairly productive in terms of medals. British men's water polo teams were almost assured a medal in the Olympic tournament in each games prior to the war, and the swimmers usually acquitted themselves well. The Olympic Games of 1908 were staged in London, with a hundred-metre-long outdoor pool being built in the centre of the Olympic Stadium in Shepherd's Bush erected especially for the games. The men's water polo team took the gold medal, the men's swimming team took four of six gold medals, as well as two silver medals and a bronze. During the 1908 games a conference of international swimming nations was held at the Manchester Hotel, London. The conference resulted in the formation of the International Amateur Swimming Federation (better known under its French title and acronym; FINA – *Federation Internationale de Natation Amateur*), with George W. Hearn, an English swimming administrator, named its first general secretary. This period of British swimming development is important, because much of the early rules and policies adopted by FINA were taken straight from the ASA handbook. [47] As with many other sports that the British had pioneered, British rules and regulations were passed around the wider sporting world through their later adoption by international organizations.

This initial spurt of English swimming success and influence in the world of international swimming was not to last, however. Although the summer of 1914 began like any other of the previous 20 to 30 years, it would not end so. Like almost every other facet of English life, swimming was dramatically changed by the First World War. Most importantly for swimmers and swimming clubs, the outbreak of war meant that club memberships were diminished, and many locations used for swimming were taken over for war use or made inaccessible in other ways. In Brighton, the Brighton Swimming Club's clubhouse of the period was located on Brighton beach. Although the clubhouse remained open, and the club active for the duration of the First World War, swimming was continued at a much reduced level. The club was maintained by the most senior members, because many of the younger members were on active duty. The war can be seen as a blow to the health of the club: in 1913 it had posted its highest ever membership, at 256 men and boys, but the war caused a crash to an unspecified low that was not recovered from for years afterwards. [48]

At the end of the First World War England began to assess her losses. The terrible wartime loss of life and the 1919 influenza epidemic inevitably had an impact on all social and sporting activities. The ASA could record 1,468 affiliated clubs in 1914, and 1,423 affiliated clubs in 1915. By 1920, however, when post-war records resume, there were only 875 clubs affiliated to the association. It was not until 1929, a full decade after the close of the First World War, that the number of affiliated clubs would rise above the 1914 level. [49]

The transformation in swimming in the years between 1800 and 1918 was far-reaching and universal. Swimming pools were ubiquitous across the face of urban England. Competitive swimming was highly organized and had, in recent years, taken on a new international dimension. More important still perhaps, the role of swimming as a pleasurable activity which was both good for the individual and for society as a whole had become widely accepted.

Notes

[1] Orme, *Early British Swimming*, 1–7, 107.
[2] Strutt, *Glig-Gamena Angel Ðeod*, ii, xx, 66–7.
[3] ASA, *Successful Swimming with the ASA*, 5. Keil and Wix, *In the Swim*, 4. Neither source cites an original source for the 1743 foundation date.
[4] Dudgeon, *The Swimming Baths of London*, 9.
[5] *The Harrovian* 4, no. 4 (19 May 1891), 38; Hort, 'The School Bathing Place', 256; Sinclair and Henry, *Swimming*, 366.
[6] Sinclair and Henry, *Swimming*, 366.
[7] For more on the development of spas and the seaside resort, see Corbin, *The Lure of the Sea*; Hern, *The Seaside Holiday*; Walton, *The English Seaside Resort*; Walvin, *Beside the Seaside*.
[8] Those being HRH Prince Albert, HRH Prince George of Cambridge and HRH The Duke of Cambridge. Eton College Archives, Eton, MISC/PSY/2/1, Eton Philolutic Society Members Book 1832–49.
[9] Eton College Archives, Eton, MISC/PSY/1/1, Psychrolutic Society Book 1828–57; and MISC/PSY/2/1, Eton Philolutic Society Members Book 1832–49.
[10] *Bell's Life in London*, 10 Sept. 1837, 4c. However, a later edition of *Bell's Life* lists 1836 as the NSS founding year: *Bell's Life in London*, 10 Sept. 1843, 4c. Keil and Wix give a date of 1836 for the foundation of the NSS, evidently following *Bell's Life*, but an illustration of the medal die used by the NSS on the same page of their book indicates a foundation date of 30 June 1837. No citation is given for the source of either the illustration or information given in the text: Keil and Wix, *In the Swim*, 8. On Strachan being a wine merchant see *The Swimming Magazine* 1, no. 10 (March 1915), 22. Thierry Terret also claims that Strachan was a wine merchant who attempted to develop swimming as a professional sport, but he provides no citation for this information: Terret, 'Professional Swimming in England', 21.
[11] *The Times*, 15 Aug. 1837, 2d.
[12] *The Times*, 21 Sept. 1838, 6b.
[13] *Bell's Life in London*, 4 Aug. 1839, 4b; 19 July 1840, 4e; 16 Aug. 1840, 4c; 30 Aug. 1840, 4d.; *The Times*, 31 Aug. 1840, 6c. The 19 July 1840 article in *Bell's Life* lists NSS medals as already having been sent to Aberdeen, Dundee, Hull, Perth and Plymouth.
[14] *The Times*, 6 Sept. 1843, 3f.
[15] Reference to the 'British Swimming Society' is made in *The Times*, 18 Sept. 1841, 4f; 6 Sept. 1843, 3f; and *Bell's Life in London*, 23 July 1843, 4b. Ralph Thomas in his bibliography of swimming writings records that the BSS and the NSS were the same organization, basing his claim upon the (now non-extant) title page of a published series of essays entitled 'The Handbook of Bathing' dating from 1841; Anonymous [Ralph Thomas], *Swimming: A Bibliographical List*, 7. In 1915 *The Swimming Magazine* printed an article that claimed that John Strachan was the one who had renamed the NSS the BSS; *The Swimming Magazine* 1, no. 10 (March 1915), 22. Terret follows Thomas: Terret, 'Professional Swimming in England', 21, 27. Keil and Wix claim that the BSS was a separate organization from the NSS, but that it was founded in 1840, not 1841, apparently basing this claim on information gained from an issue of *Bell's Life* which is mentioned, but not cited, and which this author has been unable to trace: Keil and Wix, *In the Swim*, 8. Aside from the three newspaper articles cited there appear to be no other contemporary sources that refer to the existence of a 'British Swimming

[16] These essays were referenced by Ralph Thomas in 1868 and 1904, and by Sinclair and Henry in 1893. They have not survived to the present day. Thomas names the authors as James Mason and A.M. Payne. Anonymous [Thomas], *Swimming: A Bibliographical List*, 7; Sinclair and Henry, *Swimming*, 21. See the footnotes above about the debate over the exact name of the organization that published these essays.

Society'. Reference to the 'National Swimming Society' explicitly by name is made in *Bell's Life* from 1839 to 1844 with the BSS only reported on once as noted above.

[17] Lambeth Archives: Minet Library, London (hereafter LAML), Newspaper Clippings File 537, cutting of 18 Dec. 1836. The source of the cutting is unspecified. One of the swimming pools in this building was said to be 210 feet by 60 feet.
[18] Cape, *Baths and Wash Houses*, 42. The only surviving copy of this work appears to be held in the Lambeth Archives, Minet Library, as the British Library does not hold a copy.
[19] Royal Humane Society, *Sixty-Ninth Annual Report*, 12–13. Royal Humane Society, *Seventieth Annual Report*, 14. These figures must, of course, be treated with extreme caution as to their accuracy. They point more towards a general trend and interest than absolute numbers of swimmers. Copies of these annual reports are housed in the Royal Humane Society's offices in London.
[20] Sinclair and Henry, *Swimming*, 413.
[21] Hansard Parliamentary Debates (H.C.), 3rd series, vol. 87 (19 June 1846), cols. 762; Parliamentary Debates (H.L.), 3rd series, vol. 88 (3 Aug. 1846), col. 277.
[22] Simply looking at *The Times* uncovers several articles on the strength of northern swimmers. See for example *The Times*, 7 Aug. 1822, 3b; 16 July 1827, 2e; 20 June 1863, 11e.
[23] *A Manual Compiled under the Sanction of The London Swimming Club*, 16–17, 26–7. The Holborn Baths had been reportedly converted into the Holborn Assembly Rooms by 1861.
[24] *The Swimming Record and Chronicle of Sport Events* 1, no. 3 (24 May 1873), 2.
[25] Otter Swimming Club, *Otter Swimming Club Centenary*, 24–6 and *passim*. The club, for example, donated the Otter Swimming Club Challenge Shield to the Boy Scouts prior to 1914 for internal competition.
[26] Keil and Wix had access to the original minute book of the proceedings of the AMSC and LSA when writing their history of the ASA in 1995–96 (See p.12 of their work for a reproduction of the first page of this manuscript). Every time this author has been to the ASA library this work has been out 'on loan' and thus unavailable for consultation. The recounting of events here is derived from Keil and Wix, *In the Swim*, 9–12. See also ASA Library (hereafter ASAL), Loughborough, Minute Book No. 2 of the Metropolitan Swimming Association, 3, Minutes of 8 Dec. 1873.
[27] ASAL, various printed programmes held loose. Several important changes have occurred to the conditions governing the mile championship since its inception, perhaps most importantly the metrification (to 1500 metres) of the race in 1971.
[28] Royal Humane Society, *One Hundredth Annual Report*, 25.
[29] See for example the case of York City Corporation running the Yearsley Baths by the 1850s and looking at supplementing those baths with new baths in the late 1860s: York City Archives, York, BC.96.4, Bathing Public Bathing Committee 1868–69, 78–82, Minutes of 28 July 1868 and 29 April 1869.
[30] Public Record Office (hereafter PRO), BT 31, various sub-class listings.
[31] HMSO, *Queen's Regulations and Orders for the Army*, 458–9.
[32] See for example, *Swimming* 1, no. 1 (13 March 1895); *Swimming & Lacrosse* 1, no. 2 (20 March 1895). See also Lowerson, *Sport and the English Middle Classes*, 225–60.
[33] ASAL, Minute Book No. 2 of the MSA, 2–10, Minutes of 11 Nov. 1873; Committee and Special General Meeting Minutes of 8 Dec. 1873; Special General Meeting Minutes and Financial Statements for 1873, 19 Jan. 1874.

[34] *Bell's Life in London*, 28 Aug. 1875, 3.
[35] See *The Times*, 14 Aug. 1875, 5f; 25 Aug. 1875, 3c; 26 Aug. 1875, 3f, 7c and d; *Bell's Life in London*, 28 Aug. 1875, 3; *Illustrated London News*, 21 Aug. 1875, 189–90; 28 Aug. 1875, 202. It is generally accepted that Webb did not write the books credited to him. Rather, his agent, A.G. Payne, seems to have been the author of the books. See Thomas, *Swimming*, 57, 63, 334.
[36] *Bell's Life in London*, 28 Aug. 1875, 5.
[37] Sinclair and Henry, *Swimming*, 281–5.
[38] PRO, ADM 7/895, Admiralty Fleet Circulars 1878–79, Fleet Circular no. 34 N. See also HMSO, *1880 Addenda to The Queen's Regulations*, 3–4.
[39] Royal Humane Society, *One Hundred and Eighth Annual Report*, 22.
[40] For the start and the finish of the PSA see *Sporting Life*, 9 July 1881, 14 Oct. 1891. A few records of the PSA can be found in the archives of the ASA, mainly in the form of racing and entertainment programmes. The vast bulk of PSA records seems to have been lost.
[41] *Illustrated London News*, 28 July 1883, 101.
[42] Bilsborough, *One Hundred Years of Scottish Swimming*, 3–5.
[43] Sinclair and Henry, *Swimming*, 341–7, 348–51.
[44] ASA, *Handbook for 1901*, 6–7, 109–14.
[45] Sinclair and Henry, *Swimming*, 352–3. Interestingly, education records held in the PRO do not mention swimming at all until 1903–04.
[46] Ibid., 300–1.
[47] ASA, *Handbook for 1910*, 131–9.
[48] Brighton Swimming Club, *1860–1960 One Hundred Years of Swimming*, 11.
[49] ASA, *Handbook for 1948*, 4–5.

References

Anonymous, *A Manual Compiled under the Sanction of The London Swimming Club for the Use of Its Members and Others; with an Account of the Progress of the Art during the last Twenty Years, and a Short Notice of The Swimming Baths of the Metropolis*. London: W.H. Leverell, 1861.

Anonymous [Ralph Thomas]. *Swimming: A Bibliographical List of Works on Swimming*. London: John Russell Smith, 1868.

ASA (Amateur Swimming Association). *Handbook for 1901*. London: Amateur Swimming Association, 1901.

———. *Handbook for 1910*. London: Amateur Swimming Association, 1910.

———. *Handbook for 1948*. London: Amateur Swimming Association, 1948.

———. *Successful Swimming with the ASA: The ASA Handbook for Swimmers*. Loughborough: Amateur Swimming Association, 1991.

Bilsborough, Peter. *One Hundred Years of Scottish Swimming*. Edinburgh: Scottish Amateur Swimming Association, 1988.

Brighton Swimming Club. *1860–1960 One Hundred Years of Swimming*. Brighton: Brighton Swimming Club, 1960.

Cape, George A. *Baths and Wash Houses*. London: Simpkin, Marshall & Co., 1854.

Corbin, Alain. *The Lure of the Sea: The Discovery of the Seaside in the Western World, 1750–1840*. Translated by Jocelyn Phelps. Cambridge: Polity Press, 1994.

Dudgeon, R.E. *The Swimming Baths of London*. London: Henry Turner and Co., 1870.

HMSO. *Queen's Regulations and Orders for the Army*. London: Horse Guards, 1868.

———. *1880 Addenda to The Queen's Regulations and Admiralty Instructions of 1879*. London: Admiralty, 1880.

Hern, Anthony. *The Seaside Holiday: The History of the English Seaside Resort*. London: The Cresset Press, 1967.

Hort, A.F. 'The School Bathing Place'. In *Harrow School*. edited by Edmund W. Howson and George Townsend Warner. London: Edward Arnold, 1898: 256–63.

Keil, Ian and Don Wix. *In the Swim: The Amateur Swimming Association from 1869 to 1994*. Loughborough: Swimming Times Ltd., 1996.

Lowerson, John. *Sport and the English Middle Classes 1870–1914*. Manchester: Manchester University Press, 1993.

Orme, Nicholas. *Early British Swimming 55 BC–AD 1719 with the First Swimming Treatise in English, 1595*. Exeter: Exeter University Press, 1983.

Otter Swimming Club. *Otter Swimming Club Centenary 1869–1969*. London: Otter Swimming Club, 1969.

Royal Humane Society. *Sixty-Ninth Annual Report of the Royal Humane Society*. London: RHS, 1843.

———. *Seventieth Annual Report of the Royal Humane Society*. London: RHS, 1844.

———. *One Hundredth Annual Report of the Royal Humane Society*. London: RHS, 1874.

———. *One Hundred and Eighth Annual Report of the Royal Humane Society*. London: RHS, 1882.

Sinclair, Archibald, and William Henry. *Swimming* (The Badminton Library of Sports and Pastimes). London: Longmans, Green, and Co., 1893.

Strutt, Joseph. *Glig-Gamena Angel Ðeod, or, The Sports and Pastimes of the People of England*. 1st edn. London, J. White, 1801.

Terret, Thierry. 'Professional Swimming in England, 1837–75'. *The International Journal of the History of Sport* 12, no. 1 (1995): 18–32.

Thomas, Ralph. *Swimming*. 2nd edn. London, Sampson Low, Marston & Company, 1904.

Walton, John K. *The English Seaside Resort: A Social History 1750–1914*. Leicester: Leicester University Press, 1983.

Walvin, James. *Beside the Seaside: A Social History of the Popular Seaside Holiday*. London: Allen Lane, 1978.

Swimming and Gender in the Victorian World

The debate over women's place in society grew ever louder in nineteenth-century England. The roles and place of both men and women in society were rigidly defined by a multitude of social conventions, and changes to these conventions proved difficult and time-consuming. The acceptance of women into areas of activity outside the home, at least for women of the middle and upper classes, was a highly contested area in English society throughout the nineteenth and twentieth centuries. Kathleen E. McCrone has written about the place of women in the sport and leisure world of that time:

> While women of various classes were never completely excluded from England's sporting life, women in sport were a social anomaly for centuries. Sport was considered essentially masculine, requiring physical and psychological attitudes and behaviour unnatural to respectable ladies, and thus beyond their proper sphere. In this as in so many other areas it was the nineteenth century that brought change. Women's entry into modern sport was related directly to the Victorian sporting revolution in which they demanded a share, and to the movement for women's rights which sought women's admission into spheres previously monopolized by men. By 1914, although participation was still limited by definitions of femininity, there was scarcely a sport that women had not tried. [1]

Swimming was one of those activities that women had become involved in, and they continued to participate up to the First World War. Not surprisingly then, as swimming reflected society in so many ways it also reflected the debate about the place of women within sport, and more generally English society, between 1800 and 1918.

Initially, swimming appears to have been a male preserve. Press reports about early swimming associations and societies uniformly refer to the members and participants in their events as being male. Women might sometimes be present for races as spectators, but often they were even absent or excluded from that role by the circumstances under which early races were organized. During the first few years of its existence the National Swimming Society, for example, held many of its races in the Serpentine. These races were usually held quite early in the morning, 6.00 or 6.30 being not uncommon starting times for such events. [2] It is highly unlikely that women were present for any of these races. Indeed, any woman found in the crowd watching such races at that hour would likely have been considered to be of dubious character. This tradition of staging races in the Serpentine, especially for male swimmers, remained a long-standing one. In 1864 the Serpentine Swimming Club was founded to provide an organization for those who enjoyed swimming in the lake. From its inception it ran an annual Christmas Day handicap race in the Serpentine that continues to this day. The club was exclusively male throughout the period under review. Women were only allowed access to the lido in Hyde Park, and thus the ability to swim in the Serpentine, in the 1930s. [3]

This general exclusion of women from organized, competitive, forms of swimming continued throughout most of the nineteenth century. To be more precise, 'respectable' women were excluded from competitive swimming for most of the century. Starting in the 1870s, and perhaps earlier, some working-class women started to break into the ranks of the professional swimming world. Invariably these were young, unmarried women, often the daughters of male swimming professionals. Initially these women acted as swimming instructors and performers in aquatic entertainments. [4]

The Question of Respectable Dress

The issue of gender was at its most obvious in the question of dress in the water. In the 1830s and earlier, when bathing at the seaside was the predominant form of swimming for people, nude bathing was common for men, and sometimes for women, although the wearing of long loose-fitting gowns akin to nightdresses by women bathers was also common. Over the course of the nineteenth century, attitudes towards nude bathing changed; it became much less acceptable and was ultimately banned outright at many bathing beaches by local authorities. For example nude bathing was banned at Margate in 1862. [5] At the same time as nude bathing was condemned, the practice of mixed bathing was also curbed. The exact extent of such mixed bathing at the seaside during the late Georgian and early Victorian periods is impossible to quantify. That mixed bathing was taking place, however, is incontrovertible; Corbin, Hern, and Walvin all make note of the practice taking place. [6] Certainly by the time of the introduction of the Baths and Washhouses Act, 1846, there was a legislative consensus against the practice, as according to schedule A of the act, any local authority implementing the act had also to enact by-laws that ensured people using baths, washhouses or public bathing places had 'adequate privacy' and further that men and boys of over the age of eight bathed separately from women, girls and children under the age of eight. [7] These provisions were further tightened and clarified with the passing of The Town Police Clauses Act, 1847. Clause 69 of that act explicitly required local authorities operating public bathing places to set limits on the areas where both men and women were allowed to bath, with adequate distance between the two areas so that there would be no 'indecent exposure' of the bathers. [8] In the context of both of these acts, bathing meant for the most part cleaning oneself in a bath, but would also have included swimming at open-air public bathing places. Thus before the middle of the nineteenth century, mixed bathing was essentially outlawed. Walvin, however, has noted that even as late as 1856 issues of decency at the seaside were still raised. In certain locations both men and women could observe the opposite sex bathing in the sea, sometimes in less than decent attire, from the beach or the promenade. Whether or not mixed bathing ever totally died out, therefore, is unknown, and unknowable. It seems likely that nude bathing continued in some locales, but convention and newly introduced legislation ensured that the practice was outlawed.

The public disapproval, at least among the middle and upper classes, that led to the suppression of mixed bathing was partly due to the rise of a highly regulated urban society, notably in the new seaside resorts, and the urge of local authorities to regulate local behaviour. [9] By the 1870s there were strict social codes in place, and sometimes legal ones as well, presumably to prevent the possibility of sexual arousal or titillation of any sort taking place when bathers of the opposite sex happened to meet each other on the way to their segregated swimming areas. Such strict enforcement, either through social codes or local regulation, was to continue in some areas until changing social forces in the mid-twentieth century brought about their reform. As shall be seen below, however, in other areas the suppression of mixed swimming was challenged as early as the 1890s, and with increasing success from 1900.

One way to ensure that public decency was preserved, aside from a strict segregation of the sexes while swimming, was the provision of swimming costumes for men and women. As has been noted by the early 1830s, provision had been made for women's attire while in the water, but men still swam in the nude. The various predecessor bodies of the Amateur Swimming Association (ASA) required the wearing of at least drawers in many of their championship races, but this practice was never made uniform and overarching for all activity promoted by these bodies or their affiliated clubs. [10]

All the ASA's predecessors, despite their claims to be national organizations, had struggled to achieve influence and control of swimming beyond London and the south of England. Once a stable governing body had been established for competitive swimming it was perhaps inevitable, given prevailing norms, that regulations governing acceptable swimming attire would be created. It was not, however, until after the formation of the Amateur Swimming Association took place in 1886 that overarching regulation of the issue was considered, and the first ASA costume law did not appear until 1890. This law was designed for men only, women not then being allowed to compete in public under ASA laws. At base, the regulation was designed to ensure public decency was maintained. The colours of a regulation costume were strictly limited to black, red or dark blue, drawers were to be worn underneath, shoulder straps were to be two inches wide or more, the front of the costume could not reach more than five inches below the base of the neck, and legs must extent at least four and half inches below the crotch. This first regulation issued by the ASA to govern the standard of swimwear provides a great deal of information about current practice in male swimming around 1890. The phrasing of the regulation strongly suggests that nude bathing, presumably among men, still continued and that swimming officialdom was concerned about this practice. The fact that it was men, not women, who swam in the nude can be deduced from a number of facts. For a start, in the 1890s the number of swimming races for women was extremely small, and they were almost uniformly private events. In addition, the drive for women covering up their bodies while swimming had been much greater from an earlier date. The tradition of independent, male, swimming clubs hosting local events in their baths during training times, with no audience present, was a tradition reaching back to the 1860s and perhaps before. In private men's competitions, men often swam in the nude with no concern for modesty or respectability, the matter being an established practice. The concern for propriety and respectability is revealed in section (b), where the requirement for drawers under the costume is noted. Early swimming costumes were notorious for their habit of clinging to the body of swimmers when wet and for the tendency of the predominantly wool costumes of the period from the early 1890s through the 1920s to become transparent when wet after a few uses. The final 'NB' of the regulation reveals another very important point of information: costumes were commercially manufactured by this time. The ASA. was attempting to impose its regulations on an already existing trade, rather than setting up regulation before there was a large established market for the product in question. Manufacturers had already seen a growing market for costumes and produced the garments accordingly. [11]

In 1899 the ASA revised the costume law to take into account female swimmers. For the most part, the regulations framed in 1890 for men were retained, with minor additions being inserted to ensure that women's costumes were 'decent'. Women's costumes were required to have a minimum of a three-inch sleeve and were required to be straight cut around the neck, ensuring that no skin on the chest was showing. [12]

Costume regulations were further refined in May 1900, when it was decided to allow only costumes that were black or dark blue from that point forward in official competitions. [13] Exactly why this change was made is unclear, but since swimwear manufacturers today still struggle to prevent transparency in red fabrics used for swimwear it is perhaps not hard to surmise. At the same time that the range of colours in approved swimwear was being restricted, the ASA was also instituting policy in regard to how swimming entertainments and galas should be conducted. One rule of the suggested competition code was designed to deal harshly with those infringing the costume regulations:

> 18. **Costumes.** – The regulation Costumes must be worn when ladies are present at Galas. (Law 61.) The leg portions must not be turned up (Law 61, Section H), and drawers must be worn underneath. (Law 61, Section B.)
>
> Any Competitor who is discovered to have swam without drawers, or with the leg portion turned up is thereby disqualified, and the promoters of the Meeting must report him to the Association. [14]

Public decency was evidently taken quite seriously, and the penalties for breaching the regulations severe. Being referred to the association could mean suspension as an amateur, the ultimate sanction that the ASA executive committee could wield. It is interesting that the regulation cited refers specifically to competitions where 'ladies' were present. This would seem to indicate that there was only concern about men swimming in the nude and thus provoking scandal in mixed company. If both men and women were swimming nude as a matter of course in private competitions, it would be expected that the regulation would have read along the lines of 'The regulation Costumes must be worn when *mixed* company is present at Galas' or something similar. Evidently, even as late as 1901, men were still able to swim in the nude, or only in drawers, in competitions where women were not present. Further, the phrasing of the rule would seem to indicate that all women by this time were swimming in costume as a matter of course, and there was no need to specify that women need wear costumes when men or 'gentlemen' came to view their competitions or entertainments.

By 1909 the ASA costume regulations had been further revised, especially in regard to the provisions for female swimmers. These were the last changes to the law prior to the First World War, and represent the most restrictive set of costume regulations set by the ASA. These regulations explicitly defined the drawers that all swimmers were expected to wear under their costume, and added the requirement that female competitors over the age of 14 had to wear a dressing gown up to the point of starting a race, and immediately upon exiting the pool after a race. [15]

It is clear therefore that throughout the period from 1890 to 1918 there was increasing regulation of what swimmers could wear, at least when swimming in competitions sanctioned by the ASA. In fact, the restrictions enacted by the ASA were widely disseminated throughout recreational swimming as well. When the Manchester Baths and Washhouses committee decided to trial mixed swimming in the city it adopted the ASA definition of costume as the only type of costume to be allowed during mixed swimming sessions. [16]

Interestingly, while the ASA was attempting to restrict the amount of choice swimmers had in their costumes, particularly for female swimmers, the trend within society at large was beginning to turn in the opposite direction. Throughout the period from the 1870s to the 1930s there was a movement demanding that women be able to dress 'rationally', and that many societal restrictions on women's dress be relaxed. This debate affected swimming as much as, if not more than, other areas of English sport. Increasingly, the debate focussed more on the style and amount of body coverage provided by women's costumes as opposed to both women's and men's dress in the water. To a degree this was part of the broader movement among women's activists for rational dress in general. [17] These debates about gender and dress did not apply solely to women, for male swimmers were also subject to certain restrictions. Initially, as has been noted, the uniform regulations for swimmers set out by the ASA made no distinction about dress between men and women. Both sexes were required to wear costumes that abided by the same regulation, and it was considered just as important for the male body to be hidden from view as much as possible as it was for the female body to be obscured. Intended to hide as much of the body as possible, approved costumes were designed with public sensibilities in mind, not performance in the water.

Just how far this concept of respectability and modesty took precedence over performance is made clear in a column on swimming from 1915. In it the author reveals the interesting fact that English female swimmers were particularly hampered when it came to competition, whether domestic or international, by the fact that ASA costume regulations required a four-inch sleeve on all women's bathing costumes – the only country in the world to impose such a requirement. [18] In fact the costume regulations of the ASA show that the minimum sleeve length was three inches, not four, as the author suggested. But there was clearly a difference between what English women were required to wear and their international rivals. [19] This distinction stands as an example of the concern for modesty at the heart of English swimming culture, and even in English society at large.

All began to change after the First World War. The social upheavals of that war – for example, in this case, the impact of women's work on women's dress – saw a swift and almost universal change in women's clothing and styles. During the 1920s and 1930s standards and practice began to diverge in what was allowed for men and women to wear when swimming. In part this was because of the cult of sunbathing, which emerged in the 1920s and which inevitably led to a change in style, with greater areas of the body exposed to the sun. [20] Increasingly, women wore what they liked when bathing at the various lidos and beaches in England. The ASA., however, maintained a strict attitude towards what was acceptable for competitors to wear. It was not until after the Second World War that there was an almost complete break from past practice for swimwear for both men and women and ASA. costume law was relaxed somewhat. [21]

Women and Competitive Swimming

Competitive speed swimming has probably always been the form of aquatic sport with the largest number of participants in England. Water polo and life-saving may have approached speed swimming's popularity, but without firm figures this is merely speculation. Certainly diving and synchronized swimming cannot ever have come close to having the same number of participants. As the dominant aquatic sport, speed swimming has also been the discipline with the most overt regulation of men and women. While regulation of the sport dates from the formation of the Associated Metropolitan Swimming Clubs (AMSC) in 1869, codification of rules and their underlying social conventions really began in earnest in the 1880s after the settlement of the amateur-professional debate in the swimming world. A clear division between men and women is immediately evident here. While swimming championships for men date to 1869 and the foundation of the English amateur men's mile championship, the first official ASA championship for women was not started until 1901. This was despite the fact that women had been engaged in recreational swimming across the country since at least the 1870s, and likely earlier, and may have been hosting their own competitions in the later 1880s and through the 1890s. The first women's championship was much shorter than the men's mile event, being only of 100 yards distance, and the prize for this first women's championship was a silver vase, donated by the Ravensbourne Swimming Club, compared to the traditional silver championship cup used for men's events. [22] By 1904 the ASA recognized 13 separate events for the purpose of ratifying sporting records: 12 of these – the 100 yards, 150 yards, 220 yards, 300 yards, 440 yards, 500 yards, 880 yards, 1,000 yards, one mile, 150 yards back, 150 yards breast and plunging – were for men only. The only women's event for which records were ratified was still the 100 yards. [23] This divergence in the number of championships recognized for each gender continued until after 1918.

Speed swimming today, like athleticism in general, is a highly scientific business, with training programmes individually designed for each swimmer so that he or she reaches peak physical condition for major competitions. Most competitive swimmers retire before they enter their 30s due to the stress and strain of constant training. In the period between 1870 and 1918 we can see the origins of the same trend. As in most of the sports and activities that appeared during the explosion of Victorian games, participation in the most demanding activities at the highest level was left for males under the age of 30. Swimming activities for those keen to compete, but not able to maintain the pace at the highest level, became necessary. This led to the eventual development in the 1870s and 1880s of diving, synchronized swimming and water polo as separate and distinct areas of aquatic activity, followed by the development of aquatic life-saving in the 1890s. Of more specialized form than simple competitive swimming, these activities attracted less interest than the dominant activity, and the development of each of these activities involved restrictions and conventions based on gender to a greater or lesser extent than had existed in competitive swimming.

Of these disciplines, it is likely that diving had the longest history, for it is probable that for as long as people have been swimming they have been diving into the water in order to begin their swims. Despite this, diving appears to have been, and continues to be, the most marginal of the aquatic sports in England. Being an activity that relies as much, if not more, on gymnastic ability than swimming skill, and requiring specialized equipment in the form of springboards and towers, it can only be properly practised in facilities with the appropriate amenities. Throughout the period under review those facilities were generally lacking in England, and the diving that did exist was initially a male-only sport, just as swimming had been earlier in the century.

Synchronized swimming provides an even more interesting study of gender relations and segregation within English society. The modern form of synchronized swimming that we know today is a product of developments in North America during the inter-war period of the 1920s and 1930s. The origins of the activity, however, can be traced to nineteenth-century England. Originally, synchronized swimming was known as 'graceful swimming', 'ornamental swimming' or 'scientific swimming', and its practitioners were exclusively male. Many of the original techniques of the discipline were created by swimming professionals in the 1850s and 1860s, if not earlier. [24] By the 1880s, however, control of the discipline was passing from professionals to amateurs, as was generally the case for the rest of the aquatic world. Scientific swimming contained most of the basic elements now associated with synchronized swimming, along with unique activities which later fell out of fashion. Some typical activities of scientific swimming would include staying in one spot without sinking (treading water), moving while floating (sculling), somersaults in the water, smoking while swimming, smoking underwater (!) and so on. Initially, the parlour-trick aspects of scientific swimming, such as eating while swimming or eating underwater, were included to impress audiences at swimming galas. These tricks, however, must have become boring after being viewed a couple of times, and this probably explains why they disappeared from the later repertoire of synchronized swimming. The fact that scientific swimming did not rely upon speed or excessive strength for most of its feats made it the ideal activity to be pursued by swimmers who were either older and unable to compete as effectively in races, or for those with no interest in racing. The activity was seen as being a less strenuous one for middle-aged males.

Over time, this reputation as a less strenuous activity, however, made scientific swimming an obvious, and increasingly popular, activity for women to take up, privately at first and then, as restrictions loosened, in public. By 1900 women could be seen providing the entertainments and demonstrations of scientific swimming at swimming club galas. By the 1920s and 1930s popular aquatic revues and films coming out of Hollywood had turned scientific swimming into synchronized swimming and into an all-female activity. The price for this takeover by women, however, was the social marginalization of the activity. While vigorously pursued within a female sphere, synchronized swimming was denied status within a male-dominated sporting and leisure world. It was not until the 1980s that the sport gained demonstration and then full medal Olympic status.

At the time when women's swimming in England was beginning to be recognized as a competitive activity, the modern Olympic Games had emerged, and the socially codified understandings of the differences between men and women in swimming were internationalized. Although there were influences from the swimming traditions of many different countries in the regulations decided upon at each Olympiad, there certainly appears to have been a dominant British influence in the general trend of framing the rules. The first games, in Athens, included four, all-male, speed swimming events. The number and type of events over the next games, in 1900, 1904, and 1908, were varied, but were also exclusively male. After the International Amateur Swimming Federation, better known as FINA, was founded in London during the 1908 Olympiad, it adopted in 1909 most of the ASA.'s regulations as the basis for international swimming regulation. [25] It was at the 1912 Stockholm games that women were admitted for the first time as competitors in aquatic events, being eligible to compete in diving and speed swimming. Significantly, in the speed swimming events, however, the men swam seven events, while the women only swam two. Even more importantly, perhaps, the two events women were allowed to participate in were the 100-metre freestyle and the 400-metre freestyle relay (100 metres each for four competitors), equivalent to the 100 yards championship distance recognized in England. Therefore no one woman competitor swam more than 100 metres at a time in this competition. The men, on the other hand, swam individual distance events of up to 1500 metres and relay distances of up to 200 metres per swimmer. Nowhere was the cultural belief in the greater strength and stamina of the male versus the general weakness and frailty of the female more clearly illustrated.

Provision for Women's Bathing

Quite early on it seems to have been decided that female swimmers did not require the same amount of space to swim in, or the same amount of swimming time, as male swimmers. In 1873, when the Clapham and Brixton Baths were under construction in London, the men's swimming pool was reported to be 150 feet by 60 feet, while the women's swimming pool was only 65 feet by 30 feet, less than a quarter of the area. [26] In Manchester, women's pools, where they were provided within baths facilities, were always smaller than the men's pools in the same facility, usually significantly so. With the sole, and notable, exception of the Leaf Street Baths, it was not until 1906 that women's pools in Manchester began to be constructed with dimensions close to those used for men's swimming pools. [27] The provision of smaller pools for women appears to have been general across England. At the Lambeth Public Baths, for example, opened in 1897, there were three swimming pools. Two were designated as male pools and one was designated a women's pool. The two men's pools were both larger than the women's pool: the first-class men's pool was 132 feet by 40 feet, the second-class men's pool was 90 feet by 30 feet, and the women's pool was only 56 feet by 25 feet. [28] When the time came to decide if all three pools were to be kept open over the winter season, it was decided to close both men's baths, leaving only the much smaller women's pool open to be used as a first- and second-class men's pool and a women's pool, in rotation. [29] Exactly what schedule was arranged for use of the women's pool in that winter is not clear. The following winter it was decided that the men's first-class swimming pool would become a hall, the men's second-class swimming pool would remain open and the women's pool would function as a women's first-class pool one day a week, as a women's second-class pool one day a week and as the men's first-class swimming pool for the other four days a week that it was open. [30] Even by the winter of 1911–12 women were still receiving less pool time than men. For that winter season, women's swimming was restricted to 9.00 to 14.00 on Tuesdays and Thursdays, and 14.00 to 21.00 on Wednesdays and Fridays in the first-class swimming pool. Men could swim in the first-class swimming pool from 8.00 to 21.00 on Mondays and Saturdays, 8.00 to 9.00 and 14.00 to 21.00 on Tuesdays and Thursdays, and 8.00 to 14.00 on Wednesdays and Fridays. For this winter, however, the men's second-class swimming pool was closed, so the difference in provision was not as great as previously. [31] The difference is shown not only in official printed material, but also in press articles that refer to the contrasts between male and female provision. In September 1915 'Lady Dorothy' wrote a column in *The Swimming Magazine* complaining about the general lack of consideration shown to women swimmers and women's swimming clubs. She noted that it was still common practice for women's swimming pools in recently-built baths establishments to be half the size of a men's pool in the same facility. When this was the case, women were also generally charged the same sum for admission as the men for entry to their bath. In facilities where men and women had to share the use of the same bath on a rotating basis, she condemned the practice of men, and men's swimming clubs, receiving preference in the allocation of hours for club and general swimming times. [32]

That there was such a restriction placed on the provision of swimming facilities for women was ironic considering the generally beneficial role swimming was increasingly believed to play in a woman's health and well-being from the 1870s onwards. This came to the fore in the issue of children's well-being. The physical education of children became an important topic in the later half of the nineteenth century, especially after the creation of the state elementary education system. Special attention was paid to the health and physical well-being of girls and young women. Sometimes complex arguments were made about the amount of exercise required by girls and young married and unmarried women, and the exact form that exercise should take. It was generally agreed that swimming was a suitable activity for females to undertake, for many different reasons. Patricia Vertinsky's comments on this subject are insightful:

> Although few women could actually swim, swimming came to be extolled as an excellent sport, always provided that the exercise was not too violent and the bathing costume was modest. From the health and character points of view, cold bathing was regarded as a particularly good tonic for the circulation. Sea bathing came to be medically recommended to women with menstruation pains and as a means of increasing fertility. With its educative effects of cultivating the willpower, its predicted possibilities of increasing fertility, the opportunity for developing muscular strength and endurance, and the added bonus of cleanliness, recreational swimming epitomized medically appropriate sportive exercise for the modern woman. [33]

Indeed, by 1870 the topic of appropriate physical education activities for girls in the newly created or supported state elementary schools was deemed important enough to be raised at election rallies for the boards created to run the new schools system. In November 1870, Dr Elizabeth Garrett, MD, later Dr Elizabeth Garrett Anderson, the famous Victorian woman doctor and medical theorist, stood as a candidate for the School Board of St Marylebone. At an election rally held on 11 November 1870 she was asked a question about physical education and swimming. Dr Garrett was a prominent supporter of physical education for girls and women, and she is reported to have responded to the question by stating, 'she thought physical education was necessary, especially for girls, and she said so strongly did she think swimming necessary that she had practised for many years to acquire facility in the art'. [34]

This belief in the special virtues of swimming for women's fitness and health was prominent from the 1870s until after the end of the First World War. In 1879 Mrs Hoggan, MD, an early female doctor, made a speech to the Women's Union Swimming Club which was later distributed in pamphlet form. Her arguments illustrate the importance that was attached to swimming as a means of promoting women's health during this period. She opened her speech by stating:

> I propose to consider the influence of swimming on the health of women, and I hope to be able to show that, so far from being of less value to women than it is men, it is, if possible, more necessary to them as a counterpoise to their more sedentary employments and physically less active life. [35]

Mrs Hoggan held that swimming was good exercise for the lungs, freed women from the constraints of stays and corset and allowed women to use their muscles in a natural, much healthier, manner. [36] These general benefits could also to a greater or lesser extent be applied to male swimmers, so Mrs Hoggan also included a list of special benefits only obtained by female swimmers. In this section of her speech she argued that women in general tended to have weaker muscles than men, so the exercise derived from swimming was of greater benefit. Also lack of exercise among women was common, especially among those idle during the day, and this promoted 'internal congestions' in these women; swimming, therefore, would work against this problem. Further, swimming also allowed the exercise of a wide variety of muscles, while women used but few muscles during their daily routines. In addition, Hoggan argued that women's chests were inferior in volume to men's and their nervous systems less stable. The general inactivity of most women's lifestyles could increase these problems. The exercise undertaken while swimming increased the chest volume of women and the water they swam in acted as a tonic to help restore balance to a woman's nervous system. Finally, Mrs Hoggan pointed out that swimming allowed a woman to wear sensible dress, freeing her from the general constraints that clothing placed upon a woman of the period. Because of all of these benefits, she argued that swimming should not be limited to men only, but opened up to women who would benefit even more from the activity. In new baths facilities there should be provision for at least one women's swimming pool alongside the men's pool or pools. Where no separate women's pool was provided in a facility, time should be set aside daily for women to be able to swim. [37] We cannot tell how widespread such views were, but it is clear enough that the medical and social virtues of swimming for females were publicly discussed. They were, in essence, part of the much broader debate about the rights and role of women in contemporary society.

By the 1890s swimming was becoming a widespread activity among women of the middle classes of English society, and Mrs Hoggan's views appear to have become widespread. Kathleen McCrone has written of the period from 1890 to 1914 as one where middle-class English women began to challenge societal expectations and engage in sporting activities in large numbers. She has noted:

> Prior to 1914 women and girls from almost all sections of English society took part in various forms of calisthenics and gymnastics. But the female dimension of the sporting revolution was primarily middle-class, for it was women of the middle ranks whose sporting consciousness was awakened first by educational and recreational experiences, who had the free time and financial means participation required, and who, despite numerous impediments related to the patriarchal nature of social relations and restrictive perceptions of femininity, began to 'play the game' by the thousands. In comparison women of the working classes were much less involved, because the requisite schooling, money, and time for leisure activities were lacking, and because of their subservient relationships with men of their own class and with women of higher classes. [38]

As late as 1914 opinion was still divided within the general medical community over exactly how much exercise women should indulge in, and what form that exercise should take. Dr Elizabeth Sloan-Chesser, MD, another early female medical pioneer, was especially active during this period. Although accepting the dominant male medical model of women being disadvantaged because of their sex, compared to many of her fellow female medical practitioners of the time, Dr. Sloan-Chesser also advocated swimming as one of the desirable exercises that would allow women to keep themselves strong and healthy. This would allow English women to bear healthy children and thus help preserve the Empire. [39] In 1915, an article in *The Swimming Magazine* reported,

> Women are realising more and more the benefits of the art of swimming. Medical and physical culture authorities regard it as one of the most health-giving, grace-producing and beneficial exercises in which a girl can indulge. One reason why swimming, although the most artificial exercise we take, is of the best is because it puts the body in an entirely different position from the normal one. It offers perfect relaxation to every part and a change of movement for practically all the muscles coming into use, while it brings into action some that are seldom taxed in ordinary daily activities. In addition to these advantages the knowledge of swimming and life saving helps to create confidence and courage, both of which are particularly essential during the boating and bathing season or in cases of accident. [40]

Mixed Bathing

The question of mixed bathing and swimming remained a very vexed one throughout the period. As has already been mentioned, prior to 1800 it would appear that mixed bathing, while not common, did take place from time to time. By the time civic corporations began to build baths and swimming pools, following the introduction of the Baths and Washhouses Act, 1846, however, mixed bathing was not countenanced.

The question of allowing mixed bathing, at least for members of the same family, was reawakened in the last decade of the nineteenth century. Between 1890 and 1918 the calls for the provision of mixed bathing, or family bathing, became increasingly frequent, and were often successful. [41] By this time the enforced segregation of men and women within public swimming facilities was an accepted norm, enforced in law in many locations. At issue was the question of whether a strict segregation of the sexes was required to maintain proper social decency and modesty, or if it was acceptable to allow mixed, or family, bathing so that a father or husband could engage in recreation with his family and teach his children or wife how to swim. By 1893 only limited success had been achieved by those who advocated mixed bathing, at the very least, for families. Sinclair and Henry could write of provision at the time,

> There are a few places in England, such as Sea View, in the Isle of Wight, where whole families bathe together in the sea, but this pleasure is almost totally prohibited, either by beach regulations or custom, throughout Great Britain. Such an absurd veto is an abuse which needs remedying. [42]

Early photographic evidence, however, suggests that families, parents and children, did bathe in the sea together at some seaside resorts.

At the end of the summer of 1898 a short news item in *The Swimming Magazine* reported that there had been a distinct lack of bathing machines compared to the number of people waiting to swim at Margate during the past swimming season. The author of the article went on to express the opinion that, because mixed bathing was now taking place almost everywhere along the coast, it was time to use tents for changing on the beach, with bathers to wear towels around themselves to the water's edge. Men should also be required to wear university-style costume as opposed to simply drawers. [43] From this article we gain an important insight into the state of mixed bathing at the time. Allowing for exaggeration on the part of the author, it seems clear that at a good number of seaside resorts mixed bathing of some form or other was common. Public decency was still catered for by the fact that bathing machines were used to transport swimmers from the shore out into the surf, but demand for access to swimming was outstripping the supply of machines, at least at Margate. Further, both men and women were wearing costumes when swimming from these bathing machines, but men were still able to offend public decency as they were only wearing drawers, rather than full costume. This was in stark contrast to the state of affairs existing in indoor swimming facilities, where strict segregation was still the order of the day. Still, it is clear that in some ways a move was being made towards an unsegregated swimming world, at least at the seaside. As Walvin has noted, Bexhill became one of the first resorts to allow mixed bathing in 1901. [44]

It was different in municipal swimming pools. Most local authorities enacted legislation quite early to prevent any undermining of public morals from occurring in their facilities. Indeed, as has already been mentioned, such regulation was required by law. Manchester City Council, for example, instituted a by-law as soon as it established baths in the city to the effect that men and women were to use all parts of the baths buildings separately. [45] Similarly, after Lambeth Borough Council in London finally opened its own baths in 1897 a similar regulation was in force no later than 1900. [46]

While some progress was made prior to the First World War in regard to the provision for mixed bathing, by and large swimming remained a sexually segregated activity. This was true of all levels of swimming, from municipal pools to competitive swimming. Swimming as a competitive activity, along with the derived activities of diving and water polo, was created for the most part as a male enterprise in England between 1800 and 1918. The participation of women in these activities was neither forbidden nor unknown, but it was effectively marginalized. Competitive swimming appears to have had the greatest number of female participants, but this did not translate into competitive excellence or widespread women's recreational swimming. Excellence and innovation in such competitive swimming was found elsewhere, notably in Australia and the United States of America, rather than in England. Richard Holt has claimed that this was due to the relative lack of class distinctions in swimming, at least in the case of the United States. [47] This may indeed be the case, but closer study would appear to be necessary. In the field of synchronized swimming, female participation appears to have been more common, but prior to 1918 the activity was a relatively minor one at best in England, for both men and women. Major development of the sport again took place away from England, in North America. It developed into a bastion of female participation, effectively becoming a women-only activity, but at the cost of marginalization in the sporting world.

Recreational swimming was the most common form of swimming for women from the 1870s onwards. Few absolute records of exact numbers of women involved in swimming exist, but Agnes Campbell's survey of municipal baths facilities published in 1918 provides a glimpse of the activity's popularity. The data tables in her appendix reveal literally tens of thousands of women were using municipal swimming pools by 1913–14. As in the case of life-saving, the number of women swimming formed a minority of those using municipal swimming pools, but the absolute numbers were large. We also cannot be certain that the published figures do not include repeat visits to the same facilities by a smaller number of women. Even if true, however, the high attendance figures given would seem to indicate that a large number of women were involved. [48]

Clearly, this sexual divide in swimming reflected more fundamental divisions in English society. Societal expectations and taboos restricted and shaped those activities that women could participate in. Studying how the Victorians and Edwardians established, structured and maintained these gender divisions provides some further illumination on gender divisions within the wider English society of the period, as well as helping reveal how swimming as an activity fitted into that whole.

Notes

[1] McCrone, 'Emancipation or Recreation?', 204–5.
[2] For the early starting of the various races staged by the NSS see *Bell's Life in London*, 19 July 1840, 4e, and 11 July 1841, 4d.
[3] Titmus, *Breaking the Ice*, 25 and *passim*. See also Sinclair and Henry, *Swimming*, 169–70.
[4] For a listing of professionals in England in 1878, including seven women, see *Bicycle Journal, Swimming and General Athletic & Pedestrian Recorder*, enlarged series, 1, no. 106 (21 Aug. 1878), 7.
[5] See Hern, *The Seaside Holiday*, 36–7.
[6] Corbin, *The Lure of the Sea*, 73–85; Hern, *The Seaside Holiday*, 5, 21–37, and plates 1, 2, and 9; Walvin, *Beside the Seaside*, 71–2.
[7] 9 & 10 Vict., c. 74, schedule A.
[8] 10 & 11 Vict., c. 89, clause 69.
[9] See Corbin, *The Lure of the Sea, passim*; Hern, *The Seaside Holiday*, 21–39.
[10] Amateur Swimming Association Library (ASAL), miscellaneous competition programmes dating from 1875 to 1882. These items are held loose and unorganized on the shelves of the library. See also, for example, Minute Book no. 3, The Swimming Association of Great Britain, 58, Minutes of 8 Aug. 1881, glued in programme of the 1881 Mile Amateur Championship, hereafter cited as Minute Book no. 3 SAGB.
[11] ASAL, ASA Minute Book no. 2, fols. 8–9.
[12] ASA, *Handbook for 1899*, 42–3.
[13] ASA, *Handbook for 1901*, 42–3, 99.
[14] Ibid., 94. Bold text is present in the original.
[15] ASA, *Handbook for 1909*, 44–5.
[16] Manchester Local Studies Archives Service, Central Library, Manchester (hereafter MLSAS), Baths and Wash Houses Committee Minutes, Vol.16, fols. 144–5, minutes of 8 July 1914.
[17] On the topic of 'rational dress', see McCrone, 'Emancipation or Recreation?', 204–29; McCrone, *Sport and the Physical Emancipation of English Women*; Park, 'Sport, Dress Reform and the Emancipation of Women'; and Vertinsky, *The Eternally Wounded Woman*.
[18] Lady Dorothy, 'The Ladies Section', *The Swimming Magazine* 2, no. 5 (Oct. 1915), 89.
[19] For example see the photographs of female competitive swimmers from the period given in Keil and Wix, *In the Swim*, 36–7, 187; and Gonsalves and LaMondia, *First to the Wall*, 29–30.
[20] For the origins of the sun worship craze see Walvin, *Beside the Seaside*, 120–1.
[21] By 1933 the ASA costume law had been relaxed from its previous rigorous enforcement of exact leg lengths and widths of shoulder straps, but there was still a requirement for costumes to be of one piece and non-transparent. Drawers or slips still had to be worn under costumes, and female competitors were required to wear bathrobes before and after competing in races. ASA, *Handbook for 1933*, 53.
[22] ASA, *Handbook for 1901*, 65.
[23] ASA, *Handbook for 1904*, 118.

[24] See Aquarius [Robert Patrick Watson], 'A Retrospect', *The Swimming, Rowing, and Athletic Record* 1, no. 1 (10 May 1873), 1–2.
[25] ASA, *Handbook for 1910*, 131–9.
[26] *The Swimming Record and Chronicle of Sporting Events* 1, no. 13 (2 Aug. 1873), 2.
[27] Campbell, *Report on Public Baths*, appendix 50–63.
[28] Lambeth Archives Minet Library (hereafter LAML), P12/80/10, *A Souvenir of the 9th July 1897. From the Clerk to The Chairman*. This is an oversized commemorative volume containing the programme of the opening ceremony and various photographs taken on the day.
[29] LAML, P12/41, Lambeth Baths and Washhouses Committee Minutes 1891–97, 216, minutes of 21 Sept. 1897.
[30] LAML, P12/38, Lambeth Baths and Cemetery Committee Minutes 1898–14 Oct 1899, 101, minutes of 19 Sept. 1898.
[31] LAML, P12/80/11/1, winter 1911–12 bathing hours and costs (a small folded card).
[32] Lady Dorothy, 'The Ladies Section', *The Swimming Magazine* 2, no. 4 (Sept. 1915), 65.
[33] Vertinsky, *The Eternally Wounded Woman*, 82.
[34] *The Times*, 12 Nov. 1870, 6d.
[35] Hoggan, *Swimming and its Relation to the Health of Women*, 1.
[36] Ibid., 2–4.
[37] Ibid., 7–8.
[38] McCrone, 'Class, Gender, and English Women's Sport', 159.
[39] Vertinsky, *The Eternally Wounded Woman*, 153–5.
[40] *The Swimming Magazine* 1, no. 12 (May 1915), 8. The title *The Swimming Magazine* was used for two separate publications on swimming, the first ran from June 1898 to May 1899 and the second ran from June 1914 to May 1918.
[41] Family bathing was the allowing of males to swim with their female relations, usually limited to wives and daughters. Mixed bathing was the provision of swimming times where males and females unrelated to each other could swim in a pool at the same time.
[42] Sinclair and Henry, *Swimming*, 185.
[43] *The Swimming Magazine* 1, no. 4 (1 Sept. 1898), 31. University costume was simply another way of describing ASA regulation costume.
[44] Walvin, *Beside the Seaside*, 92.
[45] MLSAS, Proceedings of the Baths and Wash Houses Committee, vol. 1, 131, minutes of 4 July 1878.
[46] LAML, P12/80/7, Baths By-laws, Lambeth Baths By-laws for 1900.
[47] Holt, *Sport and the British*, 130.
[48] Campbell, *Report on Public Baths*, appendix.

References

ASA (Amateur Swimming Association). *Handbook for 1899*. London: Amateur Swimming Association, 1899.
———. *Handbook for 1901*. London: Amateur Swimming Association, 1901.
———. *Handbook for 1904*. London: Amateur Swimming Association, 1904.
———. *Handbook for 1910*. London: Amateur Swimming Association, 1910.
———. *Handbook for 1933*. Gloucester: ASA, 1933.
Campbell, Agnes. *Report on Public Baths and Wash-Houses in the United Kingdom*. Edinburgh: Edinburgh University Press, 1918.
Corbin, Alain. *The Lure of the Sea: The Discovery of the Seaside in the Western World, 1750–1840*. Translated by Jocelyn Phelps. Cambridge: Polity Press, 1994.

Gonsalves, Kelly and Susan LaMondia. *First to the Wall: 100 Years of Olympic Swimming*. East Longmeadow, MA: Freestyle Publications, 1999.

Hern, Anthony. *The Seaside Holiday: The History of the English Seaside Resort*. London: The Cresset Press, 1967.

Hoggan, Mrs. *Swimming and its Relation to the Health of Women*. London: Women's Printing Society Limited, 1879.

Holt, Richard. *Sport and the British: A Modern History*. Oxford: Oxford University Press, 1989.

Keil, Ian and Don Wix. *In the Swim: The Amateur Swimming Association from 1869 to 1994*. Loughborough: Swimming Times Ltd., 1996.

McCrone, Kathleen E. 'Class, Gender, and English Women's Sport, *c.* 1890–1914'. *Journal of Sport History* 18, no. 1 (Spring 1991): 159–82.

——. 'Emancipation or Recreation? The Development of Women's Sport at the University of London'. *The International Journal of the History of Sport* 7, no. 2 (1990): 204–29.

——. *Sport and the Physical Emancipation of English Women, 1870–1914*. London: Routledge, 1988.

Park, Jihang. 'Sport, Dress Reform and the Emancipation of Women in Victorian England: A Reappraisal'. *The International Journal of the History of Sport* 6, no. 1 (1989): 10–30.

Sinclair, Archibald, and William Henry. *Swimming* (The Badminton Library of Sports and Pastimes). London: Longmans, Green, and Co., 1893.

Titmus, Alan, ed. *Breaking the Ice*. London: Serpentine Swimming Club, 1964.

Vertinsky, Patricia. *The Eternally Wounded Woman: Women, Doctors and Exercise in the Late Nineteenth Century*. Manchester: Manchester University Press, 1990.

Walton, John K. *The English Seaside Resort: A Social History 1750–1914*. Leicester: Leicester University Press, 1983.

Walvin, James. *Beside the Seaside: A Social History of the Popular Seaside Holiday*. London: Allen Lane, 1978.

Social Class and the Swimming World: Amateurs and Professionals

Victorian and Edwardian England was a highly stratified society. The English became divided into distinct social classes, each with its own appointed place and duties within the overall social system. To a certain extent these social divisions were based on older relationships of leaders and followers, masters and servants, rulers and ruled. At the same time, however, they were increasingly defined by newer forces of economic standing, as the process of industrialization created a growing and rising middle and working class. Class came to affect all features of English life, and sport was no exception. Exactly what forms of sport, recreation and physical training were appropriate for these various classes became an issue in late Victorian England. Most importantly, sport became a forum for issues of social inclusion and exclusion. Like all other Victorian and Edwardian sports and recreational activities, swimming was subject to these social conventions. The manner in which competitive swimming came to be organized and the ideas underlying the provision of, and the regulations governing, public swimming facilities are but two of the many areas that illustrate these social codes at work.

Prior to the formation of the Amalgamated Metropolitan Swimming Clubs in January 1869, there seems to have been little or no distinction made between amateurs and professionals in swimming circles. Previously, swimming was simply an unregulated traditional leisure activity that shared many similarities with other traditional pastimes and sports. Betting, for example, was commonplace. [1] As with pedestrianism, the professionalized and semi-traditional form of athletics, betting on swimming contests prior to 1869 was accepted as a normal part of the event. The swimmers themselves would often place wagers on the outcome, and large purses were not uncommon. That said, betting occupied a twilight world in Victorian society. Betting at racecourses was legal throughout the period 1800 to 1918, as it has remained to this day. Street betting also appears to have been common, and remained legal until 1906, when Parliament passed an act outlawing it. Off-course betting, however, was a matter of concern. Although legal for the first half of the nineteenth century, betting houses run by bookmakers were fundamentally viewed with suspicion. Concern over betting houses was largely a matter of class. It appears to have been thought that the presence of betting houses corrupted the working classes, distracting them from work and contributing towards poverty. In 1853 Parliament made illegal all off-course betting in betting shops. The government of the day took the view, according to Carl Chinn, that 'while off-course betting with professional bookmakers needed to be prohibited, amateur wagering between individuals was legitimate and ought to be allowed'. [2] In essence then, the propertied classes were allowed to gamble but the working classes were not.

As early as May 1791, *The Times* recorded a swimming race held in the Thames for a wager of eight guineas. The race was considered noteworthy, not because of the prize involved or the swimming feat, but rather because the winner drank himself to death immediately after winning the race. Similar peculiar swimming stories appeared in the press between 1791 and the 1830s, covering such diverse events as a soldier swimming from Deal to Ramsgate in 1805 and a sailor swimming across Portsmouth Harbour in 1810. [3] Over time such contests began to be organized by self-promoting showmen who often dubbed themselves 'professors'.

Such 'professors' were often involved in early attempts to organize swimming in a more formal manner. When the National Swimming Society was formed in the late 1830s it immediately acquired the services of several 'professors', who provided swimming lessons in the Serpentine, the Surrey Canal and the Thames. [4] Initially, all of these 'professors' were simply unknown individuals, relegated to passing notice in the press, but by 1840 there was sufficient interest in swimming for such 'professors' to be working at their trade full-time, and some were acquiring personal reputations for their activity. One such noted professional was Captain Stevens, the resident professional at the 'National Baths', Westminster Road, in Lambeth. In 1842 he ran a notice in the press about a benefit being held for himself in the National Baths. [5] This seems to be the earliest appearance of the use of the term 'benefit' to describe a swimming contest or, more usually, an entertainment, with the financial proceeds given to the designated beneficiary. Such benefits were often designed to supplement the income of a swimming 'professor', which was generally seasonal and irregular. By the late nineteenth century the tradition had developed of holding an annual benefit for the professional resident at a bath, or in the employ of a swimming club. At this early date, however, it would appear such benefits were organized by a professional whenever he felt the need to hold one. Captain Stevens clearly needed the extra money from a benefit; less than a year later he was imprisoned in debtors' prison, allegedly for financially over-extending himself while promoting swimming. He was eventually freed, perhaps because of an appeal for donations towards his release that appeared in *Bell's Life*. Whatever the case, he went on in 1844 to create the grandly titled 'Royal Universal Swimming Society', which seems to have disappeared after hosting only one swimming competition. [6] Professional status, and publicity in the press did not, however, guarantee success. Up to the middle of the 1840s the press coverage of swimming was overwhelmingly concerned with events where wagers were placed or of races promoted by showmen such as Captain Stevens. Organized swimming, therefore, could best be described as being in the hands of the professionals, and it would appear that those involved in swimming as a sport were not overly concerned with distinctions between amateurs and professionals. It was more a form of commercial entertainment.

John Lowerson has noted that it was not long before the great sporting boom of the 1870s and 1880s that the idea of the amateur athlete, as distinct from the professional athlete, was formed. [7] Swimming follows this trend, with the amateur governing body not formed until 1869. There were precursors to this development, however, and it seems likely that it was during the 1850s that an early, explicit distinction began to emerge between amateurs and professionals. As we have seen, by the late 1840s these swimming professionals, many originally oarsmen or boatmen, organized grand swimming entertainments which attracted a great deal of betting. Some professionals were extremely fast swimmers and clearly made a good living from winnings; others were only adequate swimmers but much better as showmen and promoters. Various allegations were later made about race fixing and other less than honourable activities at these meetings, but contemporary accounts rarely mention any hint of such deeds. News about betting, however, was common until well after the division of swimmers into amateur and professional ranks occurred from the late 1860s onwards.

A number of these men, 'Doctor' Isaac Bedale (Manchester), Harry Gurr (Manchester), Frederick Beckwith (Margate, eventually London), Frederick Cavill (London, then Australia), Harry Parker (London) and J.B. Johnson (Manchester, later Leeds), set themselves up as swimming professionals around the country. Frederick Beckwith, better known as Professor Beckwith, was arguably the most prolific of these professionals. According to some reports Beckwith was the foremost swimmer of his era, while according to others he was not the fastest of swimmers. [8] Whatever his level of swimming ability and speed, however, he definitely had a keen grasp of showmanship and promotion. He also seems to have been shrewd in the swimming challenges he accepted during his racing career. In 1861, for example, he arranged a swimming match against Deerfoot, a Native American running champion, which eventually was forfeited by Deerfoot before the race was swum. [9] Over time he included all four of his children – Agnes, Charles, Jessie, and William – in his spectacular shows. William was an active professional racer for a time, and both Charles and Agnes later became well-known swimmers in their own right. [10]

Frederick Beckwith's career is important in a number of respects, because it spans the main period of massive growth that occurred in sport in general and swimming in particular in the 1870s and 1880s. Beckwith also remained in the public eye throughout the entire period, eventually presenting aquatic entertainments to the

British Royal Family. [11] An advertisement for one of his entertainments would usually read much like this one from May 1873:

> PROFESSOR BECKWITH, LAMBETH BATHS, WESTMINSTER BRIDGE ROAD. This Celebrated Ex-Champion Swimming Teacher begs to inform the nobility and gentry that he is constantly in attendance at the above magnificent Establishment. Beckwith wishes it known that he has given considerably over 300 prizes towards furthering the interests of this art, and to prove the excellency of his teaching, points to the many celebrated swimmers brought out by him, both amateur and professional. N.B. – there will shortly be a great gala on the Thames, and races (open to the world) for all classes. [12]

This advertisement again reveals the division between amateurs and professionals in swimming by the 1870s. It also reveals the place of swimming professionals within the wider world of swimming. A 'professor' such as Beckwith was perfectly able to provide instruction to those who considered themselves, and who were viewed as, amateurs. Such a professional could hope for, and even expect, patronage from the nobility, provided he conducted himself in an appropriate fashion. Beckwith also positioned himself as an upright and trustworthy individual by emphasizing his generosity through the award of a number of prizes in promotion of swimming. Throughout, however, Beckwith kept an eye on his finances. Swimming was his business, and he attempted to be as shrewd as possible while conducting that business. Whether it was managing his children's careers, or promoting an entertainment, Beckwith always sought to enhance his name and image and profit from the venture. Note, for example, an advertisement Beckwith placed in the press in July 1873:

> THE LATE CHALLENGE FROM THE BOY BECKWITH TO J. B. JOHNSON, AND THOSE WHO SWAM IN THE SERPENTINE RACE.
> Professor Beckwith acknowledges having, by some means, made a great mistake. His son possesses no chance with 20 yards start in 1,000 yards, from J.B. Johnson, but he will take 100 yards in that distance for any fair stake. W. Beckwith is under 15 years of age, and his father sends this second challenge, not wishing to run down Johnson's swimming powers. The challenge is correct as regards the other men who contended, and Beckwith will swim H. Parker 400 yards with 30 seconds start. First come, first served. [13]

Clearly, with the challenge contained in this advertisement Beckwith was attempting to ensure that his son would have the best possible chance of beating J.B. Johnson in a race, which Beckwith *père* would then presumably profit from. The theory that Beckwith was quite canny when organizing races, and always attempted to ensure that the conditions of any particular race were to his advantage, is further confirmed by a comment that Robert Watson, the most prolific reporter of swimming during the period, wrote about Beckwith in *Swimming Notes and Record* on 10 May 1884: 'I mean the gentleman who has given about 4,999 prizes, including a stop watch, for the promotion of swimming. Good luck to you, old man, and may you live to give another 4,999 prizes for swimming, minus that bit of string at the end of them.' [14] Clearly the last part of this comment, about the bit of string, was Watson's way of implying that Beckwith was sometimes a bit of a shady character. Both Beckwith's advertisement of July 1873 and Watson's article of May 1884 reveal the less savoury side of swimming in the nineteenth century. When professionals arranged races against each other they always attempted to gain maximum advantage for themselves. This could be achieved in many ways, including by asking for head starts of a set distance, or a certain amount of time, from their opponent. Similarly, strict race conditions would often be drawn up in contracts before such races, and thus the results of races could often be challenged on technicalities. Frederick Beckwith was a major figure in this world. Long after his retirement from competitive swimming himself he managed his children's careers and organized swimming entertainments and competitions. For many years the Beckwith family were the top bill in the English aquatic world, performing at swimming-pool openings across the country, as in Isleworth in 1873 and Lambeth in 1897. [15] Frederick Beckwith died in early 1898, at the age of 79, while his son, Charles, died in July of the same year at the age of 33. [16]

As has been noted, Robert Patrick Watson, the sports journalist, had a keen interest in swimming, and he chronicled much about the swimming world between the late 1860s and the 1890s. He associated with both amateurs and professionals, and seems to have retained the trust of both groups throughout his career. Utilizing the pen name 'Aquarius', Watson provided a series of glimpses of the early division of swimmers into amateurs and professionals in the 1860s in a column entitled 'A Retrospect' in his 1873 publication *The Swimming, Rowing, and Athletic Record* (which later became *The Swimming Record and Chronicle of Sporting Events*). In these columns Watson was distinctly friendly in tone towards both professionals and professionalism, while at the same time providing coverage of amateur matters. One column is worth quoting at length:

> One would almost imagine that of late years swimming had become a sport into which the betting element has not entered (many look upon this as a test of purity), particularly when I remember a few years ago matches being made for £10 and contested eight hours afterwards; instanced in Mather and Peter Johnson's 500 yards race (Leaf-street Baths, Manchester), in conjunction with many others I could mention. Still, although we may deplore the non-existence of big stakes – with which no one was better acquainted than Fred Beckwith – events do occur, only seldom, I acknowledge, forcibly reminding us of old times: we allude to a recent event, wherein Harry Parker, a most unassuming and well-behaved young fellow, opposed H.G. Dunlop, another swimmer held in high esteem. It would be useless for me to recapitulate any one salient feature in connection with this encounter, which was so ably dealt with by *the* greatest authority on matters pertaining to sport, *Bell's Life*. I not only allude to it for previously explained reasons, but to express my admiration of the friendly though business-like manner which characterised every negociation [*sic*]. [17]

This text is rich in information about the early divide between amateurs and professionals. Watson reveals that swimming was formerly more noted for its associated betting than it was for the swimming times themselves. Frederick Beckwith was clearly connected with large bets, with the hint that Beckwith ensured he retained those large stakes. Watson's list of swimmers included many from the north of England, indicating a flourishing swimming culture, at least in Leeds and Manchester. Beckwith's role as swimming master at the Lambeth Baths (the private baths on the Westminster Road) confirms that such a position was commonly reserved for older professionals who were no longer competitive swimmers.

Most importantly, however, Watson noted that the lack of betting was considered 'a test of purity' in the amateur world – an indication of the early division in the swimming world, between amateurs and professionals. Watson pointed to the continued existence of betting and staking, albeit at a greatly reduced scale, within the professional swimming world. But such practice was clearly becoming marginalized, the likely cause being the increased control that amateurs were assuming over the swimming world, and the consequent decline in influence of the professionals.

Later in the same issue of the journal, Watson noted that the Metropolitan Swimming Association had recently run a series of races at the City of London Baths, Barbican, during which no fewer than 18 heats were run for a 108 yards handicap race. [18] In his survey of baths, Dudgeon recorded the size of the first-class swimming pool in the City of London Baths as being 30 yards by 11 yards. [19] This is approximately the same width as a modern four-lane 25-metre swimming pool. Assuming then either four or five competitors per heat, and also that all of the heats mentioned were first preliminary heats, rather than preliminaries, quarter-finals and semi-finals, it is evident that between 80 and 100 swimmers were involved in the event. Even if some of the races were quarter and semi-final heats, the number of initial swimmers in the races would still have been in the order of 50 to 60. Such figures confirm that amateur swimming events were quite popular at the time. These various articles and editorials by Watson confirm that amateurism was the prevailing ideology in the organized swimming world, and that amateurs were in control of competitive swimming during the 1870s.

By the early 1870s, then, a distinct division between amateurs and professional swimmers was visible to contemporary commentators. Several of Watson's comments hint at a class dimension behind this separation. Wray Vamplew's comments on the subject of amateurs and professionals, notably in team sports, are relevant to swimming as well:

> Social prejudice permeated all the major criticisms of sports professionalism. Often this masqueraded as sporting idealism, though some opponents openly admitted to class bias, believing that professionalism lowered sport to the level of a trade and that merely to play alongside players was sufficient for some gentlemen to 'hazard

their self-respect' and that it was 'degrading for respectable men to play with professionals'. Others felt that professionals did not play the game, that they had turned play into work, consumption into production, and made winning so important that in order to secure victory they would resort to foul play and sharp practice. Their lack of education meant that they had not 'the same sense of honour as the public school boy'. [20]

Further, Vamplew has also noted that the concept of professionalism itself was not something the gentlemen amateurs opposed in other facets of their lives. Indeed, the thought of using the services of an amateur lawyer or doctor would have appalled most amateurs. In the leisure sector, however, professionals were to be condemned. Professional sportsmen had to be excluded or controlled in order for amateurs to retain their place. [21]

Although organized competitive swimming was not primarily a product of the public school world, the condemnation and prejudice noted by Vamplew was clearly present within the swimming world by the later 1870s. In time, organized swimming sought to become one of the most ethically 'pure' amateur sports.

But what precisely *was* the conception of amateurism in the swimming world in 1869 when the Associated Metropolitan Swimming Clubs (AMSC) was founded? The AMSC drafted the first set of laws that clearly outlined the difference between what constituted an amateur as opposed to a professional. At this early stage, the amateur law was quite simple. Anyone accepting money for a swimming performance or race was deemed a professional. Amateurs could race against professionals provided that they either accepted no prize or other inducement for taking part in the race, or they donated any prize won in such a contest to the AMSC. [22] These rules were clear and, in theory, easy to enforce, but there was a grey area around what constituted a professional. It is easy to see how an amateur racing against a professional could publicly state that he was not going to accept any prize for the race, but then secretly pocket an inducement for taking part in the race either before or after the event.

Such considerations obviously passed through the minds of contemporary swimming administrators as well, for by 1873 the Metropolitan Swimming Association (MSA) had revised the amateur law such that any competition against a professional by an amateur rendered that amateur ineligible to compete as an amateur again. [23] These revised rules were simple but quite strict, dividing the swimming world into amateurs and professionals, with no grey area between them. The penalty for breaching law number one was clear and severe. Such certainty and severity did not last, however. The rules were, in effect, eroded by rapidly changing practice and conventions in sport at large. Indeed, by 1878 the MSA had changed its name to the Swimming Association of Great Britain (SAGB) and the laws of swimming had again been revised. The first two laws still outlined the distinction between an amateur and a professional, but were now somewhat more lenient:

I. – A person who has competed for money, for a wager, for public or admission money, or who has otherwise made the art of swimming a means of pecuniary profit, shall not be allowed to compete as an amateur.

II. – An amateur shall be allowed to compete with a professional for a prize or honour only. [24]

In fact, the 1878 revisions to the amateur law can be seen as a near return to the original amateur laws of 1869. If one is to take the minutes of the SAGB and memoirs of swimmers of the era as any indication, however, in many ways this law was noted more in its breach than its observance.

From December 1873 to around the start of 1880 the breaching of the amateur law appears to have been a recurring problem, with the executive committee of the SAGB considering at least one infraction of the amateur laws each season. Throughout the same period there were regular proposals to create a committee of vigilance to be proactive in tracking down those who were infringing the laws of swimming. [25] It is clear that the MSA/SAGB was racked with argument in these years, and at the centre of those arguments was the issue of amateurism/professionalism. The banning of all competition against professionals by the MSA appears to have been the root of later dissension within amateur ranks, but it was revisions to the amateur laws in 1878, 1881 and 1884 by the SAGB that eventually created a schism in the amateur swimming world.

The ostensible cause of the split in amateur swimming ranks in 1884 was yet another revision of the amateur laws, but one that many clubs could not agree with. Tensions, however, had been building in the clubs that made up the SAGB for some time prior to this open breach. The full details of the events leading up to the great schism in the amateur swimming ranks fill page after page in the minute books of the SAGB, and can often seem Byzantine in their nuances. One short case study will help illustrate how fraught the debate over the distinction between amateurs and professional had become prior to the split.

In November 1883 Mr Walter Blew-Jones, a delegate from the Otter SC to the SAGB and recent second-place finisher in the 220 yards amateur championship, charged that the winner of the championship, Thomas Cairns, was a professional because he was a bath attendant. In support of his case Mr Blew-Jones also presented unspecified evidence that Cairns had competed in at least six races for cash prizes in the past. Indeed, Cairns had previously been brought before the SAGB committee on similar charges, and had been suspended from amateur competition until 1 August 1883. [26] The SAGB decided to investigate the charges, and reserved judgment until its December meeting. At that meeting it was decided that Cairns had been an amateur when he raced for the 220 yards championship, and Blew-Jones's case was dismissed. Mr Blew-Jones, after his case had been dismissed, informed the meeting that legal proceedings were to be expected. [27]

This case, perhaps even more so than any other incident, was a trigger to the amateur split. At the 11 February 1884 meeting of the SAGB committee Mr Blew-Jones returned his second place medal from the 1883 220 yards amateur championship race and demanded the first-place medal which he felt was his by right. Again the SAGB committee considered the issue closed, and a further attempt to reopen the Cairns case in March 1884 also failed. In April 1884 Mr Blew-Jones's club, the Otter SC, was one of the clubs that split from the SAGB over the revision of the amateur laws. [28] Such small, apparently trivial, matters were basic to the fundamental arguments about amateurism and professionalism. Grand principles clashed in small committee meetings, and inspired swimmers to adopt principled stands about the rankings in competitions and the receipt of medals.

By the 1880s and the 1890s, despite the division between the amateur and professional ranks, most amateurs paid scant attention to the 'true' professionals. In fact, the 1880s saw the start of a terminal decline in the fortunes of professional swimmers as an organized and recognized group. Increasingly it appears that being declared a professional was seen as something to be avoided at all costs. Very few people appear to have been able to make a living as a professional during this period without recourse to other employment. Professor Beckwith, for example, during the 1880s was variously the proprietor of a cigar shop on Westminster Road and also of a hotel, with attached wash baths and a billiards room. [29]

The decline of the fortunes of swimming professionals can be at least partially linked with the rise of other, more popular, professional sports. The most obvious example of a professional sport that was massively popular during the period was football. As *the* mass spectator sport of the later nineteenth and early twentieth centuries, football catered to the need of the urban worker for sporting entertainment. The new football grounds that were built during the 1880s and 1890s were designed to accommodate thousands of spectators. Football, and to a lesser extent cricket, became the great spectator sports of the age. [30] Most swimming pools of the period, on the other hand, would have been fortunate to be able to accommodate 200 to 300 spectators. The facilities available to swimming professionals were not on the scale required to attract a large audience. In addition, it would seem likely that the predictable (and perhaps less exciting) nature of most swimming races or entertainments did not hold the same attraction for punters as the weekly football or cricket match. Thus, sidelined by the amateurs who controlled swimming, denied audiences by the size of their facilities and facing competition from other more popular spectator sports, the swimming professionals of the 1880s and 1890s found themselves with little to do besides teaching people to swim.

It was during this same period of time that the SAGB executive committee established a vigilance committee and maintained a black book for listing offenders against amateurism. When the amateur swimming community split into two factions in 1884 over the precise definition of an amateur, the provisions for the suspension of swimmers for infractions of amateur regulations were used by both sides. The SAGB and the Amateur Swimming Union (ASU) excommunicated all those swimmers who participated in the events organized by the opposite amateur body. [31] The professionals were for the most part ignored, as the arguments were now between amateurs.

When the two amateur camps were reconciled in 1886 with the formation of the Amateur Swimming Association (ASA), much of the former attention devoted to preserving the purity of the amateur ranks appears to have been lost. Exactly why this was the case is not entirely clear, although perhaps contemporary swimming administrators were more accepting of professionalism because of the existence of professionals in football and cricket. Although the amateur laws do not seem to have been weakened in any way, prosecution of those who breached the laws of amateurism appears to have taken place only in the most extreme cases. Robert Watson, as an inside observer of the swimming world throughout the period, noted during the split that many in the ASU could have been termed professionals by any strict standard. [32] By the time he published his memoirs in 1899 he was of the opinion that in the 1870s there had been a distinct difference between amateurs and professionals, while by 1899 various professional amateurs or 'shamateurs' were in actual fact full professionals, but still managed to maintain their amateur status under ASA rules. [33]

The question of the status of the amateur versus professional did not change after 1899. If anything, the debate over what exactly constituted an amateur became even more confused. The hypocrisy involved in excluding some from the definition, while including others, became more and more openly based upon ideas of class and respectability. Any conception of the division between amateurs and professionals based on a recognition of those who made their living from the activity, as compared to those who simply participated for the love of sport, was effectively eliminated. This was most clearly expressed by continued changes to the ASA definition of an amateur, but it also became an issue debated in the swimming print media.

In common with other sports, notably football, by July 1898 a major debate had erupted in the swimming world over the question of what eventually would be termed 'broken time'. [34] At issue was the question of whether or not those who were allowed time off from work, without pay, during the day by their employers to teach swimming to schoolchildren or similar groups should be allowed to receive financial compensation for the hours spent away from work. Many within the swimming world thought that the provision of compensation was fair, because those providing instruction were not earning any more money by their actions than they would have done at work, and they were also providing a useful and necessary public service. An article in *The Swimming Magazine* of July 1898 set forth the current debate over the issue by examining the response of the ASA to a recent case in Swindon of swimmers receiving 'broken time' payments for instructing swimming to schoolchildren:

> It is to be presumed that the Swimming Association through its district organizations really means what it says when it states that the objects of its existence are: (*a*) 'To promote and encourage the art of swimming', and (*b*) 'To stimulate public opinion in favour of providing public facilities for acquiring the art of swimming'. Public opinion, as represented by the Swindon School Board, *has*

been stimulated in this direction, and that body has decided that Swindon school children shall be taught swimming. One would have thought that such a decision would have called forth expressions of approval and appreciation. Not so, however. Officialism – bound up in narrow red tape – more observant of the letter than the spirit – and not *very* observant of the letter – practically forbids it, and, on a *misreading* of the laws, the members of the Swindon SC who had offered to undertake the instruction of the children, are to be penalised, if they carry out their offer, by being dubbed 'professional'. [35]

The author of the article, presumably William Henry, the editor of the journal and chief secretary of the Royal Life Saving Society (RLSS), went on to argue against the decision of the Southern Counties Amateur Swimming Association (SCASA) that the Swindon swimmers would be professionals for accepting 'broken time' payments. Key to his argument was the question of what constituted financial benefit or gain from swimming. Henry argued that there was no gain at all to the individuals who would be teaching swimming in the Swindon case. The men would only be compensated for wages lost from their employ with the Great Western Railway Company while away from work. Henry noted that there were already provisions in the ASA regulations for amateurs to collect expenses for travelling, to avoid being out of pocket. How did the Swindon case vary in any manner from that principle? Indeed, even more to the point, Henry quoted regulations that allowed schoolteachers to lead swimming lessons without losing amateur status. What then was the difference in the Swindon case? [36]

The issue of broken time was to remain an open point of dispute within organized English swimming until long after 1918. The argument presented in the article from *The Swimming Magazine* would seem to be rational and a commonsense interpretation of the situation, and one that seemingly satisfied the current definitions of what constituted an amateur. Reference to the official *ASA Rules for 1898* shows that Henry was accurate with his quotations and was not omitting any clauses that would have overtly refuted his argument. It is clear that the article in *The Swimming Magazine* was correct in its details, and also its interpretation. Under standing ASA policy there should have been no question of the members of the Swindon SC *not* being able to receive reimbursement for the time lost from work. Why then was there such a stand against such a policy? The only reasonable explanation would seem to be one based upon class. The exception made in ASA law for schoolteachers, so that they did not become professionals for teaching swimming while being paid, can be seen in the same light. Schoolteachers were likely seen as professional people. The cult of amateurism was very much a middle-class creation, and could not easily exclude teachers from the amateur ranks simply for undertaking their professional obligations. Based on the evidence given in *The Swimming Magazine* article, however, the members of the Swindon SC appear to have been of a humbler rank. They were mentioned as being given time off from offices and workshops. Thus they were probably clerks and mechanics or technicians.

John Lowerson has written that during the period between 1870 and 1914 the idea of the amateur athlete became the middle-class ideal. Further, a certain tension existed *within* this idea, however, as the middle classes were increasingly made up of the members of the new professional classes of the period, who were in essence opposed to professional practice within their sport and recreation. [37] At the same time, however, as Wray Vamplew has written, when the payment of expenses began to appear in sports, it was the death of true amateurism. [38] Robert Watson had commented on the rise of the 'shamateur' earlier in the 1880s and 1890s, but by 1898 the status was perhaps almost confirmed with the institution of policy by the ASA on the subject of expenses for amateurs. Between 1898 and 1918 the ASA regulations that governed the definitions of amateurs and professionals were continually changed, it would appear, to preserve class divisions in the competitive swimming world. It is important to note that as the ASA was the sporting body in control of water polo and diving up to 1901, the ASA definition of what constituted an amateur applied equally to those disciplines. Life-saving also fell under the amateur definition issued by the ASA, as noted in article 2(c), of the 1898 laws. By 1901 a further amendment to the amateur laws had been made to strengthen the exemption that allowed instructors of life-saving to be paid or reimbursed for their efforts, while at the same time regular instructors of swimming were still deemed professionals for their activities. Of course, class was not mentioned *explicitly* in the notice issued about the change, but it can be seen to be implicit in the statement:

SPECIAL NOTICE.
LIFE SAVING AND PROFESSIONALISM
None of the standing laws of Amateurism laid down by the ASA, AAA, NCU and NSA, apply to Life Saving, either in the matter of learning, teaching, exhibiting, competing, prizes, payment, or any other branch, the ASA being of opinion that the Life Saving land and water drills (including resuscitation) form a higher and combined development of gymnastic exercise, swimming ability and medical knowledge for the benefit of the race, and as such cannot be classified as 'Sport,' or be considered to come within the term 'Athletic Exercises,' specified in Laws 1 and 2 of the ASA. [39]

By 1898, schoolteachers and life-saving instructors were exempted from some aspects of the amateur provisions legislated by the ASA, and these exceptions were reinforced in 1901. Further, joint suspensions were in force between the ASA, the AAA, the National Cycling Union (NCU) and the National Skating Association (NSA). That is, an amateur suspended or declared a professional by one of these bodies was suspended or declared a professional by all of them. Further change of the amateur definition was necessary, however, because it became harder to exclude those of 'undesirable' class from the swimming world. Changes to the amateur law were made on a regular basis between 1901 and 1918, with major revisions appearing in 1906 and 1910. Starting in 1902 the amateur law was amended to allow the acceptance of expense money in certain circumstances by swimmers or swimming officials. [40] These provisions became more and more comprehensive, and by 1910 had become quite detailed. Where once the amateur definition had only filled a paragraph on a page, it now filled several pages in the ASA annual handbook. The change in length alone indicates that the amateur laws were becoming increasingly complex.

Whatever the social divide along the lines of amateur/professional, swimming provision *also* illustrated divisions within the swimming world. From before the introduction of the first Baths and Washhouses Act in 1846 there had been differences in the level of provision of swimming facilities. Early private baths facilities inevitably catered for the more prosperous. The Baths and Washhouses Act, 1846 (9 & 10 Vict., c. 74) reinforced these divisions by authorizing local authorities to provide three or more separate classes of baths within facilities they built.

Looking at early privately-run swimming pools, it is clear that the separation of swimmers by class was not a new concept when the Baths and Washhouses Act, 1846, formalized it. In his survey of the sanitary conditions in London, published in 1842, Edwin Chadwick noted that in the City Road there were a pair of swimming pools open to the public at a charge. One of these pools was more expensively appointed, charging a shilling for entry. The other pool was not so well provided for and cost only sixpence for entry. In addition to these two baths, Chadwick also mentioned that there was a private establishment in Westminster that contained an unspecified number of swimming pools. These pools had been specifically constructed for the use of the working class. A charge of threepence was made for their use. [41] Later, in 1854, George Cape, the secretary of the Lambeth Baths and Wash-House Company, a private company, issued a small book on the subject of baths and washhouses. He noted that the Lambeth Baths contained two swimming pools, one designated as first-class, the other as second-class. Even in the language used – class – the issue of social class was evident. [42] The first-class bath had a fountain in its centre, and was considered to be the more opulent of the two pools. [43] Thus even *after* the introduction of the Baths and Washhouses Act, there was a continued division of swimmers in those pools not covered by the provisions of the act.

This division of swimmers into different classifications of swimming pools continued throughout the nineteenth century and into the twentieth. In those areas where larger baths establishments could be built, multiple swimming pools were constructed on the same site, as was the case in Islington, Marylebone, Paddington and St Pancras in London, and also in Manchester and other provincial cities. After accounting for the fact that facilities with multiple swimming pools often set one aside for use by women, the remaining pools were divided into first-, second- and sometimes third-class swimming pools. The lower the class of the pool, the cheaper the entry charge made for its use, and thus the lower the social tone of the experience for swimmers. In places where it was either physically or financially not possible to build multiple pools at a location, then a rotating schedule of use of the pool was drawn up, specifying when each class of swimmers could use the pool. [44]

It is also important to note that the level of technology available for keeping a pool clean affected when certain classes of people could use a swimming pool. Generally speaking, there was no filtration of swimming pool water between 1800 and 1918. This meant that the water remained dirty until the pool was either partially or completely refilled with fresh water. Clean water days, therefore, were generally reserved for use by higher-class patrons.

Over time, as architects became more adept at building swimming pools and baths buildings, the distinctions between the various classes of baths became somewhat standardized. By 1894 Robert Owen Allsop, an architect known for building several civic baths establishments, produced a textbook on the subject of designing and constructing a bath and washhouse. Very early on in his work he states: 'The question of *class* naturally requires consideration at an early stage. Much in this way depends upon the place and position, and the neighbourhood where the baths are erected.' [45] This concentration on class was a continuous theme in swimming-pool design manuals up to the First World War. In 1906 Alfred W.S. Cross, a noted architect of the period, produced his own handbook on the design of public baths and washhouses. [46] He recommended that there should be at least two swimming pools in any public bath facility, one for first-class use and one for second-class use. If no provision could be made for a women's bath, then time should be set aside for women's use of the other baths as appropriate. He recommended that the first-class swimming pool should measure 100 feet by 40 feet to best conform to standard racing distances. The second-class and women's baths, should they exist, need not be this size. He suggested that a second-class bath need only be 75 feet by 35 feet, and a women's bath 60 feet by 30 feet. [47] Clearly Cross was suggesting here that users of the first-class pool took priority over the users of all other swimming pools within a baths facility. By the start of the twentieth century there was clearly a market for the books being produced by Allsop and Cross.

Increasingly from 1878 onwards, when amendments to the Baths and Washhouses Act allowed municipalities to construct and operate indoor swimming pools, the number of municipal swimming pools had grown at a great rate. Ready-made plans for swimming pools, with all the considerations surrounding social regulation already addressed, were in demand. Clearly, organized swimming came heavily laden with various forms of social division and regulation. Though not unique to swimming, these forms of social regulation remained present and obvious in the swimming world for much longer than in other areas of sport and recreation, notably cricket, football and rugby.

The divide between amateur and professional swimmers was most strongly observed in 1918, but had been developing since 1869. The laws implemented to enforce the amateur and professional division became increasing complex between 1869 and 1918, the better to maintain the class divide in organized swimming. In theory anyone who made money from swimming was deemed a professional. Certain groups of amateur swimmers, however, had little trouble in securing payments (prizes and expenses), especially after 1898. Behind the entire issue lay the ubiquitous issue of social class.

Notes

[1] For more on the history of betting, see Chinn, *Better Betting with a Decent Feller*; Clapson, *A Bit of a Flutter*; Dixon, *From Prohibition to Regulation*; Munting, *An Economic and Social History of Gambling*.
[2] Chinn, *Better Betting with a Decent Feller*, 71.
[3] *The Times*, 19 May 1791, 3b; *The Times*, 24 Sept. 1805, 3d; *The Times*, 7 Sept. 1810, 4c.
[4] *The Times*, 21 Sept. 1838, 6b.
[5] *Bell's Life in London*, 2 Oct. 1842, 4d.
[6] *Bell's Life in London*, 27 Aug. 1843, 4c; *Bell's Life in London*, 3 Sept. 1843, 4f; *Bell's Life in London*, 14 July 1844, 4e.
[7] Lowerson, *Sport and the English Middle Classes*, 155.
[8] See Watson, *Memoirs*, 116–19; *The Times*, 12 Aug. 1863, 9a; Anonymous, *London Swimming Club Manual*, 16.
[9] *The Times*, 18 Oct. 1861, 10a.
[10] For more contemporary accounts about the Beckwiths see *The Times*, 7 Oct. 1863, 12b; Anonymous, *London Swimming Club Manual*, 24, 28, 34; Keil and Wix, *In the Swim*, 185; *Illustrated London News* 67, no. 1882 (4 Sept. 1875), 227; *The Swimming Magazine* 1, no. 3 (1 Aug. 1898), 24.
[11] Watson, *Memoirs*, 122.
[12] *The Swimming Record and Chronicle of Sporting Events* 1, no. 4 (31 May 1873), 1.
[13] *The Swimming Record and Chronicle of Sporting Events* 1, no. 11 (19 July 1873), 4.
[14] *Swimming Notes and Record* 13 (10 May 1884), 2.
[15] *The Swimming Record and Chronicle of Sporting Events* 1, no. 15 (16 Aug. 1873), 3; Lambeth Archives Minet Library, P12/80/10, *A Souvenir of the 9th July, 1897. From the Clerk to The Chairman*.
[16] *The Swimming Magazine* 1, no. 1 (1 June 1898), 10; *The Swimming Magazine* 1, no. 3 (1 Aug. 1898, 24.
[17] Aquarius [Robert Patrick Watson], 'A Retrospect', *The Swimming, Rowing, and Athletic Record* 1, no. 1 (10 May 1873), 2.
[18] Ibid.
[19] Dudgeon, *The Swimming Baths of London*, 14–15.
[20] Vamplew, *Pay Up and Play the Game*, 196–7.
[21] Ibid., 198–9.
[22] Sinclair and Henry, *Swimming*, 335–6.
[23] 'Laws of Amateur Swimming', *The Swimming Record and Chronicle of Sporting Events* 1, no. 29 (22 Nov. 1873), 4.
[24] Amateur Swimming Association Library (hereafter ASAL), *Minute Book no. 2 of the MSA*, 104, Minutes of the Annual General Meeting 14 Jan. 1878.
[25] ASAL, *Minute Book no. 2 of the MSA*, passim; *Minute Book no. 3, The SAGB*, passim.
[26] ASAL, *Minute Book no. 3, The SAGB*, 104–10, Minutes of 14 Sept. 1882, 9 Oct. 1882; *Minute Book no. 4 The Swimming Association of Great Britain*, 207–11, Minutes of 12 Nov. 1883. Hereafter cited as *Minute Book no. 4, SAGB*.
[27] ASAL, *Minute Book no. 4, SAGB*, 212–14, Minutes of 10 Dec. 1883. See also, *Sporting Life*, 11 Dec. 1883.
[28] ASAL, *Minute Book no. 4, SAGB*, 219–27, 231–3, Minutes of 11 Feb. 1884, 10 March 1884; Minutes of SAGB AGM, 7 April 1884.

[29] *Notes* 3 (1 March 1884), 7; *Swimming Notes and Record* 13 (10 May 1884), 2.
[30] For the history of football as a popular entertainment, se Holt, *Sport and the British*, 281–6; Mason, *Association Football*, 138–74; Walvin, *The People's Game*, 75.
[31] See ASAL, *Minute Book no. 3, SAGB*, and *Minute Book no. 4, SAGB*, passim.
[32] *Swimming Notes and Record* 17 (7 June 1884), 1.
[33] Watson, *Memoirs*, 282.
[34] See, for example, Holt, *Sport and the British*, 98–117.
[35] *The Swimming Magazine* 1, no. 2 (1 July 1898), 16. Italics are in the original.
[36] *The Swimming Magazine* 1, no. 2, 1 July 1898, 16–17.
[37] Lowerson, *Sport and the English Middle Classes*, 155.
[38] Vamplew, *Pay Up and Play the Game*, 199.
[39] ASA, *Handbook for 1901*, 26.
[40] ASA, *Handbook for 1902*, 20–1.
[41] Chadwick, *Report on the Sanitary Condition of the Labouring Population*, 317.
[42] See Briggs, 'The Language of "Class" in Early Nineteenth-Century England', 3–33.
[43] Cape, *Baths and Wash Houses*, 48 and frontispiece.
[44] See for example the hours of the Moss Side Baths in Manchester for 1906; Manchester Local Studies Archives Service, Baths and Wash Houses Committee Minutes 12, fols. 98–9, glued-in report on hours of operation of Victoria Baths and Moss Side Baths.
[45] Allsop, *Public Baths and Wash-Houses*, 8.
[46] Cross, *Public Baths and Wash-Houses*, passim.
[47] Ibid., 46, 58.

References

Allsop, Robert Owen. *Public Baths and Wash-Houses*. London: E. & F. N. Spon, 1894.

Anonymous, *A Manual Compiled under the Sanction of The London Swimming Club for the Use of Its Members and Others; with an Account of the Progress of the Art During the Last Twenty Years, and a Short Notice of The Swimming Baths of the Metropolis*. London: W. H. Leverell, 1861.

ASA (Amateur Swimming Association). *Handbook for 1901*. London: Amateur Swimming Association, 1901.

——. *Handbook for 1902*. London: Amateur Swimming Association, 1902.

Briggs, Asa. 'The Language of "Class" in Early Nineteenth-Century England'. In *The Collected Essays of Asa Briggs*, Vol. 1. Brighton: The Harvester Press, 1985: 3–33.

Cape, George A. *Baths and Wash Houses*. London: Simpkin, Marshall & Co., 1854.

Chadwick, Edwin. *Report on the Sanitary Condition of the Labouring Population of Great Britain*. Edited by M.W. Flinn. Edinburgh: Edinburgh University Press, 1965 [first published 1842].

Chinn, Carl. *Better Betting with a Decent Feller: Bookmaking, Betting and the British Working Class, 1750–1990*. Hemel Hempstead: Harvester Wheatsheaf, 1991.

Clapson, Mark. *A Bit of a Flutter: Popular Gambling and English Society, c. 1823–1961*. Manchester: Manchester University Press, 1992.

Cross, Alfred W.S. *Public Baths and Wash-Houses*. London: B.T. Batsford, 1906.

Dixon, David. *From Prohibition to Regulation: Bookmaking, Anti-Gambling, and the Law*. Oxford: Oxford University Press, 1991.

Dudgeon, R.E. *The Swimming Baths of London*. London: Henry Turner and Co., 1870.

Holt, Richard. *Sport and the British: A Modern History*. Oxford: Oxford University Press, 1989.

Keil, Ian and Don Wix. *In the Swim: The Amateur Swimming Association from 1869 to 1994*. Loughborough: Swimming Times Ltd., 1996.

Lowerson, John. *Sport and the English Middle Classes 1870–1914*. Manchester: Manchester University Press, 1993.

Mason, Tony. *Association Football and English Society 1863–1915*. Brighton: Harvester Press Limited, 1980.

Munting, Roger. *An Economic and Social History of Gambling in Britain and the USA*. Manchester: Manchester University Press, 1996.

Sinclair, Archibald and William Henry. *Swimming* (The Badminton Library of Sports and Pastimes). London: Longmans, Green, and Co., 1893.

Vamplew, Wray. *Pay Up and Play the Game: Professional Sport in Britain 1875–1914*. Cambridge: Cambridge University Press, 1988.

Walvin, James. *The People's Game A Social History of British Football*. London: Allen Lane, 1975.

Watson, Robert Patrick. *Memoirs of Robert Patrick Watson: A Journalist's Experience of Mixed Society*. London: Smith, Ainslie & Co., 1899.

Local Aquatic Empires: The Municipal Provision of Swimming Pools in England, 1828–1918

The provision of plunge or swimming baths, as swimming pools were familiarly known to the Victorians and Edwardians, was initially a matter of private investment. Right up to the end of the nineteenth century the building of swimming pools was funded by local public subscriptions, joint stock companies or non-profit bodies. The first swimming pool in York, for example, was opened in 1837 as a privately funded bath on the Manor Shore of the River Ouse. Over time, however, Victorian cities came to be characterized by the lavish provision of public facilities and buildings. Town halls, libraries, railway stations, schools, even the construction of sewers, all became features of the distinctive Victorian urban landscape. Swimming pools were a late addition to this list. [1] After the introduction of the Baths And Washhouses Act, 1846, privately-financed pools soon gave way to municipal involvement in swimming provision. [2] In 1828 the Corporation of Liverpool opened the first municipal swimming pool in England, the 'St George's Baths', on the banks of the River Mersey. This was an example that other towns wished to copy. Throughout the century civically built public baths, funded by local authorities from their rates, came to form the great bulk of swimming-pool provision in England. Baths appeared particularly rapidly in major areas of population, especially in many northern towns where swimming was a common activity in the natural environment.

Municipal provision was accelerated by the passing of the 1846 act, which provided an impetus for cities and towns to build their own baths. The act was of course only one of many pieces of legislation from that period concerned with the sanitary condition of towns and the living conditions of the urban poor. Although the act itself was not championed by the great sanitary reformer of the period, Edwin

Chadwick, it was clearly consistent with his views on improving the sanitary environment of cities and towns. In his famous 1842 *Report on the Sanitary Condition of the Labouring Population of Great Britain*, Chadwick had made passing reference to swimming pools by noting that there existed at least two pools on a site in the City Road, London, as well as an unspecified number in Westminster. [3] Overall, however, he was more concerned with the provision of water and the proper construction of sewers, the existence of which were necessary for the proper supply of wash and swimming baths and laundries to the populace at large.

The Baths and Washhouses Act, 1846, was concerned only with the provision of wash baths for individuals and washing facilities for clothing and house linen. This was obviously intended to address shortages and inadequacies in housing facilities. Urban people had few (and inadequate) places at home in which to wash themselves or their possessions. The act also made provision for the regulation of public bathing places, in essence large open-air pools. While the wording of the act seems to indicate that its authors were thinking of providing such facilities simply for their sanitary function, they could also be seen as authorizing the setting up and regulation of open-air swimming areas. [4] Early amendments to the initial act were made by the Baths and Washhouses Act, 1847 (10 & 11 Vict., c. 61), which allowed for charges to be made at what were termed 'open bathing places', in essence outdoor swimming pools. Other amendments and additions to the act were contained in the Towns Improvement Clauses Act, 1847 (10 & 11 Vict., c. 34) and the Towns Police Clauses Act, 1847 (10 & 11 Vict., c. 89). By the end of 1847, then, municipal authorities with responsibility for collecting the poor law rate were empowered to set up boards of commissioners to provide baths and washhouses in their district. These facilities could include wash baths, laundries and outdoor swimming areas. Provision was made that if these establishments proved too expensive to maintain they could be sold off. Most importantly, however, these facilities were to be supported by contributions from the local rates, and had a maximum charge set for the various services they provided. For the period immediately following 1846, the only charge of concern to swimmers was the ½d (halfpenny) maximum charge for use of 'open bathing places'. The 1846 act and the amendments made to it in 1847 did not include explicit provision for indoor or covered swimming pools. The provision of such pools, however, seems to have figured in the early plans of most of the larger centres. It would appear that municipal authorities circumvented the wording of the Baths and Washhouses Act by terming these swimming pools 'plunge baths' and justified their construction on the grounds that they were meant to bathe large numbers of people at cheaper costs and in less time than individual wash baths. Victorian city-fathers were, as ever, anxious to get the best deal for their money. In this case, more people could be cleaned communally than by individual baths.

Adoption of the Baths and Washhouses Act, 1846, and its various amendments was not a uniform practice among English urban authorities – i.e. provincial town councils and urban district councils, London vestries and then, later, London boroughs. As a piece of permissive as opposed to mandatory legislation, municipal authorities had to decide to adopt the act for their area of authority, rather than having it automatically put into force. Furthermore, as the act was concerned with baths, washhouses and also laundries, even those authorities which *did* adopt the act did not have to erect the *full* range of facilities allowed by the act. This led to a widely varied patchwork of arrangements in civic provision of swimming facilities throughout England. For example, in 1847 when the Corporation of Leeds Council adopted the Baths and Washhouses Acts they immediately sent off a subcommittee of investigation to Liverpool and Manchester, to view the baths there before deciding to build baths in Leeds. [5] Assuming that this committee of investigation visited the St George's Baths, they would have been viewing public (i.e. municipal) baths in Liverpool. In Manchester, however, they would have been viewing private facilities, as that corporation was not to adopt the Baths and Washhouses Acts until 1876. [6] Further, in Liverpool they would likely have seen the swimming pool at the St George's Baths, while no swimming pools are known to have existed in Manchester at this time. The Leeds committee, therefore, were faced by two rather different models of provision of baths to the populace. This might partially explain why Leeds, although it adopted the Baths and Washhouses Act in 1847, did not actually erect any swimming pools or baths facilities, and therefore make use of the powers of the act, until the 1890s. [7]

Most of the surveys of bathing facilities in the nineteenth century date from the 1850s and 1860s, and provide an informative illustration of the provision of swimming pools during that period. The surveys concentrate most of their attention on the state of affairs in London. Enough provincial evidence exists, however, to provide an outline of bathing and swimming provision outside the capital. In 1854, George A. Cape produced his general survey on baths and washhouses, in which he also included some information on swimming and swimming pools. Cape was the secretary of the Lambeth Baths and Wash-House Company, a private business running the 'National Baths' in Lambeth at this time, and he claimed to have been moved to write the work to provide information to the public on a subject for which information was lacking. [8] He reported that when the Baths and Washhouses Act, 1846, was passed there were two private baths establishments in London, neither of which contained a swimming pool. [9] Aside from these private facilities, Cape recorded which London parishes had also begun to operate swimming pools, with St Marylebone (two pools), St Margaret and St John, Westminster (one pool), Greenwich (two pools), Poplar (two pools) and St Giles in the Fields and St George, Bloomsbury (two pools). Beyond the capital he noted that in 1854 there were bath facilities in Bilston, Birmingham, Coventry, Hereford, Hull, Liverpool (three baths sites), Maidstone, Nottingham, Plymouth, Preston, Sunderland and Wolverhampton. Almost all these locations also had at least one, and sometimes more than one, swimming pool available for general use. Cape recorded the distribution of swimming pools as Bilston (one pool), Birmingham (two pools), Coventry (one pool), Hull (one pool), Liverpool (three baths sites, five pools), Maidstone (one pool), Nottingham (two pools), Preston (one pool), and Wolverhampton (one pool).

[10] He did not, however, specify if these baths and swimming pools were municipally owned and operated or privately run. The Liverpool examples were almost certainly civic baths, as the city had possessed a municipal swimming pool from 1828. We also know that the list is incomplete if it is supposed to contain both municipal and private bath facilities. It does not, for example, include the Manor Shore or Marygate Baths in York, which dated from 1837, nor does it include the Peerless Pool mentioned by Chadwick in his report.

Cape's survey of baths was followed in 1861 by a survey of swimming locations undertaken by members of the London Swimming Club. This work dealt only with London swimming locations, and does not differentiate between municipal and private ventures. It lists a total of six open-air swimming locations and nine establishments in London that had covered swimming baths by 1861. Of the outdoor swimming locations, four could be considered to be municipal (although only in the broadest sense), these being the Serpentine; the bathing pond in Sion Park; the Thames; and the Victoria Park bathing lake. Of the nine indoor swimming pools listed, only three are definitely municipal facilities: the Bloomsbury; the Marylebone; and the St George's Baths, Davies Street. A fourth facility, the St George's Baths, Pimlico, Upper Belgrave Place, might possibly have been municipal. The remaining five facilities were most certainly private. [11]

In 1870 Dr R.E. Dudgeon, MD, conducted his own survey of London swimming pools. A proponent of swimming as an exercise that promoted health, Dudgeon seems to have undertaken his survey in order to provide his readers with the best possible advice on which baths were healthy to swim in, and which were substandard and unhealthy, and thus to be avoided. Altogether, Dudgeon surveyed 22 bathing facilities in London that possessed swimming pools. For the most part he does not differentiate between municipal and private facilities in his survey. However, he makes the occasional comment about a certain bath being more 'select' or another being of 'inferior quality', which might indicate a difference between municipal and private provision. [12]

Dr Dudgeon was the first author to provide extended information about the actual extent of swimming provision within the new facilities that London vestries were building. He reported, for example, that although the combined vestries of St Giles and St George, Bloomsbury had two swimming pools, in the Endell Street Baths, these pools were both extremely small and hardly suited for swimming at all. Both were irregularly-shaped oblong pools of 12 yards length and ten yards width at one end, and eight yards width at the other. [13] Some of the other baths were not much better. Dr Dudgeon's survey included measurements for almost all the metropolitan baths, whether publicly or privately owned. He recorded the Bermondsey Bath as being 13 yards by nine yards, the first-class swimming pool in the Marylebone Swimming Baths as 15 yards by eight yards, both swimming pools in the Poplar Baths (All Saints parish) as being 15 yards by nine yards, and the St James' Swimming Bath as 13 yards by nine yards. [14] Only the St George's Swimming Baths, Buckingham Palace Road, at 20 yards by eight yards, and the St Pancras Swimming Baths, at 19 yards by eight yards for both swimming pools, came close to the measurements of the standard 25-metre swimming pools of the later twentieth century. There was no standard format or agreement about the size a swimming pool should be at this time. Indeed, the standardization of pools came much later, and was a function of the need to be able to compare distances and times in competitive swimming. [15] As Dudgeon commented,

> With few exceptions the London swimming baths are too small. When any considerable number of bathers are in the water, then there is hardly room for the swimmers, who are consequently continually butting against, or kicking, or even scratching one another in a manner anything but favorable [sic] for the preservation of good temper – a most essential requisite in a hygienic point of view. [16]

He goes on to point out that the majority of baths in the capital, both public and private, were ill provided with lighting of any sort, making them quite dark. They also suffered from a lack of proper air circulation, making them humid and stuffy. [17]

It seems clear, therefore, that up until the early 1870s at least, while London had swimming pools, the provision of swimming facilities within the capital were not built with serious swimmers in mind. The sizes of most public baths of this period suggest that London parish councils focused more on the wash baths and laundry aspect of the facilities, allocating more space and resources for these functions. There was very good reason for this, of course – notably growing contemporary concerns about personal and communal hygiene. There were, however, exceptions to this rule, in particular the parishes of Marylebone, of St George, Hanover Square, and of Paddington. Either through the provision of a greater than average number of swimming pools, or through the provision of larger swimming pools, these facilities were of greater use to swimmers of the time.

Bathing and swimming was, like most aspects of Victorian urban life, periodically transformed by new Parliamentary legislation. The great Public Health Act, 1875, produced critical change. [18] It was a sweeping act that regulated many areas of life not previously touched by the hand of government. Importantly, the act also included clauses that specifically referred to swimming and to the provision of swimming facilities. The act allowed new urban local authorities (other than parishes and vestries) to adopt the provisions of the Baths and Washhouses Act. It further allowed local authorities to supply water to baths and washhouses on terms to be negotiated by the authority involved. These authorities were also empowered to provide water, free of charge, to baths and washhouses that were not run as private profit-making ventures or were not already supported by the local poor or borough rates. Finally, the act incorporated all the clauses related to public out-of-doors bathing from the Towns Police Clauses Act, 1847.

Three years later further legislative changes were made to the laws governing baths and washhouses with the enactment of the Baths and Washhouses Act, 1878. [19] It was this set of amendments that finally set out in law the ability of local authorities to construct or purchase covered (i.e. indoor) swimming baths. It also decreed that the authority controlling a facility containing covered swimming baths could close the pools for a period not exceeding five months, between 1 November and 30 March. During this time the closed pool could be turned into a gymnasium or other type of facility designed to provide a means of 'healthful recreation'. The closed swimming baths were explicitly *not* allowed to be used for music performances or dancing. The schedule of charges attached to the act allowed for a maximum charge of 8d per person for use of a first-class bath, 4d per person for use of a second-class bath, and 2d per person for use of a third or any lower class of bath. This act, allowing both swimming and gymnastics under the same municipally-financed roof, was clearly intended to tackle the broader problems of the physical well-being of the urban population. Swimming had clearly come of age; being viewed as an important element in the development of the masses' physical condition. That this legislation was passed less than three years after Captain Webb's famous cross channel swim may also indicate that the government was responding to the swimming craze created by that event.

Three further sets of amendments to the Baths and Washhouses Act, 1846, were passed during the nineteenth century. The amendments of 1882 were concerned with clarifying some of the language introduced in the 1878 amendments, and they did not introduce any new powers. Amendments in 1896 specifically repealed, for the County of London only, the restriction on not using pools closed for the winter months for music or dancing (provided that the required licence was applied for and granted). The amendments of 1899 repealed the same restriction for the rest of England. [20] After this time, no further changes to the act were made prior to 1918.

After the introduction of the 1878 amendments to the Baths and Washhouses Act, one further survey of the baths of London survives. Published in 1885, William Smith's *The Swimming Club Directory* detailed not only indoor and outdoor swimming pools across London, but also listed swimming clubs in London and the provinces. [21] Smith was the secretary of the Llandudno Swimming Club, and appears to have been attempting to provide a service to swimmers who were looking for baths while travelling across the country. [22] He may also have been trying to break into the world of sports publishing (a growing publishing industry at the time). Like Dudgeon, Smith did not specify whether the baths he was reporting on were municipally or privately owned. In total he names 43 swimming pools, indoor and outdoor, plus the Thames, that were either then open for use in London or soon to be completed. [23]

Clearly, municipal swimming had become a notable feature of life in English cities on the eve of the First World War. This had emerged for a complexity of reasons; including physical recreation, education provision and concerns about cleanliness. But we need to know how *extensive* such provision was. Perhaps the most comprehensive survey of municipal provision of swimming facilities in England was the report compiled by Agnes Campbell during the First World War for the Carnegie

United Kingdom Trust. Part of the deed establishing the trust recommended the provision or support of public baths, and this survey was therefore undertaken to determine the current provision of baths facilities across the United Kingdom. [24] It was a massive survey of over 300 pages and provides unprecedented detail about swimming-pool provision within the United Kingdom, and especially England. It also includes a cursory, and very generalized, history of swimming since ancient times, and a review of the history of baths and washhouses legislation since 1846.

Most importantly, however, Campbell's work reveals that by 1914 almost *all* swimming pool provision within England was offered by municipal governments. As the author herself noted, this was a vast change from the recent past when there had been a much larger amount of voluntary or private provision. [25] According to her own analysis of the data she had collected, Campbell observed a tendency for industrial and shipping (port) centres to adopt the act much more readily than mining areas. The most densely populated areas of Lancashire and Yorkshire, therefore, had larger numbers of baths than other areas. In London all the boroughs, except for Finsbury, had provided baths of some sort by 1914, and in every English population centre of over 100,000 inhabitants there was *some* form of bathing provision. In centres of population of 50,000 to 100,000 inhabitants every city or town, again, had bathing facilities, with the exceptions of Hornsey and Yarmouth, although Oxford's facilities were singled out as being rather 'minor'. [26] For the large number of population centres with between 20,000 and 50,000 inhabitants, a total of 108 were recorded as providing some form of bathing establishment. The other 40 such centres of population had no municipal provision. The majority of the smaller towns providing baths establishments only provided outdoor baths. [27] The particular case of London deserves special attention. On the eve of the First World War swimming had clearly become a deeply entrenched and widely popular pastime in the capital. By 1914 there were 101 municipal swimming pools, both indoors and outdoors, spread among 51 locations in the boroughs that made up the London County Council. [28] This was a huge change from 1846 when there were no municipal swimming pools in London.

Analysis of the data that Campbell collected, in particular a graph that charted the building of municipal baths buildings in England from just prior to the introduction of the Baths and Washhouses Act, 1846, until 1915, reveals interesting trends. It is clear after reviewing this material that, after an initial period of low interest (between roughly 1845 and 1850), the response of local authorities to the Baths and Washhouses Act was to begin building baths and washhouses. This was followed by a second period of low interest in building, from roughly 1860 to 1875. The period after 1875 was one of continuing, sustained and increasing interest in building new baths. These two periods of building may be attributed to the introduction of the initial Baths and Washhouses Act of 1846 and the amended act of 1878 which specifically allowed covered swimming pools to be built as part of baths establishments. The introduction of further amendments in the 1890s, which allowed swimming pools to be turned into dance halls or other places of entertainment over the winter months subject to certain conditions, is also likely to have helped spur on later growth. [29]

The importance of the increase in number of municipal baths establishments, and the change from privately owned and operated baths to publicly owned and operated baths should not be underestimated. Campbell's study is almost totally concerned with municipal provision, as she herself points out in her foreword, and depended a great deal on provision of information from local authorities themselves, thereby potentially influencing her conclusions. [30] Even if we treat Campbell's results with due caution, it seems clear that the scale of change from one extreme of provision to the other was great. As one example, she records that by 1915 over £2 million had been spent by local authorities of over 200,000 inhabitants, excluding London, on the provision of baths establishments. The conclusion that the number of private baths establishment providers was declining seems to be at least partially backed up by Board of Trade papers which record the dissolution of no fewer than 40 private swimming and wash bath companies between 1866 and 1935, with the majority of these companies going out of business in the period between 1870 and 1900. [31] This period does not exactly coincide with the explosion of local authority provision of baths, as illustrated above, and clearly other economic factors were involved to a greater or lesser extent. Nevertheless, this decline in private baths companies must have been at least partially affected by the ability of public baths to levy part of their costs on the local rates, and by the cap on admittance charges to the public baths that was part of the Baths and Washhouses Act, 1846, and its various amendments. Here is an unmistakable example of municipal provision pushing aside, or taking over from, private provision. Town and city authorities now had economic (and social) clout and muscle and could provide for their inhabitants – especially the poorer sort – in ways not thought possible or suitable by private enterprise. It was an important example of the emergent success of municipal enterprise for the benefit of local citizens.

The period between 1800 and 1918 saw a complete reversal in the role that municipal authorities fulfilled in the promotion of swimming and the provision of swimming facilities. In 1800 there was no municipal involvement in the promotion of swimming or the provision of facilities. By 1918 municipal authorities were the largest providers of swimming facilities in England, and generally also great supporters of swimming as an activity. Of course there were regional variations in the exact levels of provision made and the amount of support that local swimmers could expect from their municipal authorities. Be that as it may, the overwhelming trend was for greater and greater municipal provision of baths facilities, and a relative decline in the private provision of swimming pools. The extent of this change should not be underestimated, as the repercussions from it influenced the development of school swimming, at least in the state school sector.

Indeed, the development of municipal swimming facilities with low entry charges allowed access to swimming facilities by numerous groups that previously would have found it difficult. As has been noted, the original Baths and Washhouses Act and its various amendments capped the charges that could be made for admittance to municipally provided facilities. This certainly allowed the working classes greater access than ever before to the chance to swim. The provision by certain municipalities of special admittance prices for selected groups meant that, over time, many facilities were opened up for use by local state schools so that pupils could be taught how to swim. Municipal pools helped to fuel the increase in popularity of swimming in England in the later nineteenth and early twentieth centuries.

Notes

[1] For more on the development of the Victorian city see, for example, Briggs, *Victorian Cities* and Dyos and Wolff, *The Victorian City*.
[2] For purposes of this article the term 'municipal' will be used generally to refer to all local governmental bodies in England, whether they be civic corporations, parish councils or urban district councils. In cases where only one single type of local governmental authority is referred to, the appropriate term will be used.
[3] Chadwick, *Report on the Sanitary Condition of the Labouring Population*, 317. For more on Chadwick and the debate over sanitation and cleanliness from the period see Finer, *The Life and Times of Sir Edwin Chadwick*; and Hamlin, *Public Health and Social Justice in the Age of Chadwick*.
[4] 9 & 10 Vict., c. 74, The Baths and Washhouses Act, 1846, schedule B.
[5] West Yorkshire Archives Service (WYAS), Sheepscar, Leeds, LC/TC1/2, *Leeds Borough Council Municipal Report Book*, vol. 2, Report of the Baths and Washhouses Committee, 26 Oct. 1847.
[6] Manchester Local Studies Archives Service, *Proceedings of the Baths and Wash Houses Committee*, vol. 1, 1, minutes of 17 Aug. 1876.
[7] See Campbell, *Report on Public Baths*, appendix, 164–75, where she reports on the construction dates of civic baths in Leeds. The first bath was not built by the council until 1895.
[8] Cape, *Baths and Wash Houses*, 3, 5–6.
[9] Ibid., 39.
[10] Ibid., 47–8.
[11] Anonymous, *London Swimming Club Manual*, 39–41. The private facilities were the Albion Bath, the Lambeth Baths, the Metropolitan Baths, the North London Baths and the 'Wenlock'.
[12] Dudgeon, *The Swimming Baths of London*, 12–22. For specific examples of Dudgeon's rating of baths for their 'class' see his description of the Kensington Baths on p. 17, and his description of the Wenlock Baths on p. 18.
[13] Ibid., 20–1.
[14] Ibid., 14, 17, 19, 21.
[15] Ibid., 20–1. The standardization of competitive swimming course distances at 25 metres and 50 metres, thus making 25-metre and 50-metre swimming pools the standard sizes of pool built, was a development of the internationalization of swimming competition begun with the first modern Olympic Games in Athens in 1896, and based on a need to be able to compare times, and thus records, over set distances. It was eventually mandated by FINA, the international governing body of swimming, after the Second World War. Prior to 1918, however, swimming competitions were generally held in whatever sized body of water was available and the standardization of course distances was barely an issue, and thus forms no part of this study.
[16] Dudgeon, *The Swimming Baths of London*, 25.
[17] Ibid., 25.

[18] 38 & 39 Vict., c. 55.
[19] 41 & 42 Vict., c. 14.
[20] 45 & 46 Vict., c. 30; 59 & 60 Vict., c. 59; 62 & 63 Vict., c. 29.
[21] Smith, *The Swimming Club Directory 1885, For the United Kingdom*. The title would appear to indicate that this was intended to be one in a series of works, but it seems to have been a one-off production. A copy is held in the British Library.
[22] Ibid., 3.
[23] Ibid., 36–7.
[24] Campbell, *Report on Public Baths*, iii.
[25] Ibid., 7.
[26] Ibid., 7–8. Campbell admitted, however, that when it came to population centres of over 100 000, Willesden provided only open-air baths.
[27] Ibid., 8. These numbers were based upon total UK returns, so of the 148 population centres of 20,000 to 50,000 inhabitants, some were in Ireland, Scotland and Wales, as well as England.
[28] Ibid., 9.
[29] Ibid., 6 and facing.
[30] Ibid., v–vi.
[31] PRO, BT 31, various sub-class listings. Of the sample of 42 private baths companies wound up by the Board of Trade between 1846 and 1945 that I traced in the Public Record Office (now the National Archives) only one went out of business prior to 1870 (in 1866) and eight were wound up after 1900.

References

Anonymous, *A Manual Compiled under the Sanction of The London Swimming Club for the Use of Its Members and Others; with an Account of the Progress of the Art during the last Twenty Years, and a Short Notice of The Swimming Baths of the Metropolis*. London: W. H. Leverell, 1861.
Briggs, Asa. *Victorian Cities*. London: Odhams Press, 1963.
Campbell, Agnes. *Report on Public Baths and Wash-Houses in the United Kingdom*. Edinburgh: Edinburgh University Press, 1918.
Cape, George A. *Baths and Wash Houses*. London: Simpkin, Marshall & Co., 1854.
Chadwick, Edwin. *Report on the Sanitary Condition of the Labouring Population of Great Britain*. Edited by M.W. Flinn. Edinburgh: Edinburgh University Press, 1965 [first published 1842].
Dudgeon, R.E. *The Swimming Baths of London*. London: Henry Turner and Co., 1870.
Dyos, H.J. and Michael Wolff, eds. *The Victorian City: Images and Realities*, 2 vols. London: Routledge & Kegan Paul, 1973.
Finer, S.E. *The Life and Times of Sir Edwin Chadwick*. New York: Barnes & Noble, 1952.
Hamlin, Christopher. *Public Health and Social Justice in the Age of Chadwick: Britain, 1800–1854*. Cambridge: Cambridge University Press, 1998.
Smith, William. *The Swimming Club Directory 1885, For the United Kingdom*. Llandudno: William Smith, 1885.

Holborn, Lambeth and Manchester: Three Case Studies in Municipal Swimming Pool Provision

After the introduction of the Baths and Washhouses Act, 1846, local authorities began to construct baths facilities across England, and by 1918 municipal authorities were the largest providers of swimming pools in the country. However, there was no uniform development among all municipal authorities. Indeed, some municipal governments were much more keen on swimming provision than others. The London boroughs of Holborn and Lambeth and the city of Manchester provide contrasting examples of municipal development, in areas that differed in the size of their populations and their public policies towards the provision of swimming pools.

Prior to the reorganization of London into boroughs in 1900–01, the majority of what became Holborn consisted of the parishes of St Giles in the Fields and St George, Bloomsbury, which for purposes of enacting the Baths and Washhouses Act had formed a joint vestry. The joint vestry adopted the act early in 1850; commissioners were appointed and held their first meeting in March of that year. [1] In contrast to the experience in Lambeth, detailed below, the commissioners of the joint vestry formed in Bloomsbury very quickly set about their work and arranged for the provision of a baths establishment for the people in their district. Initially, the commissioners considered purchasing the existing 'National Baths', a private concern that existed in Holborn. This idea was not pursued, however, and by December of 1851 tenders were being issued for the construction of a municipal bath establishment on Endell Street, near Lascelles Court. [2] Provision was made for the inclusion of two plunge baths, basically swimming pools but so named, perhaps, to conform to the letter of the Baths and Washhouse Act, 1846. The construction of the two swimming pools may have been the most problematic aspect of the project, as they were the last areas of the baths establishment to be completed. Eventually, however, the facility opened to the public at the end of June 1853. [3] The two swimming pools were, however, quite small; Dr Dudgeon reported on their small size and irregular shape in his survey of 1870. [4] Their primary use, initially, seems to have been as large multi-person baths, rather than as swimming spaces. Almost immediately after the opening of the baths establishment, for example, the commissioners resolved that boys of the Ragged School be allowed half-price entrance to the second-class plunge bath on Wednesdays from 9.00 to 11.00. There were to be no concessions, however, on the charge for individual wash baths. Charges were on the higher end of the scale for the time, with the normal admission charge to the second-class plunge bath being 2d. [5]

Although the baths commissioners for the joint vestry of St Giles and St George had been quite active in the rapid provision of baths for the district, they were also quite conservative when it came to any innovation in the use of the establishment. It appears that the commissioners saw the provision of the Endell Street Baths as essentially a hygienic enterprise. In 1890 the Metropolitan Police 'E' Division Rowing and Swimming Club, based at the Bow Street police station, wrote to the commissioners asking if it was possible to obtain a concessionary rate to the baths for members, understanding that a minimum number of tickets might have to be purchased. This request was refused by the commissioners because they felt granting such a request would be contrary to the objects for which the baths were established. A similar request was received in 1891 in regard to the students of Vere Street Board School, Drury Lane. Again, the commissioners declined to grant the request, citing the fact that such an undertaking would be against the objects of the baths. [6] After a long series of negotiations, students from the School Board for London were admitted to the swimming pools, beginning in late 1891, at a reduced charge of 1d, but only on Tuesdays, Wednesdays and Friday mornings from 9.00 to 11.00. [7]

Starting in January 1892 the baths commissioners began to close the swimming pools for various periods of time over the winter. Initially, the closure was only for a period of two months, from the start of January to 1 March 1892. [8] By 1894, however, the winter closure was running until the end of March, and by 1895 the closure was starting at the beginning of November and continuing until the end of March. [9] These closures were consistent with the powers of closure granted by the Baths and Washhouses Act, 1878. At no point, however, was the establishment of a gymnasium or other facility as authorized by those same amendments considered by the baths commissioners. Its seems likely that the commissioners were either not prepared to spend the money required to convert the swimming pools into gymnasiums over the winter months, thereby simply saving money by closing the pools, or considered that there were already enough local facilities that allowed for the practice of gymnastics.

It is apparent that the baths commissioners for the joint vestries of St Giles in the Fields and St George, Bloomsbury, were inherently conservative in their approach to managing the baths establishment. Although they were early adopters of the 1846 Baths and Washhouses Act, they adhered to the strict letter of the law when it came to operating the baths. Swimming pools may have been included as part of the original design of the baths, but they were termed 'plunge baths' and seem to have been regarded by the commissioners as large pools for the washing of large numbers of people, rather than as places to swim. Even after 1878, when amendments to the act allowed for covered swimming pools to be supported by local rates, there was little change. The commissioners may have used the term 'swimming baths' rather than plunge baths, but the continued emphasis seems to have been on cleanliness rather than swimming. In 1892, when structural improvements had to be made to the baths (in order to prevent part of the building from collapsing), the suggestion was made that the existing pools should be renovated, either making them larger or combining them into a single pool. Nothing came of this. [10] The suggestion was evidently kept in mind, however, because in 1918 Agnes Campbell could record that the Endell Street Baths, still the only municipal baths facility in what had then become Holborn, had been extended in 1902. [11] The measurements of the swimming baths after this extension were 90 feet by 28 feet and 50 feet by 40 feet. These were significantly changed from the measurements given by Dr Dudgeon when he surveyed the pools in 1870 [12].

A great deal of the conservatism among the commissioners was likely due to financial concerns. The commissioners, it would seem, wanted to provide minimal facilities, at the cheapest cost to the ratepayers, while levying high admission charges and spending as little as possible on operations at the baths. By 1913 the admission charges for the Endell Street Baths were still quite high, at 6d for adult entry into the first-class swimming pool, although only 2d for entry into the second-class pool. [13] There was clearly a concern both for the financial stability of the baths and for social exclusion between the classes. Very few of the working class would be able to afford the 6d fee for swimming in the first-class swimming pool on a regular basis.

In contrast to the other districts surveyed, in the vestry (later the borough) of Lambeth in London there was long-standing opposition to the implementation of the Baths and Washhouses Act, 1846. Exactly *why* there was opposition is not made clear. After the first attempt to introduce the act was blocked by ratepayers in a parish council meeting in 1876, a period of almost 15 years was to pass before the act was actually adopted in 1891. This suggests that the process for the adoption of the act faced stiff opposition. It seems likely that opposition to the adoption of the act was based on the possibility of an increase of several pennies to be added to the vestry rates on the act's adoption, in order to pay for the construction allowed under the act. The first attempt to have the legislation implemented by the vestry council was made in March 1876, when a group of ratepayers in the parish petitioned the vestry to hold a vote on whether or not the act should be adopted. [14] However, it was not until another vote was held in November 1890 for the purpose of adopting the Baths and Washhouses Act and its various amendments that the act was finally adopted. [15]

On 20 November 1890, the vestry of Lambeth finally adopted the Baths and Washhouses Act. [16] The new baths commissioners went about their work slowly and it was not until 17 November 1892 that they produced their first proposal to provide municipal baths for Lambeth. These plans, however, were quickly abandoned after it was discovered that there would be many legal problems in securing the manorial rights to the land being considered for construction. Instead, attention was turned to purchasing the site of the Lambeth Polytechnic on Ferndale Road in Brixton. This site already had a private swimming pool on the site, in addition to a well to supply water to the bath. It seemed an ideal solution to the provision issue. In actual fact, however, the bath on this site was never to be opened under the management of the vestry. The purchase of the polytechnic took place, but within three months of the purchase, the vestrymen and ratepayers of the parish were questioning the wisdom of the transaction, especially the cost of it. [17]

For the next year the purchase of the polytechnic seems to have been the subject of quite vigorous debate within the vestry. The full extent of the ensuing debate about the baths is revealed in the next surviving report of the commissioners from 26 July 1894. The terse report detailed that, after extensive legal opinion had been sought, it had been determined that the site of the Lambeth Polytechnic could be sold, provided the proceeds of the sale were used for the provision of equivalent baths elsewhere in the parish. A piece of land at the corner of the Lambeth and Kennington Roads was proposed as the site for vestry baths, and this was approved in principle, provided the Lambeth Polytechnic was sold off to provide the funding for purchase. [18] Debate over the purchase of this piece of land also dragged on for nearly a year. At a contentious vestry meeting in April 1895 final approval was given to the plan to purchase the land at the intersection of the Lambeth and Kennington Roads, and to sell the polytechnic site. As negotiations for the sale of the polytechnic were still ongoing, a loan application to the Local Government Board was to be made to cover the cost of purchasing the Lambeth and Kennington Road site. Although not explicit in the minutes, it seems likely that this loan request was part of the reason there was opposition to the entire plan. Local ratepayers would have been concerned about having to pay higher rates to cover the repayment of the loan. Nevertheless, construction of the vestry baths was begun at some point in 1896, though the sale of the Polytechnic site continued to be delayed. By September 1897 it had been resolved by the vestry that the baths commissioners were to sell the polytechnic site at a loss, if necessary, to the Technical Education Board. A technical school on the site would clearly be of benefit to the district, and would make up for any immediate financial loss suffered from the sale. [19]

After all the arguments over money and property sales, the long-proposed baths were finally opened. On 9 July 1897 the new Lambeth Public Baths were opened at the corner of the Lambeth and Kennington Roads, in a ceremony presided over by the Prince and Princess of Wales. The new facility contained three swimming pools; a 132 foot by 40 foot first-class men's pool, a 90 foot by 30 foot second-class men's pool, and a 56 foot by 25 foot women's pool. [20] Although the construction of the baths had been dogged by political arguments, mainly about expense, support for the baths, once erected, seems to have increased. A continued concern for the cost of operating the baths is evident in the decision to close both men's baths over the winter months, leaving only the much smaller women's bath open, but the decision to provide electric lighting in the baths must have been a costly one, at least initially. [21] The Lambeth Public Baths were clearly a major addition to the local civic amenities in Lambeth. Despite the cost of construction and operation, the facility was a testimony to what could be provided at the municipal level.

The initial charge for access to the first-class swimming pools for both men and women was 6d. Debate over whether this should be reduced to 4d occurred in September 1898, but the decision was taken to leave the charges at the original level. [22] Evidently there was concern among some members of the committee that the pricing structure of the baths was excluding some potential users. The entry charges to the baths were finally changed, and by the winter of 1911 the charge for adult entry to the men's and women's first-class swimming pools was 4d, and to the men's second-class swimming pool 2d. [23]

The provision of municipal swimming facilities in Lambeth was quite late compared to many other local authorities, both in London and in the provinces. This seems to have stemmed from several causes. The fact that private facilities already existed within the Lambeth area, most notably the Lambeth Baths (Westminster Bridge Road), probably reduced popular agitation in the vestry for such facilities. Also there seems to have been an underlying conservatism in the ratepayers of the vestry, as registered in the minutes noted above, towards any innovation or expenditure that might necessitate an increase in the rates paid to local government. This theory is reinforced by the use of the smaller women's swimming pool during the winter season as a pool for all classes of swimmers. The decision to close the two larger pools meant a reduction in costs, with smaller inputs of water, and fuel for heating the water. In addition fewer attendants were required to watch the pools. The later decision to maintain a 6d admission charge to the first-class swimming pools until some point after 1900 also points to financial caution. Higher user charges, especially for the more exclusive areas of the facility, meant less needed to be paid by ratepayers to maintain those facilities.

London was, of course, a special case. But what was the situation in England's rapidly expanding industrial cities? Perhaps the most famous of these was Manchester. There, links to swimming went back to the early nineteenth century, and it is perhaps no surprise that once the building of swimming pools was undertaken on a large scale across England, Manchester was part of the trend. Manchester is also a useful case to study because the development of swimming provision within the city was markedly different from that in London. It is clear, however, that some of the same trends witnessed in other locations held true here as well. Initially, private bath companies provided washing, laundry and swimming facilities to the populace of the surrounding urban districts.

Manchester City Council established a Baths and Washhouse Committee in August 1876 even before it had adopted the Baths and Washhouses Act. By January 1877 the committee had determined that Manchester required a minimum of four baths buildings (including swimming and wash baths). The company that owned the private facilities on Mayfield and Leaf Streets was willing to sell the properties to the committee for a price of £19,000. This price seems to have been deemed too high at the time, for by the end of January the committee was no longer seeking to negotiate the purchase of the two existing baths, and instead was looking for land that could be purchased for the construction of civic baths buildings. [24] By April 1877 the committee had changed its position on the purchase of existing private baths buildings, and had resumed negotiations with the private company that owned the Leaf Street and Mayfield Baths. In June the committee recommended to the council to purchase these properties at the previously rejected price of £19,000. From February 1877 onwards the committee also continued to look for suitable sites for baths within Manchester, and eventually recommended the purchase of a site on Henry Street, New Islington. By July of 1877, plans were being drawn up for the construction of a baths building including two swimming pools on the New Islington site. With all of this work taking place on baths and washhouses within Manchester, the council decided that it was necessary to ensure that everything was done legally, and on 1 August 1877, The Baths and Washhouses Act, 1846, along with its various amendments, was adopted by the council. With these legal powers then in place, the corporation would take possession of the private baths it was purchasing on 29 September 1877. [25]

It is clear then that, after a somewhat hesitant start, Manchester Council very quickly became committed to the large-scale provision of baths facilities within its area of jurisdiction. The large initial payment for the purchase of the private baths, even after a six-month period of indecision, was a precursor of the council's continuing commitment, until well after 1918, to provide bathing, and especially swimming, facilities within the city. In order to ensure that the newly purchased Manchester baths compared favourably to others in the country, a subcommittee of the Baths And Washhouses Committee toured various baths and washhouses in Eastbourne and London in December 1877. [26] It is unclear whether or not councillors were deliberately attempting to equal or surpass the programmes already undertaken by other councils, but between the current and planned projects in Manchester, the result would be the provision of more baths, especially swimming pools, than any single parish in London and probably most other provincial cities and towns.

By 1878, the first year that the council would be operating swimming pools through the Baths and Washhouses Committee, local innovations in the use of the baths were well under way. In May it was decided to reserve the second-class swimming pool at Leaf Street for an hour every Thursday afternoon for the use of males aged 12 and under, at a charge of 1d. The water in the pool was to be specially lowered for the use of these customers, and the new policy was to be advertised in local newspapers and circulated to Manchester School Board schools and local public school heads. In addition, parties of 12 juveniles accompanied by a teacher or other responsible person were to be admitted to both the Leaf Street and Mayfield Baths at the price of a halfpenny. [27] This innovation is important, because it was voluntarily proposed and adopted by the baths committee roughly a decade *prior* to the extension of similar privileges for students being available in London after prolonged campaigning by the ASA and School Board for London authorities. [28]

The swimming pools in Manchester seem, from the evidence, to have been effectively a male preserve at this time. This view is further reinforced by a minute of 26 June 1879, about the need for a women's swimming pool to be established in Manchester. [29] At that same meeting the by-laws to be enforced within the corporation's baths were revised, and several more regulations were enacted that were aimed at ensuring a proper social tone was maintained within the baths. Notable among these new regulations were those prohibiting any bather from using a bath of a higher class than he had paid for, and a prohibition against using any bath, including the swimming pools, for more than 30 minutes at a time without paying for a second admission. [30] Clearly, these regulations were aimed, in part, at keeping the social classes apart, with the working classes pretty much relegated to the cheaper second-class facilities, while the wealthier middle and upper classes used the first-class facilities. In the extraordinary case that a working man managed to save enough money to be able to afford access to the first-class facilities, he would not be able to enjoy them for long, more than likely not being able to come up with a second admission fee after 30 minutes.

Throughout the 1880s and 1890s the number of baths containing swimming pools in Manchester continued to increase as the Baths and Washhouses Committee continued to support widespread access to such facilities for its citizens. Between 1878 and 1913 the committee built or took control of 14 separate baths facilities containing a total of 33 swimming pools. As can be clearly seen, throughout this period the corporation was undertaking a building programme that was greater than any single borough in London and which rivalled most of the other large cities in England of the period. By 1918, Manchester had the largest number of swimming pools of any city in England, excluding the combined total for all of the boroughs of London. [31]

Besides being a large provider of swimming facilities to its population, and the populations of surrounding districts, Manchester was also in the forefront of other developments in the swimming world. In 1880 the Baths and Washhouses Committee appointed two swimming masters, at a salary of 20 shillings per week, to provide free instruction in swimming in the baths of the corporation from 13.00 to 20.30 daily. These instructors would be allowed to take on private students from the opening of the pools in the morning until 13.00. [32] By 1881 professional swimmers such as J.B. Johnson of Leeds were running swimming entertainments in the corporation baths that could attract up to 1,100 spectators. [33] While professionals usually had to hire the baths for their entertainments, on occasion the Baths and Washhouses Committee engaged noted professionals to give displays. In July of 1881, for example, Captain Matthew Webb, the first man to swim the English Channel, was engaged for six performances in Manchester. He performed twice at each of the three baths facilities with swimming pools at the time between 13 July and 16 July 1881, and was paid £18 18s and his return rail fare from London. [34] After Webb's death in July 1883, during his misguided attempt to swim the rapids below Niagara Falls, the corporation allowed another professional, James Finney, to use the civic baths free of charge for the purpose of running a series of four swimming exhibitions or entertainments as benefits in aid of Mrs Webb and her children. [35] Besides being places to clean one's body or engage in some physical activity, from an early period the Manchester swimming pools were also places of entertainment, where people could witness the abilities of superior and professional swimmers.

The Baths and Washhouses Committee in Manchester was also interested in promoting swimming as a recreational activity. Obviously, the more swimmers using their facilities, the better the financial situation of the baths would be. But there seems to have been even more than a simple financial motive behind the committee's promotion of swimming. In 1886 the committee set the charges for use of its swimming baths at 4d for the use of the first-class baths, and 2d for the use of the second-class baths. Youths aged between 12 and 15 years of age were admitted at half price prior to 13.00 each day. [36] By 1888 the committee had authorized the sale of lots of 250 tickets at the price of 1d per ticket to girls' schools, mill girls and other similar groups. [37] This was half the usual price for use of the second-class swimming pools in the city. In the same year the committee also decided that members of recognized swimming clubs were to be admitted to first-class swimming pools on club practice nights at a charge of 2d, rather than the usual 4d. [38] Perhaps most interestingly, however, in 1890 the Baths and Washhouses Committee proposed that at each of the establishments in the city housing swimming pools there should be free admittance to a designated pool after 16.00, Monday and Saturday, between 1 October 1890 and 1 March 1891. This proposal was rejected by the city council when it was brought forward to that body for approval. [39] The original proposal is the clearest evidence that a significant portion of the Manchester Baths and Washhouses Committee was interested in promoting swimming in the corporation's baths for the broader social good.

That the members of Manchester's Baths and Washhouses Committee were committed to the promotion of swimming, often without great concern over the financial cost of such promotion, was further reinforced by their actions through most of the 1890s. It has already been noted how the committee made provision for reduced charges for school swimmers starting in 1878, and club swimmers starting in 1888. These provisions were further developed and supported over time. By 1893 lots of 250 tickets were being provided to schools, allowing entry to the swimming pools at reduced rates. First-class tickets were to be sold for 1d, while second-class tickets were to be sold for a halfpenny. There were restrictions on exactly when these tickets could be used, but the terms were fairly generous, being two mornings or afternoons a week, plus Friday afternoons and Saturday mornings. [40] In the following year, all members of the Manchester Police Swimming Club were allowed to swim at the club rate in any Manchester swimming pool on production of their club membership card. The usual practice of the time was for club members only to receive the club membership rate on club nights at the swimming pool where their club was based. [41] Also by 1894 the Manchester Baths and Washhouses Committee was providing a dedicated women's swimming pool, or designated women's swimming times, at all its facilities. [42] It is clear enough that there were numerous swimming groups in the city (schools, police, private clubs) keen to use the local municipal facilities. How far these clubs had been encouraged to form and become active *because* of the existence of local municipal facilities is, of course, hard to tell. Yet it seems reasonable to claim that by the 1890s the City of Manchester's authorities had supervised and encouraged a marked expansion of swimming in that city.

In 1898 Manchester Council adopted a resolution calling for the Baths and Washhouses Committee to examine the possibility of offering free second-class wash bath and swimming bath facilities to the citizens of the city, an interesting development considering the council had blocked a similar idea on a smaller scale in 1891. The committee responded to the council's resolution with a pamphlet dated 17 May 1898. The committee had to argue that such a plan was not feasible, notably on the question of public order. It was considered that if such a course were adopted, there would be a crush of people wanting to enter the baths at very restricted periods of time, such as early morning and early evening. The baths would not be able to handle that crush. The safeguarding of property and the maintenance of public decency would also become quite difficult. [43] In the same year, however, the committee extended free bathing privileges to school students, as long as they were accompanied by a teacher, between 6.00 and 16.30 daily from 1 April to 30 September, and between 9.00 and 16.30 daily from 1 October to 31 March. [44] Clearly, the members of the Baths and Washhouses Committee were more concerned with the maintenance of order, rather than being dead set against the idea of providing free swimming sessions. There is also more than a hint here that the baths might be overwhelmed by popularity. There was no guarantee that the staff and facilities could cope with the potential demand. Those closest to the swimming world in Manchester clearly knew that there was a very large constituency of swimmers keen to gain access to their facilities – if they were free.

This commitment to the provision of free swimming in Manchester was further demonstrated in 1900, when the Baths and Washhouses Committee instituted a programme of free swimming for students in the corporation's pools during the summer vacation. During the restricted period of the programme, a total of

136,174 students were allowed to swim for free. The vast majority of these were boys, constituting 117,355 of the total. [45] This was the first year that the programme was run, but not the last. In fact, the programme was to run through to at least the start of the First World War, although due to other more pressing concerns, returns of bathers were not always presented in the minutes. [46] Starting in 1903, free season tickets to the swimming baths were awarded to all school swimming competition winners, all students at Manchester schools possessing a Life Saving Society proficiency certificate and all members of the Manchester Police swimming club who possessed a Life Saving Society proficiency certificate. [47] These concessions were followed by the implementation of a plan to introduce free instruction in life-saving techniques at corporation pools. [48] This programme ran until at least 1911, although at no point prior to the end of the First World War is there any official notice of its being discontinued.

In 1912 the question of mixed bathing in the swimming pools of the corporation was raised for discussion in the Baths and Washhouses Committee. A petition in favour of mixed bathing, consisting of 287 signatures, was presented to the committee on 18 September 1912. From this the general superintendent of the baths was requested to gather more information about the subject. [49] The end result was that a pilot programme was run to see if mixed bathing could be run without any social problems taking place. By 1915 the experiment in mixed bathing was considered to have been a success, but implementation of the innovation across the corporation's facilities was delayed due to the war. [50]

Manchester Corporation, then, was a great promoter of swimming from its adoption of the Baths and Washhouses Act, 1846, in 1877 until the First World War. While restrained by concern for public order and decency from being too innovative, the city's Baths and Washhouses Committee was in the forefront of providing enterprising programmes to promote the use of the civic swimming pool and the adoption of swimming in the population at large. In particular, its relatively generous provision of facilities for women's swimming, and its early experimentation in the provision of mixed bathing, were ahead of much of the rest of England. It is impossible to know for certain why there was this great support for swimming, but a strong pre-existing tradition of swimming in Manchester and the vicinity seems evident from the source material; this tradition coupled with civic pride may well have been the impetus for so much emphasis on swimming in the city.

Notes

[1] Camden Local Studies and Archives Centre (hereafter CLSAC), London, CO/GG/BA/2/1 (B/7C23), St Giles and Bloomsbury Baths and Washhouses Rough Minutes March 1850, fols. 2–3, minutes of 15 March 1850. Holborn Borough Council destroyed the majority of its committee minutes, including the baths and washhouses papers, prior to amalgamating with the Borough of Camden in the 1960s. The surviving papers, however, provide an insight into

developments in the provision of swimming in the area that became the borough from 1850 to 1897: email from Aiden Flood, archivist, Camden Local Studies and Archives Centre, 1 November 2001.
[2] CLSAC, CO/GG/BA/2/1 (B/7C23), St Giles and Bloomsbury Baths and Washhouses Rough Minutes March 1850, fols. 2–3, 60, minutes of 15 March 1850 and of 12 Dec. 1851.
[3] CLSAC, CO/GG/BA/2/1 (B/7C23), St Giles and Bloomsbury Baths and Washhouses Rough Minutes March 1850, fols. 118–19, 127, minutes of 10 June 1853 and 1 July 1853.
[4] Dudgeon, *The Swimming Baths of London*, 20–1.
[5] CLSAC, CO/GG/BA/2/1 (B/7C23), St Giles and Bloomsbury Baths and Washhouses Rough Minutes March 1850, fol. 143, minutes of 29 July 1853.
[6] CLSAC, CO/GG/BA/1/1 (B/7D1), St Giles Bloomsbury Baths and Washhouses Minutes, 3–4, 74–5, minutes of 5 June 1890 and 30 April 1891.
[7] CLSAC, CO/GG/BA/1/1 (B/7D1), St Giles Bloomsbury Baths and Washhouses Minutes, 80–1, 133, 215–17, 312, minutes of 14 May 1891, 27 Nov. 1891, 28 July 1892 and 27 April 1893.
[8] CLSAC, CO/GG/BA/1/1 (B/7D1), St Giles Bloomsbury Baths and Washhouses Minutes, 139, minutes of 31 Dec. 1891.
[9] CLSAC, CO/GG/BA/1/2 (B/7D2), St Giles Bloomsbury Baths and Washhouses Minutes, 16–17, 109, 166, 220–1, 272–3, 327, 380, minutes of 27 March 1894, 21 March 1895, 17 Oct. 1895, 19 March 1896, 15 Oct. 1896, 18 March 1897, and 21 Oct. 1897.
[10] CLSAC, CO/GG/BA/1/1 (B/7D1), St Giles Bloomsbury Baths and Washhouses Minutes, 215–17, 236, minutes of 28 July 1892 and 29 Sept. 1892.
[11] Campbell, *Report on Public Baths*, appendix, 86–91. For Dudgeon's measurements, see above.
[12] Dudgeon, *The Swimming Baths of London*, passim.
[13] Ibid.
[14] Lambeth Archives Minet Library (hereafter LAML), P12/80/1/2, Petition by Ratepayers to the Vestry on the issue of the Baths and Washhouses Act.
[15] LAML, P12/41, Lambeth Baths and Washhouses Committee Minutes 1891–97, 1, minutes of 5 Feb. 1891.
[16] LAML, P12/80/3, Baths Committee Reports 1890–1901, report of 20 Nov. 1890. This entire file box consists of various copies of the printed reports of the Baths Committee clipped from the printed minutes of the vestry and then simply boxed. Some excerpts still retain their binding, while others are loose or pinned together.
[17] LAML, P12/80/3, Baths Committee Reports 1890–1901, reports of 17 Nov. 1892, 30 March 1893, and 24 June 1893.
[18] LAML, P12/80/3, Baths Committee Reports 1890–1901, report of 26 July 1894.
[19] LAML, P12/80/3, Baths Committee Reports 1890–1901, reports of 4 April 1895; 9 July 1896; 8 July 1897; and 16 Sept. 1897.
[20] LAML, P12/80/10, *A Souvenir of the 9th July, 1897. From the Clerk to The Chairman*.
[21] LAML, P12/41, Lambeth Baths and Washhouses Committee Minutes 1891–1897, 216, 253–4, minutes of 21 Sept. 1897 and 28 Dec. 1897.
[22] LAML, P12/38, Lambeth Baths and Cemetery Committee Minutes 1898–14 Oct. 1899, 98, minutes of 19 Sept. 1898.
[23] LAML, P12/80/11/1, Winter 1911–12 Bathing Hours and Costs. This item is a small folded card detailing the winter arrangements for the use of the baths.
[24] Manchester Local Studies Archives Service (hereafter MLSAS), Proceedings of the Baths and Wash Houses Committee, vol. 1, 1, 12–13, 16, minutes of 17 Aug. 1876; 16 Jan. 1877; 30 Jan. 1877.
[25] MLSAS, Proceedings of the Baths and Wash Houses Committee, vol. 1, 20, 23–4, 31, 34, 47–8, Minutes of 27 Feb. 1877; 10 April 1877; 5 June 1877; 3 July, 1877; 28 Aug. 1877.

[26] MLSAS, Proceedings of the Baths and Wash Houses Committee, vol. 1, 73, minutes of 3 Jan. 1878. Baths and washhouses in the parishes of Brixton, Clapham, Kennington, Marylebone, Paddington, Pimlico and St George's were toured during the visit to London.
[27] MLSAS, Proceedings of the Baths and Wash Houses Committee, vol. 1, 102–6, minutes of 2 May 1878.
[28] For information on the campaigns undertaken by the School Board for London and the ASA, through SCASA, to have swimming allowed as an activity of official instruction for students see the following: Amateur Swimming Association Library, ASA Minute Book no. 2, fol. 33, minutes of the ASA Annual General Meeting, 23 April 1892; LAML, P12/80/2/2, School Board for London, Report of the Physical Education Subcommittee on Bathing Accommodation and Swimming Classes (Public Elementary Schools), 1–12; Sinclair and Henry, *Swimming*, 352–3.
[29] MLSAS, Proceedings of the Baths and Wash Houses Committee, vol. 1, 252, minutes of 26 June 1879.
[30] MLSAS, Proceedings of the Baths and Wash Houses Committee, vol. 1, 253–4, minutes of 26 June 1879.
[31] Campbell, *Report on Public Baths*, appendix, 50–63.
[32] MLSAS, Proceedings of the Baths and Wash Houses Committee, vol. 1, 391, minutes of 29 April 1880.
[33] MLSAS, Baths and Wash-Houses Committee Minutes, vol. 2, 38, minutes of 26 May 1881. For Johnson's entertainment on 19 May 1881 a total of 1,156 tickets were sold.
[34] MLSAS, Baths and Wash-Houses Committee Minutes, vol. 2, 61, minutes of 30 June 1881.
[35] MLSAS, Baths and Wash-Houses Committee Minutes, vol. 2, 344, minutes of 26 Sept. 1883.
[36] MLSAS, Baths and Wash-Houses Committee Minutes, vol. 3, fol. 97, minutes of 31 March 1886.
[37] MLSAS, Baths and Wash-Houses Committee Minutes, vol. 4, fol. 18.
[38] MLSAS, Baths and Wash-Houses Committee Minutes, vol. 4, fol. 32, minutes of 29 Aug. 1888.
[39] MLSAS, Baths and Wash-Houses Committee Minutes, vol. 4, fol. 178–9, minutes of 21 May 1890.
[40] MLSAS, Baths and Wash-Houses Committee Minutes, vol. 6, fols. 11–12, glued-in handbills dated 22 March 1893.
[41] MLSAS, Baths and Wash-Houses Committee Minutes, vol. 6, fols. 186–7, secretary of the Manchester Police Swimming Club to Manchester Baths and Washhouses Committee, n.d. The letter is interpolated between minutes of June and July 1894.
[42] MLSAS, Baths and Wash-Houses Committee Minutes, vol. 6, fol. 140, glued-in handbill of 31 March 1894.
[43] MLSAS, Baths and Wash-Houses Committee Minutes, vol. 9, fol. 15, glued-in pamphlet of 17 May 1898.
[44] MLSAS, Baths and Wash-Houses Committee Minutes, vol. 9, fols. 32–3, glued-in typescript, n.d. These sheets are placed between minutes for May and Aug. 1898.
[45] MLSAS, Baths and Wash-Houses Committee Minutes, vol. 10, fol. 74, minutes of 19 Feb. 1901.
[46] The last recorded set of returns prior to 1918 for student swimmers dates to October 1915. MLSAS, Baths and Wash-Houses Committee Minutes, vol. 17, fols. 24–5, minutes of 20 Oct. 1915.
[47] MLSAS, Baths and Wash Houses Committee Minutes, vol. 11, fols. 35–6, minutes of 15 April 1903.
[48] MLSAS, Baths and Wash Houses Committee Minutes, vol. 11, fols. 45–51, 70, 95, 125, minutes of 19 May 1903, 17 June 1903, 19 Aug. 1903, 18 Nov. 1903, and 17 Feb. 1904.

[49] MLSAS, Baths and Wash Houses Committee Minutes, vol. 15, fols. 195–6, minutes of 18 Sept. 1912.
[50] MLSAS, Baths and Wash Houses Committee Minutes, vol. 16, fols. 222–3, minutes of 21 April 1915.

References

Campbell, Agnes. *Report on Public Baths and Wash-Houses in the United Kingdom*. Edinburgh: Edinburgh University Press, 1918.
Dudgeon, R.E. *The Swimming Baths of London*. London: Henry Turner and Co., 1870.
Sinclair, Archibald, and William Henry. *Swimming* (The Badminton Library of Sports and Pastimes). London: Longmans, Green, and Co., 1893.

Swimming at the Clarendon Schools

Prior to the last quarter of the nineteenth century there was no mass educational system in England. A formal education was limited to a quite small minority of the population who attended private institutions, mostly termed 'public schools', up and down the country. Within these institutions sports, games and physical activities became increasingly important over the course of the nineteenth century.

The major public schools were prime movers in the development of many of today's games and recreations. But this was not the case with swimming. Indeed, swimming was often a very minor activity at most public schools, and even when it was recognized it received a great deal less support than other sports and recreations. Similarly, and by extension, the great universities of Cambridge, London and Oxford, whose sporting trends followed those of the Public Schools, also did not adopt swimming as a sporting activity until late in the nineteenth century. This was in sharp contrast to other sporting activities that developed within the public schools and which received active support from the public school establishment, such as athletics. As T.M. James pointed out in 1977,

> It is interesting to note that the Amateur Athletic Association never had to argue a case for inclusion: this was for the simple reason that the Amateur Athletic Association had its origins within the educational sphere whereas the Amateur Swimming Association did not. This demonstrates the substantial difference which existed between the two sports and their contribution to nineteenth-century education, in that the one emanated from within the educational world whilst the other was the product of the wider society. [1]

While we must bear James's statement in mind, it is important to reconsider the contribution of the public schools to the development of swimming. As J.A. Mangan and others have pointed out, the public schools were responsible for fostering

Victorian sporting activity in general. [2] Archibald Sinclair and William Henry, the chroniclers of the swimming world for the late 1800s, recorded in 1893 that a large number of public schools were engaged in some form of swimming: 'At Winchester, Cheltenham, Sherborne, Tonbridge, Shrewsbury, Merchant Taylors [*sic*], Highgate, Charterhouse, Dulwich, Royal Naval School, Marlborough, Wellington, Clifton, Royal Military College, Oundle, Weymouth, Surrey County, Newton, &c., &c., swimming competitions are carried out and the pastime is encouraged.' [3] This list is in addition to the detailed surveys that Sinclair and Henry made of swimming at Eton, Harrow, Rossall, Rugby and Uppingham. [4] It is evident then, despite James's caution, that important developments in swimming were made at some of the public schools.

Not all the public schools across England were equally well known, nor were the practices of each school equally influential. To focus this examination, then, it is necessary to select a set of schools that were well-known and considered influential in their practices. The schools surveyed by the Clarendon Commission serve well in both categories. By focusing on these schools, however, there will be certain omissions that will need to be taken up by future studies. Coverage of smaller provincial schools in general will suffer, as will any coverage of the practices of public schools for women. This is not to say that such examinations are unimportant, indeed such studies are likely to reveal many details that add to the understanding of swimming within the broader English society of the later nineteenth century.

It was in 1861 that Parliament established the Public Schools and Colleges Commission, more commonly known as the Clarendon Commission. In the same year the commission began its survey of Charterhouse School, Eton College, Harrow School, Merchant Taylors' School, Rugby College, St Paul's School, Shrewsbury School, Westminster School and Winchester College. Although primarily set out as an examination into the financial affairs and management of the schools, the commissioners also inquired into the manner and content of teaching within the schools, and the sport and recreational provision for students. It submitted its report to Parliament in 1864. Questions number 35 to 41 of part three of the written survey circulated by the commissioners were concerned with play, games and exercise within each of the schools. Swimming was mentioned specifically in question 41 as part of a query if any activities or games were compulsory within the school, such as a swimming requirement for being allowed to row. [5] From the responses the commissioners noted:

> Swimming is taught at Eton and Westminster. It is taught also at Shrewsbury. The desire to go on the river, which no boy is allowed to do till he has shown himself able to swim, operates at these schools, especially at the two former, as a sufficient inducement with a large number of boys; and we believe that at Eton almost every boy learns to swim, even if he does not row. At Winchester, indeed, where boating is not found practicable, it appears that a very large majority of the upper boys can swim; and this is probably the case at other schools having good bathing-places. It is much to be wished that every boy who goes to school should, if possible, learn to swim. [6]

By surveying the schools examined by the Clarendon Commission, an attempt can be made to determine the effect they had, if any, on the dissemination of swimming into the wider world of English society. In addition, depending on when swimming became organized in a specific school, it may become clear whether the schools were responding to outside pressure or were creating a new trend of their own, and then exporting it outwards.

Although its claim may be open to challenge by Rugby, Harrow School seems to have been the first educational establishment of any type to have a dedicated swimming pool, with the construction of what was known as the 'Duck Puddle' or 'Ducker' sometime in 1810 or 1811. This pool was the successor of an earlier 'Duck Puddle,' a local natural pond, which had been in use by the boys of the school for bathing and swimming from at least the late 1780s or early 1790s. [7] Although only a muddy hole dug in the ground and subject to being filled with frogs, ducks and other wildlife, the 'Duck Puddle' was a step removed from the previous English tradition of only natural bodies of water such as rivers, lakes and the sea being used for swimming. By the 1870s and 1880s, however, the existence of a swimming pool within a public school was becoming much more common, and by the mid-twentieth century, any of the larger public schools that did *not* have a swimming pool was an unusual school indeed. Public schools may not have created a cult of swimming, but they helped promote the activity. In the 1870s and 1880s most schools seem to have viewed swimming as a valuable skill that should be encouraged as a precaution against the danger of drowning when students were out on the river with the boating club, or otherwise playing around the various natural bodies of water in the vicinity of many of the public schools of the time. Exact records of the numbers of students able to swim at public schools are usually scattered and incomplete, but it seems likely that a large percentage of students at public schools were able to swim by the time they left their schools.

The first record of a swimming test being applied at one of the Clarendon schools appears to be at Eton, where a school swimming test was instituted in 1836, apparently in response to various drowning incidents. The administration of this test has continued in one form or another until the present. The same report which records the decision to institute the swimming test also reveals that there were attempts to establish a series of swimming prizes around 1853, but due to poor weather conditions these efforts had been suspended. [8] The Clarendon Commission recorded that 350 boys in the school could swim in 1862, and that the swimming test was then roughly 100 yards in distance. [9] The existence of a test indicates that swimming was not wholly ignored at Eton, although it was not a major sporting activity. What swimming there was prior to 1853 seems to have been the continuation of a long-standing school tradition of using the Thames and other local bodies of water for recreation purposes. In his history of Eton College, Sir H.C. Maxwell Lyte claimed that as early as 1727 there were at least seven locations along the Thames where boys went to bathe, and by 1840 official school bathing places had been established at 'Athens', Upper Hope and Cuckoo Weir. [10]

Eton also holds the distinction of hosting what were perhaps the first two swimming clubs in English history, the two school clubs known as the Philolutic Society (1832) and the Psychrolutic Society (1828). Both were designed as clubs for Eton and Cambridge students and masters who enjoyed bathing. It appears that the Cambridge members of the two societies were all old Etonians, though this is not explicitly stated in the records. While it is not clear whether bathing in this instance included swimming, it seems plausible that it did. The Philolutes had been organized to promote general bathing, while the Psychrolutes were dedicated to cold water and out-of-doors bathing in winter. By 1832, in order to be a Psychrolute one also had to be a Philolute. While no record of the Philolutes' activities has survived, it is possible to sketch a broad picture of the Psychrolutes' activities. The club book contains a list of all of the places where club members bathed, including the Serpentine, various Scottish Lochs, most of the major English rivers, various Continental rivers and the Hellespont. It seems likely that the members of these clubs were following, at least in part, the example set by Lord Byron when he swam the Hellespont in 1810. [11] Though it is doubtful that anyone copied the idea of forming a swimming club from the existence of the Philolutic and Psychrolutic Societies at Eton, it is just possible that the men who joined with John Strachan in 1837 to form the National Swimming Society in London may have heard of these groups or even had been ex-members or old Etonians.

At Harrow, swimming was not organized on the same scale as other sports. Internal contests in the school only began in 1857, 46 years after the construction of the school pool, when competition began for the 'Elvington Prize'. [12] The Clarendon Commission noted that there were prizes for swimming at Harrow and that there was systematic teaching of swimming at the school, though it was not compulsory to learn to swim. [13] The first surviving edition of the *Harrow Almanack*, from 1865, provides information about the form races at the school took, listing swimming as one of the activities that were part of the house competitions. The almanac also records that one of the objects of the Harrow Philathletic Club on its founding in 1853 was the promotion of 'all manly Sports and Exercises', including swimming. [14] A school swimming test was instituted in 1876, and became known as the 'Pass in Swimming'. School procedure was to print the names of all boys who could not swim at the beginning of each July, and their names were removed from this list as students passed the test. [15] The actual content of the test, as in the Eton case, is not recorded for the early years, although by 1898 it consisted of a swim of 70 yards. Those who wished to excel in swimming and gain the privilege of bathing in the 'Duck Puddle' more than once per day could become 'Dolphins' by completing a special swim test. This consisted of swimming roughly a half mile in distance, and included back, breast and side swimming, a running dive, swimming under a hurdle and climbing out and diving back into the pond, all while being timed. On a separate day, a candidate also had to rescue a submerged wooden dummy from the bath. [16] However, coverage of swimming at Harrow in the various school magazines was sporadic at best, and often completely absent; but when the magazine mentioned swimming, it provided a snapshot of what was clearly considered an important activity. For example, in 1903 *The Harrovian* recorded that a swimming committee of the Philathletic Club had been formed in 1902, that races were now organized by this committee and were held in 1903. A swimming match was also held against Charterhouse, which Charterhouse won. [17]

When the Clarendon Commission surveyed Charterhouse, however, there was evidently little swimming activity at the school. The commissioners made a single comment about the situation at the school: 'We would suggest to the Governors the propriety of considering whether some arrangement cannot be made for teaching swimming.' [18] The first mention of swimming as an organized activity at Charterhouse – indeed the first mention of swimming at the school at all after the Clarendon Commission report – occurs in 1873. At that time a system of ranking the swimming ability of students was instituted, and an annual series of swimming races in the River Wey was begun. [19] Beyond that scant information, however, virtually nothing was mentioned about swimming in the school for another decade, until in 1883 the school swimming baths were built. [20] Even after this time, photos in school albums reveal that swimming for many school contests still took place in the River Wey. [21]

The details about swimming at Shrewsbury School in the Clarendon Commission were, like the report on swimming at Charterhouse, quite sparse. It simply records that rowing was allowed to those who could swim, and that swimming was taught by a 'bathing master' at the school. [22] The headmaster in his submission to the commission indicated that there were bathing men (professional watermen) on the river at certain times, evidently to supervise the boys while swimming, and that there was a bath where swimming could be learnt. He felt that the boys could teach each other how to swim, and none of the teaching staff were assigned to supervise or otherwise involve themselves with swimming. [23] The link between the need to swim and rowing, indicated by the Clarendon Commission, is reinforced by the Shrewsbury School Boat Club rules of 1866. Rule VI outlines a swimming test of 40 yards that students had to undertake for entry into the rowing club. [24] The first mention of swimming as a sport in its own right in school records occurs in an article in *The Salopian* of November 1880. This article records the presentation to the school of a cup for junior swimming earlier that year. Clearly this implies that there was a pre-existing tradition of swimming races within the school, and that senior swimming in some form had been taking place before the 1880 swimming season. Whatever the exact year that swimming was established as a separate sport at Shrewsbury, all swimming was taking place in the River Severn at this time. [25] A school swimming bath was built in the late 1880s and was in operation by July 1887. [26] As was the case at Charterhouse, however, swimming in the river continued long after the school swimming bath had been opened. [27]

No mention of swimming is made at all in the Clarendon Commission's discussion of St Paul's School, London. The first mention of swimming there is to be found in the first issue of *The Pauline* from July 1882 which records the existence of a swimming club in the school. When this club had been founded, and exactly what sort of activities it pursued, however, are not recorded, although a later issue of the magazine hints that the club was formed in 1877. [28] The case of St Paul's was somewhat different from other public schools, however, as it was situated in London and was a day school, not a boarding school. The second issue of the school magazine, from October 1882, dealt more fully with swimming. The results of the annual swimming races were recorded, and it was noted that the school used the Charing Cross Baths for practices and competitions. [29] As at other schools, entry to the rowing club also required a swimming test to be completed. In the case of St Paul's it was a distance of 45 yards, which was the length of the Charing Cross Baths. [30] When the school moved to new premises in south-west London in 1884, the swimming club had to switch to more convenient baths, but still continued to operate. Occasional races were held against other schools or organizations, but for the most part swimming appears to have been internal to the school. [31] The biggest boost to the swimming club seems to have occurred in 1900 when the school's own swimming pool was opened. This also seems to have sparked an interest in water polo. In October of that year, at a gala between St Paul's and the St Mary's Swimming Club, a water polo match was included as one of the two events. [32] From the opening of the swimming baths at St Paul's School, swimming against outside teams increased, although the organization of fixtures never reached the same level as the main school sports, notably cricket and football. The most regular fixture on the swimming calendar seems to have been a series of races held against Charterhouse, beginning in 1903 and continuing, with only occasional lapses, until after the First World War. Matches against Bedford Grammar School and Dulwich College were also started at the same time. [33]

At Merchant Taylors' School the headmaster, the Revd J.A. Hessey, told the Clarendon Commission that in some past years a swimming club had been formed. [34] Evidently the fact that the club had not been in *continuous* existence is a strong indication that swimming was treated indifferently at best during this period at the school. There is no mention of any official policies towards swimming being in place at the school. Organized swimming here seems to have originated at some time in, or just prior to, 1879 when races were first swum at the Charing Cross Baths. [35] Because Merchant Taylors' was a day school within London until the 1930s, its swimming club changed its home pool on a regular basis, just as had been the case at St Paul's prior to the building of their own baths. No competitions outside Merchant Taylors' were undertaken until 1910, when boys from the school participated in the first ever 'Bath Cup' competition for public schools. [36] The school did not acquire its own swimming pool until 1933, after it had moved to its present site in Sandy Lodge on the outskirts of London. By then, swimming was seen as being an important part of the physical education curriculum of the school, and in society at large.

Rugby School could perhaps lay claim to being the first public school to possess a school bath, except for the fact that the bath in question does not seem to have been used for swimming. Two early chroniclers of the history of the school, the Revd W.H. Payne Smith and W.H.D. Rouse, provide dates of 1779 and 1777 respectively for the construction of a small plunge bath dug into the turf of 'The Close', the famous field where rugby football was later claimed to be invented. [37] Both authors note that the pool was quite small. Rouse further recorded that in 1784 a movable bathing shed was built on the banks of the Avon for the use of boys of the school, and that 'bathing men' were assigned to watch over the pupils while they were swimming. [38] No measurements of this early bath survive, but it would appear likely that it was only used as a bath, and not as a place to swim. Both books by Bradby and Rouse include references to swimming, and all of those references indicate that boys from the school swam in the River Avon at locations known as 'Aganippe', 'Sleath's' and 'Swift's'. [39] The earliest issues of the school magazine, *The Meteor*, also record that swimming took place in the Avon, and go on further to state that the school bath in The Close was small, dirty and often avoided by the boys. [40] The Clarendon Commission also commented on the presence of this pond on the school grounds, calling it a 'cold bath'. The report of the commission specifies two locations in the River Avon used by boys from Rugby for swimming. One of these was a shallow-water location for the small boys and non-swimmers to practice in, under the watchful eyes of watermen, while the other was at the confluence of the Avon and the Swift, used by the experienced swimmers. Further, the Commissioners reported, 'the swimmers have full opportunity of perfecting themselves in this art, the possession of which is almost universal in the highest forms of the School'. [41]

Organized swimming at Rugby, then, dates from a relatively early period but, as with the other great public schools, it was not one of the main sports or physical exercises of the school. The first recorded swimming competition at Rugby dates from 1870, when *The Meteor* reported on the 'School Swimming and Diving', which consisted of two events, a swimming race and a diving for eggs contest. There were only about a dozen competitors for the swimming race, divided into two heats, and even fewer for the diving for eggs. [42] While organized competition appears to have come late to swimming at Rugby, likely in the mid to late 1860s, it is apparent that swimming had a long history as a recreational activity at the school. Compared to other activities within the school, especially cricket, rugby football and shooting, the swimming races were clearly not a major part of school life. Swimming at Rugby stayed in this continuing, but ill-supported, manner until a proper school swimming bath was constructed in 1875–76, opening for use in June 1876. At the same time that the bath was opened, a swimming club was also founded to promote swimming in the school and to run the school swimming competitions. [43] In 1883 two life-saving events were added to the swimming calendar at Rugby, when competition for the Royal Humane Society medal and Dukes' Cup for Resuscitation first took place. [44]

It was not until after 1900 that swimming began to attract more widespread attention and support within Rugby. Starting in 1906 a further series of changes and additions were made to the swimming competitions. Silver medals were substituted for cash prizes in all swimming races, and a house team relay race was instituted. At the same time water polo was introduced to the school as a team sport to be competed for between houses. [45] The addition of a team dimension to swimming, and a link to the school's houses, may have helped expand swimming's popularity. It was, after all, team games that characterized public school recreational life and forged such fierce attachments among the students. In 1907 the school swimming competitions were expanded to eight events, plus the life-saving competitions, and the first outside matches were organized, with Rugby competing in matches against Old Rugbeians and King Edward's School, Birmingham. The following year saw the first match between Harrow and Rugby, the most regular of the external matches organized by Rugby before 1919. [46] Such inter-school swimming competitions, however, came *many* years after traditional sporting rivalries had already been formed, and indicate very clearly how swimming lagged behind the major team sports. Various other external matches were organized over the following decade, and water polo continued to develop in the school. Perhaps the best gauge of the improvement of swimming in the school during this period was the change in entrance requirements to the swimming club. In 1906 the requirement was for a candidate to swim 220 yards in five and a quarter minutes or less. By 1908 the entry test was a 220 yards swim in four and a half minutes or less. [47]

The story of swimming at Westminster School followed a similar pattern. As previously noted, the Clarendon Commission recorded that swimming was being taught there prior to 1864. According to the evidence gathered by the commissioners at the school, swimming was under the control of the head boy of the school. The school had no swimming pool of its own, so boys went out for general swimming and lessons, with the commissioners finding the school 'had many boys who could swim very well'. [48] The headmaster, the Revd C.B. Scott, reported that boys from the school were taught to swim in the Great Peter Street Baths. He also informed the commission that those boys who wished to go boating first had to learn to swim. [49] But after the commission's report, the trail runs out. A combination of lack of interest, neglect, the passage of time and the effect of two world wars on a London school prevent any further serious research on school swimming at Westminster. No swimming records survive at the school from before the end of the Second World War.

What the Clarendon Commission uncovered at Winchester College was quite different. There swimming was fairly widespread, despite the fact the school had no real boating activities. Although swimming was not systematically taught at the school, the commissioners revealed that 36 out of 41 boys in the sixth form could swim, and 149 out of 216 boys in the school as a whole could swim. [50] As with Westminster, almost no records of swimming survive at the school today.

What then can be said about swimming at that small grouping, the elite of the nineteenth century English public schools? No one doubts their overall attachment to sporting activity, and few scholars dispute the increasing importance that most schools came to attach to team games. Yet their interest in swimming was curiously weak. The most elite of the boys' public schools, while not great promoters of swimming, did not *ignore* it as a sporting activity either. Indeed, the fact that swimming could be a competitive sport probably ensured that it was not ignored. But, at best, it was viewed as a second- or third-class sport in all these schools. Its role as a *leisure* activity, however, is much harder to trace. Anecdotal comments in all the sources cited indicate that, beyond the competitive events, recreational swimming normally took place at the schools. The extent of this is left unrecorded, however, and beyond the fact that it clearly took place, it is impossible to be sure about the number of boys involved or the exact form of swimming they engaged in.

Swimming pools were, of course, costly to build and operate. Maintaining sports fields on the other hand was relatively cheap. Only the better-off public schools, therefore, could afford the cost of installing and running a swimming pool. Indeed, they were often the only schools that had the *space* for such a luxury. Westminster School, in the centre of London, has never had a swimming pool and probably never will due to its location. It is worth speculating about how swimming may have grown in less prestigious public schools. It would be expected that in places where there were local bodies of water that could be used for swimming, a local and informal tradition of swimming was established at some point in the nineteenth century. Over time this would develop into a more formal system, perhaps requiring a swimming test, especially if rowing was undertaken as a sport at the school. In locations where there was no nearby natural body of water in which to swim, it would be expected that there was little to no tradition of swimming. Over time as swimming pools were built at these public schools, it would be expected that swimming would become a more important activity, as a sport, a recreation and as part of physical education.

Notes

[1] James, 'The Contribution of Schools and Universities', 158.
[2] See Mangan, *Athleticism in the Victorian and Edwardian Public School*.
[3] Sinclair and Henry, *Swimming*, 377.
[4] Ibid., 366–76.
[5] Royal Commission on Public Schools and Colleges, vol. II, 92.
[6] Ibid., vol. I, 41.
[7] *The Harrovian* 4, no. 4 (19 May 1891), 38; Hort, 'The School Bathing Place', 256; Sinclair and Henry, *Swimming*, 366.
[8] Eton College Archives, Eton, SCH/SP/SW/2/1, Eton School Swimming 1853. This is a typed sheet inserted in the back of the first volume of alphabetical listings of boys who had passed the swimming test. The volume was begun in 1842.
[9] Royal Commission on Public Schools and Colleges, vol. III, 185.
[10] Maxwell Lyte, *A History of Eton College*, 323, 484.
[11] Eton College Archives, Eton, MISC/PSY/1/1, Psychrolutic Society Book 1828–57; MISC/PSY/2/1, Eton Philolutic Society Members Book 1832–49.
[12] Harrow School Archives, Harrow, 48C, Major R.O. Bridgeman, 'Harrow Records Vols. 1 & 2', c. 1976. The title of this item is misleading; it is actually a one-volume handwritten compilation of school sporting records drawn from a variety of sources, including the school magazines and actual trophies. It is inaccurate in places, but seems to be correct on swimming matters for the period up until the start of the First World War.

[13] Royal Commission on Public Schools and Colleges, vol. I, 223.
[14] *The Harrow Almanack 1865*, 40 and *passim*.
[15] *The Harrow Almanack 1876–77*, 84.
[16] Hort, 'The School Bathing Place,' 261–2.
[17] *The Harrovian* 16, no. 7 (8 October 1903), 97–8.
[18] Royal Commission on Public Schools and Colleges, vol. I, 183.
[19] Charterhouse School Archives, Godalming, 98/4 (ACC 10502/1), 'Charterhouse Bathing 1872 to 1881', fols. 4, 9, 10–12.
[20] *The Carthusian* 3, no. 97 (June 1883), 248.
[21] Charterhouse School Archives, Godalming, 'The Roskill Album/The Leighton Album'. This album contains two photographs of the school river bathing site, one of which pictures the 1906 competition for the Royal Humane Society's life-saving medal.
[22] Royal Commission on Public Schools and Colleges, vol. I, 320–1.
[23] Ibid., vol. II, 327.
[24] Shrewsbury School Archives, Shrewsbury, GB5/18, Shrewsbury School Boat Club Rules 1866.
[25] *The Salopian* 4, no. 1 (November 1880), no. 23, 151. *The Salopian* is the official school magazine of Shrewsbury School. A complete run of the magazine is housed in the school archives.
[26] *The Salopian* 10, no. 5 (June 1887), no. 63, 1052.
[27] Swimming in the Severn continued until after the Second World War. See Shrewsbury School Archives, Shrewsbury, 'School Swimming Records 1932–39,' and 'School Swimming Records 1940–48'.
[28] *The Pauline* 7, no. 36 (June 1889), 189. *The Pauline* is the official magazine of St Paul's School. A complete run of the magazine is housed in the school library.
[29] *The Pauline* 1, no. 2 (Oct. 1882), 44–5.
[30] *The Pauline* 2, no. 9 (March 1884), 210.
[31] For example, races were held against University College Hospital in 1896 and in the Thames against other public schools in 1899. In the latter case the other schools competing were not specified, and the races were organized by an unspecified outside body and billed as a 'Thames Swimming Meet'. See *The Pauline* 14, no. 83 (July 1896), 126; *The Pauline* 17, no. 105 (21 July 1899), 130.
[32] *The Pauline* 18, no. 114 (Dec. 1900), 219.
[33] *The Pauline* 21, nos. 132–3 (July 1903), 104–5.
[34] Royal Commission on Public Schools and Colleges, vol. II, 264.
[35] *The Taylorian* 2, no. 1 (Oct. 1879), 32; *The Taylorian* 2, no. 2 (Dec. 1879), 53–4. *The Taylorian* is the official school magazine for Merchant Taylors' School. A complete run of the magazine is housed in the school archives.
[36] *The Taylorian* 32, no. 6 (July 1910), 227. The Bath Cup competition was organized by the Bath Club, one of London's important social clubs of the period. The races for the cup were swum in the club's own pool. Most of the other major public schools participated in the event.
[37] Rouse bases his claim for construction of the bath in 1777 on documents detailing the transfer of the school to its present site in that year and the opening of the bath on 6 Sept. 1777. Rouse, *A History of Rugby School*, 119. Payne Smith does not link his claim for construction of the bath in 1779 to any documentation. Payne Smith, *Rugby: The School and Neighbourhood*, 3.
[38] Rouse, *A History of Rugby School*, 135–6.
[39] Bradby, *Rugby*, 137–8. Rouse, *A History of Rugby School*, 135–6. Rouse only mentions 'Sleath's' or 'Sleet's'; all three are mentioned by Bradby. 'Swift's' is mentioned in *The Meteor* 30 (19 July 1869), 7–8.

[40] See *The Meteor* 7 (4 July 1867), 6; 20 (8 Oct. 1868), 7–8; 30 (19 July 1869), 7–8. *The Meteor* was first published on 7 Feb. 1867: it has been the school's official magazine ever since. A complete run is housed in the school library.
[41] Royal Commission on Public Schools and Colleges, vol. I, 245–5.
[42] *The Meteor* 42 (27 July 1870), inside front cover. No distance is given for the swimming race.
[43] *The Meteor* 102 (28 June 1876), 493–4.
[44] *The Meteor* 193 (6 Oct. 1883), 111–12.
[45] *The Meteor* 476 (30 June 1906), 93–4; 478 (31 July 1906), 126–7.
[46] *The Meteor* 490 (22 July 1907), 89–90; 491 (30 July 1907), 110–12; 502 (27 June 1908), 97–8.
[47] *The Meteor* 476 (31 July 1906), 93–4; 504 (28 July 1908), 122–3.
[48] Royal Commission on Public Schools and Colleges, vol. III, 441.
[49] Ibid., vol. II, 205.
[50] Ibid., vol. I, 41, 152.

References

Bradby, H.D. *Rugby*. London: George Bell & Sons, 1900.
Hort, A.F. 'The School Bathing Place'. In *Harrow School*. edited by Edmund W. Howson and George Townsend Warner. London: Edward Arnold, 1898. 256–63.
James, T.M. 'The Contribution of Schools and Universities to the Development of Organized Sport up to 1900 (with Special Reference to Athletics and Swimming).' PhD diss., University of Leicester, 1977.
Mangan, J.A. *Athleticism in the Victorian and Edwardian Public School: The Emergence and Consolidation of an Educational Ideology*. Cambridge: Cambridge University Press, 1981.
Maxwell Lyte, H.C. *A History of Eton College (1440–1910)*. 4th edn. London: Macmillan, 1911.
Payne Smith, Revd W.H. *Rugby: The School and Neighbourhood*. London: Whittaker & Co., 1889.
Rouse, W.H.D. *A History of Rugby School*. London: Duckworth & Co., 1898.
Royal Commission on Public Schools and Colleges [Clarendon Commission]. 4 vols. Parliamentary Papers 1864 XX. London: UK Parliament, 1864.
Sinclair, Archibald, and William Henry. *Swimming* (The Badminton Library of Sports and Pastimes). London: Longmans, Green, and Co., 1893.

State Schools, Swimming and Physical Training

In the later nineteenth century the existing educational model was that of the public schools, institutions where a student had to pay fees, although sometimes scholarships were provided, in order to secure an education. Students from these schools went on to the universities and became members of the ruling classes of English society. When a state educational system for the mass of the population was set up in the last quarter of the nineteenth century it was organized by men who were products of this public school system, and there was, therefore, a transfer of many ideas from one system to the other. [1]

Public schools, of course, catered to the smallest of minorities. Even the largest schools seldom had more than 500 students enrolled at any one time. The new state educational system, on the other hand, was designed to provide mass education for millions of students. But the emergence of state and locally-financed schooling for all did not fully emerge until the last quarter of the nineteenth century. Those various schools were clearly influenced by the ideals of and by personnel from public school backgrounds. It was inevitable that many features of public school athleticism would find their way into these new schools, and the same was true of swimming.

In order to understand the difference in experience between the public schools and the various state schools which began to appear in the late nineteenth century it is first necessary to understand the broad outline of state involvement in education in England from the early 1800s until 1918. Beginning in 1833 Parliament began to make sums of money available to voluntary and secular schools that were providing elementary education in both England and Wales. This was followed in 1839 by the formation of the Committee of the Privy Council on Education which became responsible for distributing such funds. In 1856 an Education Department was set up to assist the Committee of the Privy Council. This new department also incorporated the former Science and Art Department of the Board of Trade. Throughout this early period the number of schools supported by the funds voted by Parliament was limited. This changed in 1870 with the passing of the 1870 Elementary Education Act, which authorized municipal authorities to construct and support schools out of local rates, increased the level of grants provided by Parliament for educational purposes, and set out how school boards were to be established across England to carry out the purposes of the act. The Education Department continued to be the main instrument of state involvement and control over local school boards until 1899, when the Board of Education was created as the single authority with responsibility for all aspects of education in England. [2] It was therefore, first under the Education Department, and then under the Board of Education, that state schools negotiated their involvement with swimming between the 1870s and 1918.

From the 1840s onwards an increasing number of privately owned and operated baths opened across England. Later, after the enactment of the permissive legislation of the Baths and Washhouses Act, 1846, and its various amendments, many municipal baths were also built. The increase in the number of facilities with swimming pools allowed the newly-established state schools to start thinking about sending their students out for instruction in swimming. For a long time, however, the ability of state schools to send students to a pool for instruction in swimming was limited. Contemporary education rules prevented state schools from spending money on swimming, as it was not listed as an activity on which education grants could be expended. Starting in 1890, however, that situation began to change. Schools under the jurisdiction of the School Board for London were the first to be allowed to include swimming as part of their curriculum. In December 1890 the Education Department granted permission to London board schools to add swimming to their school timetables and to count student attendance at swimming lessons as being school attendance. A School Board for London circular memorandum to parish councils from May 1892 summarizes the decision as part of a review of school swimming within the London parishes and boroughs. [3] By the 1891 summer season, then, swimming was an activity that had official approval, within London at least, and educators wasted no time in spending part of their education grants on providing swimming for their students. The provinces, however, would have to wait some time longer to be able to do the same.

This development of swimming in London schools did not come out of a vacuum, however. For many years prior to the official recognition of swimming by the Board of Education, various efforts had been made to promote swimming within London schools. In May 1890 the School Board for London printed and circulated a report on the current and historical status of swimming within its area of responsibility. The authors of this document traced interest in swimming in the School Board for London back to 1872. The works committee of the School Board for London had in that year asked about obtaining time in local swimming pools for lessons for students. They also enquired about the position of the Education Department on the matter of providing swimming instruction for students. Because the Elementary

Education Act of 1873 was being prepared, the School Board for London lobbied to have a clause included that would allow school boards to spend education funds either on the teaching of swimming at local baths, or to erect swimming pools attached to schools for the purpose of teaching swimming. Such a clause was not, however, included in the final legislation, and swimming was not included as an activity upon which education funds could be expended. [4]

This failure to secure recognition of swimming through official means was followed by an attempt to promote swimming through a voluntary organization linked to schools, but not restricted by Education Department regulations. In 1875 the London Schools Swimming Club (LSSC) was founded. Its purpose was the promotion of swimming for both male and female students. This was to be achieved through assisting the formation of clubs, securing permission for clubs to use the various lakes in parks around London, negotiating favourable entry fees to local bathing facilities, arranging voluntary instruction by board school teachers and obtaining and awarding prizes to both teachers and children. This club managed to survive for nearly a decade, finally folding in 1884. It does not appear to have been very successful, however, as its entire existence was plagued by funding difficulties. It seems to have survived through the extraordinary efforts of a core of very dedicated volunteer organizers. An attempt was made to revive the club in 1887, but this soon failed. The school board blamed the failure of the LSSC on a lack of funding; most people apparently believed the club was supported out of board funding and therefore declined to make voluntary donations to it. [5]

The task of providing school swimming thus returned to the School Board for London, which, between 1887 and 1890, continued to press for the inclusion of swimming in a revised education code. With this in mind it commissioned several surveys of either specific swimming provision within the areas around London schools, or more general surveys of physical training or physical education provision within London schools. During this three-year period the School Board for London placed continued emphasis on the sanitary nature of bathing, and the fact that swimming was a physical exercise that was the equal of military drill for promoting students' fitness. The board also consistently argued that taking students to the swimming baths not only taught them a useful skill, but also exposed them to habits of cleanliness and sanitation that would last long after their time at school. These were, after all, years which saw an increased concern about the 'condition of England', about fears of sickness and physical problems – all apparently related to the broader issue of individual and communal hygiene and cleanliness. These concerns reached a peak among elite and government circles during the time of the Second Boer War and the following years. [6] Swimming, it was argued, contributed to the important development of personal hygiene. However, throughout the same period, the Education Department was firm in its opposition to education funds being allocated to swimming provision, or for the building of baths, even when an inspector of schools complained, for example, of the continued dirtiness among some girl students in the Orange Street School, Southwark, where he had recommended bathing facilities some years before. [7]

By early 1890, then, swimming was being actively promoted within London, but it was not officially approved as a subject of instruction within schools. According to information collected by the School Board for London, a total of 16 parishes in the capital had adopted the Baths and Washhouses Act of 1846 and its various amendments, and provided swimming pools for public use. Three of these, Lewisham, St Pancras, and St George's, Hanover Square, had two separate bath sites within their parishes. The total number of swimming pools within these 19 baths buildings was 41. In addition, there were 25 private bath companies operating in London, providing a total of 36 swimming pools. Charges for admittance of school students, usually taken to the baths after school hours by an enthusiastic teacher, varied from 1d to 3d, sometimes including a towel and bathing costume, other times not. In certain areas, notably Battersea, Bermondsey, Lambeth, Peckham and Poplar, local funds to support swimming instruction had been set up. These districts were overwhelmingly poor working-class communities, with their own mix of serious social urban problems. They were, in effect, the kind of city communities whose children were most likely in need of access both to physical recreation and to the hygienic lessons that swimming encouraged. [8] The Serpentine was technically available for student use as a swimming site, but its hours of availability were such that it was considered unsuitable. The bathing ponds in Victoria Park, however, were thought to be much more useful for the provision of swimming instruction for both boys and girls. Overall, however, by early 1890 swimming was not well supported throughout London, and even where it was, provision for male students vastly outstripped provision for female students. [9] This was, again, a reflection of the different attitudes towards physical education for boys and girls.

In 1893 the London Schools Swimming Association (LSSA) was founded as the first schools swimming association in England. In many ways the new association was a continuation of the London Schools Swimming Club, though it seems not to have identified in any way with the previous organizational body. It was definitely more successful than the LSSC, running a series of London schools championships in 1893 and every year thereafter to the present, even through both world wars, with a few minor problems here and there. It is clear from the long-term survival of the LSSA that the organization very quickly surmounted the issue of funding that had crippled the LSSC throughout its existence. [10] It is unclear, however, whether or not the existence of the LSSA acted as some sort of catalyst for swimming activity within London schools, but the years following its formation seem to have been ones of great swimming activity in schools in the capital. The December 1890 decision of the Education Department to allow schools to spend money on swimming probably helped, but the organizational assistance of the LSSA to individual schools was also likely important. By the end of 1905 the LSSA had 924 schools affiliated to it, and roughly 7,000 certificates of proficiency in swimming were issued by the association in that year. [11] The involvement of a third organization, the Life Saving Society, in promoting swimming assisted all the other efforts taking place. It is certain that life-saving instruction was being offered by 1897 in at least some of the schools covered by the London School Board. This is demonstrated by the Life Saving Society Annual Report issued in 1897 for 1895–96, which contained printed photographs of massed groups of London board schoolgirls demonstrating the society's life-saving techniques. [12] Life Saving Society records indicate that official discussions to legitimize the teaching of life-saving to students in School Board for London schools took place in 1898, and in that year a total of 216 students were awarded certificates of proficiency by the society. [13]

At around the same time the question of the provision of swimming pools *solely* for the use of students was being raised in London. In 1897 or 1898 the School Board for London was investigating the possibility of building a swimming pool in the Dalston area of London. In March 1899 a letter was received at the offices of the Board of Education in London about this topic:

> In a letter dated the 16th November, 1898, their Lordships approved the proposal of the Board to provide a swimming bath in the neighbourhood of Dalston for the use of the Day and Evening Schools named therein, viz, Enfield Road, Haggerston Road, Sigdon Road, Queen's Road and Tottenham Road. An opportunity has now occurred of purchasing, by private treaty, the leasehold premises known as the Albion Hall and Swimming Baths, situated in Albion Square, Dalston, lying to the west of the Board's School in Queen's Road, and containing an area of about 11,325 square feet, as shown coloured pink on the accompanying plan.
>
> The Board are of opinion that [these premises should be acquired for the purpose of a swimming bath, under the sanction already given by their Lordships;] and I am accordingly instructed to ask for the Department's sanction to this proposal. [14]

The correspondence between the School Board for London and the Board of Education reveals that the School Board for London took possession of the Albion Hall and Swimming Baths, and ran them for the use of board schools. Final refurbishment of the premises was still taking place in 1903, and it does not appear that they were in use before that year. [15] Despite these delays, this represents a shift in policy by the Board of Education. Only a decade before, the board was forbidding any expenditure of money at all on swimming instruction for students. Officially, however, there was still no authorization for the instruction of students within the education acts of the period. The Education Act of 1901 was criticized by the Life Saving Society for the fact that it did not recognize swimming as a subject of instruction. Despite that, however, with the permission it had received for its area the School Board for London was offering both swimming and life-saving instruction. In 1901, 12,555 students in evening continuation classes offered by the board took part in such lessons. [16] Interestingly, Agnes Campbell in her survey of baths and washhouses in the United Kingdom claimed that local educational authorities gained the right to expend funds on the instruction of swimming to students in 1898. [17]

The discrepancy between this statement and the other, confused, evidence collected would bear further investigation.

By 1904 there was still no official authorization for swimming in the current education legislation of the day. School boards outside London were prevented from spending education funds on the teaching of swimming, or the provision of swimming baths, even though London board schools had been able to do so for over a decade. However, swimming was widely viewed as a useful skill to be learned. In addition there were health arguments raised in support of the principle of allowing students to go swimming as part of their education. In June 1904 the Borough of Newark Education Committee asked the Board of Education if it was legal under the 1902 Education Act for the committee to pay out education funds to the Newark Swimming Association in order to provide the students of the district with swimming instruction. The Local Government Board, which had evidently also been consulted on the matter, felt that this was *not* an acceptable use of funding, feeling that this expenditure was against any statutory authority granted by the law. The ultimate decision of the Board of Education, however, was that the funding arrangement *could* be undertaken. The funding was subject to the provision that the swimming lessons were included on the timetables of the schools concerned. This decision, in July 1904, was referred to as the 'Newark precedent' in later internal memoranda of the Board of Education. [18] Later in the same year, on 22 November 1904, the Hastings Education Committee submitted a similar query to the Board of Education, asking if it was within the committee's authority to pay for swimming lessons on one or two evenings a week for students. Confidential minutes from the Board of Education, dated 29 and 30 November 1904, indicate that the Board of Education felt that under Article 44 (1) and the provisions for physical exercise in the 1902 Education Act, and based on the Newark precedent, these payments *could* be made, again provided the swimming instruction was placed on the school timetable. [19]

Gradually, then, the regulations governing the expenditure of education grants were being interpreted to allow for the provision of school swimming. This change emerged not so much as a policy, but on the back of a series of small ad hoc changes and requests from a number of different education authorities, all anxious to know the legality of spending educational funds on the provision of swimming. And gradually the point was conceded: swimming *could* be incorporated into the school curriculum. By 1904 the first authorized expenditure of education funding on swimming lessons for elementary-school students was taking place outside London. This authorization, however, seems to have been given on a case-by-case basis, and the ability of local educational authorities to spend money on this subject of instruction does not seem to have been widely broadcast by the Board of Education.

Indeed, the whole state of affairs over permission for swimming instruction in schools was a confused one. According to a near contemporary press account by Harold E. Fern, then the honorary secretary of the Southern Counties Amateur Swimming Association (SCASA), but later to become the honorary secretary of the ASA, the ASA had sent a deputation to the Board of Education in 1907 on the topic of swimming as part of the education of English children. According to Fern this deputation had secured recognition of swimming as a permissive subject to be allowed in the school curriculum, and he argued that the effect of the change 'gave a great impetus to the teaching of swimming in the schools'. [20] As has been stated, however, this change of policy was not widely publicized. Throughout 1907 and into 1908 further questions about the legality and propriety of spending education funds on the provision of swimming instruction to students were received by the Board of Education in London. In March of 1907 the clerk of the Borough of Chelmsford Education Committee sent the Board of Education a letter which read, in part,

> I am directed by the above Education Committee to enquire whether it would be legal for the Committee to pay out of the Education funds:
> <u>1</u> A sum of £20 to the Corporation for the exclusive use of the swimming Bath for one hour each day for 4 days a week during 3 months of the year, for the purpose of teaching swimming to the older boys and girls attending the Elementary schools: and,
> <u>2</u> The salary of an efficient Instructor in Swimming for the above purpose. [21]

Again, internal confidential minute papers from the Board of Education reveal the thinking of what we can only assume were the most important or influential senior civil servants in the Board of Education on this issue. One of the minutes in the file, initialled 'GNR' and dated 12 March 1907, reads as follows (note the section marked off with Xs in the original text, one assumes for extra emphasis in the response),

> Please see this letter and the two attached precedents. I propose to reply as in the Hastings precedent, slightly altered –
> X Note that if arrangements for the instruction of scholars in swimming are shown on the approved time-tables of the schools affected, such instruction would be recognised as part of the ordinary school curriculum (Art. 44 of the Code), and any expense incurred in respect of it would properly be included in the expenditure required for maintaining the schools. X
> The difference in wording is due to the fact that in Hastings swimming lessons were to be given in the evenings, those proposed at Chelmsford are presumably to be in the day time, during school hours. [22]

The principle of paying out education funds for swimming instruction for students continued to be a live one. In April 1908 the Local Government Board sent a request for advice to the Board of Education on another issue related to swimming and schools. In March of that year the Heston and Isleworth Urban District Education Committee had requested approval from the Local Government Board in the matter of the expenditure of £50, payable to the schools' athletic association of the same district, for the provision of swimming instruction to local students. In support of this payment it was estimated by the education committee that roughly 800–900 students would be trained in the coming year. The circulated minute papers from the Board of Education reveal concern that the proposed swimming lessons were scheduled outside school hours and were not included on the school timetable. Overall, however, there was sympathy from the members of the Board of Education who commented on the matter, and they agreed that the proposed payment could be made, subject to the swimming lessons being placed on the school timetable. [23] Lying behind all this bureaucratic coming and going was an interesting social change. It is clear that more and more students were keen, or at least willing, to take swimming instruction. Ever more schools, and the authorities controlling them, were equally anxious to make provision for swimming in their school system. [24] What they needed was clarification from the appropriate government department of the *legality* of their actions.

The Newark decision of July 1904 was the first official recorded instance of swimming being allowed as a subject of instruction in a state-funded school outside London. In essence, government legislation had been interpreted by those responsible for the implementation of the legislation to allow funding to be allocated to an activity not *explicitly* set out by law, but which was considered to be acceptable for inclusion. This decision hinged on notions of what was socially beneficial and acceptable. The written comments made by the civil servants reviewing the applications for funding permission in all these cases are powerful illustrations of the social attitudes of the period. Although not specifically referred to as an activity for which schools could claim funding, civil servants reviewing the requests for funding were inclined to interpret physical education funding guidelines so as to include swimming as an activity that could receive funding. As an activity in general, swimming was viewed favourably by *all* the civil servants writing minutes on forms attached to the requests for funding. Perhaps most revealing is a comment made in relation to the Heston and Isleworth case. One of the senior civil servants, as he must have been to be commenting on such an application, especially a referral from the Local Government Board, although unidentifiable because of his illegible initials on the minute paper, wrote of the application: 'I cannot see how I can officially approve of any subject outside the ordinary school time, Tho', of course, I will gladly do anything possible to encourage such a useful & practical subject as swimming.' [25]

Swimming had clearly established itself as a useful form of healthy physical education for England's schoolchildren. Interest in swimming now began to extend to include senior civil servants and also members of Parliament. In 1908 a series of short letters were exchanged between T.J. MacNamara MP and Sir Robert L. Morant, the then permanent secretary of the Board of Education. MacNamara began the correspondence with the following request:

> I am going down to Plymouth the middle of next week to distribute the prizes for a Swimming Association.
> Have you got any figures in the Office showing the increase in the teaching of swimming throughout England and Wales, say, during the last 10 years? If so, I shall be obliged if you will let me have them. [26]

Morant's response to MacNamara's request is very complete and shows a desire to encourage swimming in schools. He began: 'I am sorry that we have no figures in the

Office showing the increase in the teaching of swimming throughout England and Wales during the last ten years. So far, no statistics on this point have been collected.' [27] Morant continued by pointing out that article 2 (9) of the Education Code of the day authorized swimming as a subject, and his personal belief was that many schools had included swimming in their timetables. Further, article 32 of division VI of the regulations, which covered physical training in technical schools, also authorized swimming. He believed that there had been an increase in the use of this regulation, although he was not sure of the exact extent of usage. He concluded his letter by stating: 'The particular question of instruction in swimming is being very carefully considered by the persons responsible for the administration of these Regulations at the present time, and I have hopes that there will be a considerable development within the next few years.' [28]

The progress Morant hoped for was clearly under way, because in January of 1909 a memorandum was issued to Board of Education inspectors on the subject of swimming and life-saving. The memorandum is marked 'Confidential' and was ostensibly issued because technical schools had been reporting difficulties in arranging swimming courses of the required length (a minimum of 20 hours) to obtain Board of Education funding to cover the cost of the courses. The Board of Education was of the opinion that the difficulties expressed were without merit or inconsequential, and could be easily overcome. But the main aspect is that the document signalled a strong belief in the usefulness of swimming and life-saving. At one point the memorandum reads: 'It is desirable to disseminate a practical familiarity with the theory and practice of life-saving and resuscitation, but it need hardly be said that it is useless to proceed to instruction in life-saving, except with students who are already tolerable swimmers.' [29] The text of the memorandum goes on to recommend a two year course of swimming instruction for students. Once lifesaving is mastered, 'further lessons in plunging and diving from the surface will now be particularly valuable, while there is no reason why fancy swimming should not also be taught. Such instruction is valuable not so much for the utility of fancy swimming as for the confidence which the learner insensibly acquires.' [30] At the same time the Board of Education Welsh Department was inquiring into the provision of swimming facilities within Wales and the number of schools taking advantage of these. [31]

By 1910 there was solid support behind the promotion of swimming in schools within the Board of Education, and an increasing number of local education authorities seem to have been sending their students to local swimming pools for instruction. Certainly, by this time the provision of swimming instruction by civic baths and washhouses committees within municipal baths was widespread in England. This is revealed in a report commissioned by the Manchester Baths and Washhouses Committee in 1911. The Manchester committee had asked its general superintendent of baths, J. Derbyshire, to survey a selection of boroughs, cities and towns across the United Kingdom to see what financial contributions were made by various education committees towards the teaching of swimming to students. At that time the local baths and washhouses committee was attempting to persuade the Manchester Education Committee to provide funding for student swimming lessons; the baths and washhouses committee was then covering all the costs related to instruction. Surveys were sent to a total of 46 boroughs, cities and towns and 41 replies were received. While some of the responses were short and lacking in detail, more complete responses were received from locations such as Birmingham, Bradford, Glasgow, Leeds, Leicester, Liverpool, Newcastle-upon-Tyne, Nottingham and ten London boroughs. In all 41 cases where responses were received there was some provision of funding for student swimming lessons within the authority concerned, but in only 26 cases was the funding provided by the education committee of the jurisdiction involved . In the remainder of cases funding for student swimming lessons was provided by the baths committee or by payments derived from the students. [32] It is evident from this small survey alone that the provision of swimming lessons for school students was widespread by 1910. Although exact financial arrangements varied between jurisdictions (unsurprising in Victorian local government circles where financial constraints were always a concern), the principle of providing swimming as an element of physical training for school students seems well established.

In the case of Manchester itself the superintendent noted, in his report of 17 May 1911, that between 1 April 1910 and 31 March 1911 a total of 464,963 students bathed for free in Manchester baths under the various regulations of the Baths and Washhouses Committee. A total of 337,179 students bathed for free after being brought to the baths by their schools during school hours, while a further 127,784 students bathed for free during special free bathing days arranged during the school summer-holiday period. The use of the term bathing here is deliberate, and important. Consistent with the idea of swimming as an activity that promoted cleanliness and hygiene, and with the idea of baths establishments being centres of the promotion of the public good, in Manchester all those students who attended the swimming pools during the free period were first bathed thoroughly before being allowed in for their free swim. The routine of the enjoyable activity of swimming (at least more so than school for the majority, one suspects) was explicitly linked with being clean. In all likelihood the bath that some of the students were given prior to their free swimming session was the first, or one of the first, they had ever been subjected to, and most likely the most thorough they had experienced as well. [33]

The majority of the civic authorities who provided responses to the survey also provided information about total student swimmer numbers for a similar period of time to that covered by the latest Manchester figures, and Manchester had by far the largest total of student bathers. The next six largest providers of student swimming, in descending order of provision, were Liverpool (207,640); Islington, London (164,069); Bradford, Yorkshire (137,544); Leeds (123,064); Blackburn (95,000); and Bristol (83,975). While these figures are far from definitive (we do not know, for example, if they count total individual students bathed or simply total student visits to the baths, nor do we know how the figures were collected), they do give a general overview of the extent of student swimming across England. Provision for student swimming instruction was therefore in place in at least the 41 localities that responded to the Manchester survey. Although how long such provision had been extended in the other locations described in the survey is unknown, in Manchester free bathing for students in the manner described above had been in place since 1900. [34] Over 130,000 students were given a bath and allowed to swim on an annual basis for free.

It is clear that, much more so than public schools, the newly established state schools of the last quarter of the nineteenth century were great promoters of the use of public baths and swimming, especially in London and Manchester. The amount of attention paid to the subject by the Manchester Baths and Washhouses Committee, the School Board for London and other educational authorities indicates that a great deal of importance was placed by local educationists on being able to take their students to the local swimming pool to learn to swim or practise swimming. To some, swimming would be a welcome substitute to the drill commonly used for physical education purposes in schools of the time, while others had visions of the activity promoting health and cleanliness.

Notes

[1] See for example, Mangan, *Athleticism in the Victorian and Edwardian Public School.*
[2] 'Administrative History of Records Created or Inherited by the Department of Education and Science, and of Related Bodies 1818–2000'. In Public Record Office Online Catalogue, available at http://catalogue.pro.gov.uk, accessed 13 Nov. 2002. See also 'Education Departments: Administrative History'. In National Digital Archive of Datasets, available online at http://ndad.ulcc.ac.uk/datasets/AH/13.htm, accessed 13 Nov. 2002. Please note the Public Record Office (PRO)'s website uses 'frames' and as such does not give direct web addresses to all of its pages; the citation in question can be found by searching under the 'ED' class mark.
[3] Lambeth Archives and Minet Library (hereafter LAML), P12/80/2/3, School Board for London circular to Lambeth Vestry, 19 May 1892.
[4] LAML, P12/80/2/2, School Board for London, Report of the Physical Education Sub-Committee on Bathing Accommodation and Swimming Classes (Public Elementary Schools), 1–2.
[5] LAML, P12/80/2/2, School Board for London, Report of the Physical Education Sub-Committee, 2.
[6] See, for example, Searle, *A New England?*, 375–86.
[7] LAML, P12/80/2/2, School Board for London, Report of the Physical Education Sub-Committee, 2–10.
[8] It is likely that such support funds were contributed to by local citizens, and interested local patrons, of both the working and other classes, but there is no firm evidence for this.
[9] LAML, P12/80/2/2, School Board for London, Report of the Physical Education Sub-Committee, 8. In the appendices attached to this report, where figures are given for the number of students attending the baths for swimming instruction, there are always more male students listed as attending than female students.
[10] London School Swimming Association, *Report For the year ending December 31st, 1923*, 6 and front cover.

[11] Royal Life Saving Society, *Annual Report of the Central Executive Committee for 1905*, 19.
[12] Life Saving Society, *Annual Report of the Central Executive Committee 1895–96*, 10, 40, 66.
[13] Life Saving Society, *Annual Report of the Central Executive Committee 1897–98*, 10.
[14] PRO, ED 21/11971, Dalston: Albion Square Swimming Baths. The square brackets are in the original. The plan mentioned as accompanying the letter is not appended to the file.
[15] Ibid.
[16] Life Saving Society, *Annual Report of the Central Executive Committee 1900–01*, 12.
[17] Campbell, *Report on Public Baths*, 5.
[18] PRO, ED 111/126, Donation to a Swimming Association, Borough of Newark Education Committee to Board of Education, 10 June 1904; also Local Government Board to Board of Education, 18 July 1904; also, attached minutes 12 July 1904 and 13 July 1904. This file contains an unnumbered bundle of documents, attached together, on assorted Board of Education topics. Roughly a third of the file refers to the Borough of Newark and swimming. Exactly why the Local Government Board was involved in the matter is not made clear by any of the minutes and correspondence in the file.
[19] PRO, ED 111/213, Hastings Swimming Question, attached minutes of 29 Nov. 1904 and 30 Nov. 1904. This file contains an unnumbered sheaf of memos, attached together, on assorted Board of Education topics. Roughly in the centre of the bundle are to be found the papers dealing with the Hastings swimming question. No copy of a final letter from the Board of Education authorizing the expenditure of funds by Hastings is appended to the file.
[20] Harold E. Fern, 'The Amateur Swimming Association, Its Aims and Work', *The Swimming Magazine* 1, no. 1 (June 1914), 15.
[21] PRO, ED 111/41, Exclusive Use of the Pool, Letter from Borough of Chelmsford Education Committee to the Board of Education, 8 March 1907.
[22] PRO, ED 111/41, Exclusive Use of the Pool, attached minute of 12 March 1907. The minute paper and the letter referred to above are the first items in this unnumbered collection of files. The 'X' marks are in the original.
[23] PRO, ED 111/111, Expenditure on Swimming Instruction, Isleworth. This entire file pertains to the Heston and Isleworth Urban District Education Committee in general. There is no numbering of parts or pages in the file, although the files are organized somewhat chronologically.
[24] Exactly why each school chose to pursue swimming is, of course, unknowable. The swimming craze started by Captain Webb in 1875 was likely part of the impetus for swimming in the curriculum. Of more importance, however, was likely the growing concern among many in the elites and government about the health of the nation, as is covered in the article about health and cleanliness in this volume.
[25] PRO, ED 111/111, Expenditure on Swimming Instruction, Isleworth, undated minute on attached minute sheet. The underlining is present in the original.
[26] PRO, ED 24/411, Morant to MacNamara concerning Swim Instruction, letter, 14 Oct. 1908.
[27] PRO, ED 24/411, Morant to MacNamara concerning Swim Instruction, letter, 15 Oct. 1908.
[28] 1. PRO, ED 24/411, "Morant to MacNamara concerning Swim Instruction," Letter from Morant to MacNamara 15 October 1908.
[29] PRO, ED 22/52, Grants Related to Swimming, memo to Inspectors T. no. 19, Jan. 1909.
[30] Ibid.
[31] PRO, ED 22/83, Swimming, Boating & Navigation, untitled memorandum of 10 June 1909. This file consists of unsorted memoranda from the Board of Education Welsh Department.
[32] Manchester Local Studies and Archives Service (hereafter MLSAS), Baths and Wash Houses Committee Minutes, vol. 15, fol. 9, minutes of 17 May, 1911; fol. 27, minutes of 13 July, 1911; fol. 36, minutes of 16 Aug. 1911. The Manchester Education Committee seems to have been dead set against granting any funding for swimming instruction, considering the current

funding arrangement as entirely appropriate. This attitude appears not to have changed prior to the end of the First World War.

[33] MLSAS, Baths and Wash Houses Committee Minutes, vol. 15, fol. 9, minutes of 17 May 1911.
[34] MLSAS, Baths and Wash Houses Committee Minutes, vol. 10, fol. 74, minutes of 19 Feb. 1901.

References

Campbell, Agnes. *Report on Public Baths and Wash-Houses in the United Kingdom*. Edinburgh: Edinburgh University Press, 1918.

Life Saving Society. *Annual Report of the Central Executive Committee 1895–96 and Prospectus for 1897*. London: Life Saving Society, 1897.

———. *Annual Report of the Central Executive Committee 1897–98 and Prospectus for 1899*. London: Life Saving Society, 1899.

———. *Annual Report of the Central Executive Committee 1900–01 and Prospectus for 1902*. London: Life Saving Society, 1902.

London School Swimming Association. *Report For the year ending December 31st, 1923*. London: London Schools Swimming Association, 1924.

Mangan, J.A. *Athleticism in the Victorian and Edwardian Public School: The Emergence and Consolidation of an Educational Ideology*. Cambridge: Cambridge University Press, 1981.

Royal Life Saving Society. *Annual Report of the Central Executive Committee for 1905 and Prospectus for 1906*. London: Royal Life Saving Society, 1906.

Searle, G.R. *A New England? Peace and War 1886–1918* (The New Oxford History of England). Oxford: Oxford University Press, 2004.

'Whomsoever You See in Distress': Swimming, Saving Life and the Rise of the Royal Life Saving Society

The connection between swimming and humanitarian values is a long-standing one. When the Royal Humane Society (RHS) was founded in 1776, it was dedicated, among other things, to the resuscitation of the apparently drowned. [1] This did not imply, however, that the person skilled in resuscitation also needed to be able to swim. Rather, as boatmen or others could recover the bodies of the apparently drowned, it simply implied that a person with resuscitation skills should work or be stationed near areas of water in case of accident. From this early concern to save life, a link was forged between humanitarianism and water.

The concern among many members of English society towards the plight and welfare of their fellow human beings was at the core of much Victorian humanitarian thought and action. Certainly during the Victorian and Edwardian periods broadly-based humanitarian ideas became widespread in English society. By the middle of the nineteenth century, as Edward Royle has pointed out, large amounts of money were being spent on voluntary philanthropic ventures, and the amount of money available for such ventures continued to increase to the end of the century. Exact figures on charitable expenditure are hard to determine, but by the 1860s amounted to between £5.5 million and £7 million for London alone. [2] Most of the historical research on humanitarianism and philanthropy has focused on the obvious topics, notably voluntary efforts to relieve the plight of the poor through the provision of almshouses, educational foundations, hospitals and similar institutions, as well as on the campaign to eliminate cruelty to children. [3] Scant attention has been paid to the humanitarianism expressed by those among the Victorians and Edwardians who provided first-aid and life-saving treatment to people in need. It was concern over the high number of annual drownings in England, for example, that persuaded a group of gentlemen to found the Life Saving Society in 1891.

One of the strongest and earliest reasons advanced by proponents of swimming was its importance as a humanitarian skill. A person able to swim was one who could save his own life as well as potentially that of someone else. The origins of this idea are unknown, but it was present in the eighteenth century, when the Royal Humane Society had first linked humanitarianism and water with its resuscitation methods. By 1837 the idea that swimming was a humanitarian skill had certainly gained currency. When the National Swimming Society (NSS) was founded in that year, it sought to promote swimming and provided lessons for boys who wanted to learn. It was greeted by the press as providing a useful service. *Bell's Life*, for example, noted that 'A society, we hear, is proposed to be established for the teaching of youths the *necessary* art of swimming'. [4] At around the same time, the British Swimming Society aimed 'to promote health, cleanliness, and the preservation of life by the practice of bathing and by teaching and encouraging the art of swimming'. [5] We know that as early as 1843 the Royal Humane Society was providing boatmen to supervise swimmers in the Serpentine during the summer months, and to rescue swimmers in trouble. There was, clearly, an increased sense that swimming should be taught for humanitarian and safety reasons. [6]

However, between the late 1840s, when the NSS appears to have disbanded, and 1873 little formal progress seems to have occurred in terms of promoting swimming for humanitarian reasons. During the period, notices about drownings, or rescues of people from drowning, appeared on a regular basis in *The Times*. [7] Until 1869, however, there was no organized body that promoted swimming, either as a sport or recreational activity, in the same manner that the NSS had operated in the 1830s and 1840s. Even when the Amalgamated Metropolitan Swimming Clubs, later the London Swimming Association, was founded in 1869 it did not include life-saving among the activities that it promoted.

A change began to occur from 1873 onwards, as in that year the Royal Humane Society instituted the Stanhope Medal, which was to be awarded to the person who performed the most gallant rescue of someone drowning during the previous year. The first recipient was Captain Matthew Webb, later to be famous as the first man to swim the English Channel in 1875. [8] The medal has continued to be awarded to the present day. This first award specifically dedicated to the saving of life from the water was followed in 1882 by the introduction of what became know as the Royal Humane Society Swimming Medal. Instituted to encourage swimming, and therefore reduce the number of drownings, the medal was to be awarded through a competition open to all of the boys at a participating school. The competition consisted of three tests, all involving the retrieval of a wooden dummy under varying conditions. The RHS Committee selected the schools allowed to take part in the competition, and among the schools that ran trials for the medal in the first year of its existence were Charterhouse School, Marlborough College, the Royal Naval School, Rugby School and Winchester College. [9] The number of schools selected to compete for these medals was always a very tiny minority of the number of English schools, both state and public. Participation in the competition peaked during the period immediately before the First World War, when around 40 schools and training ships were involved annually. [10]

In addition to the major awards already listed, the Royal Humane Society has maintained the awarding of medals and certificates for the saving of life from drowning to the present day. In 1905 ten students from schools involved with the London Schools Swimming Association (LSSA) were honoured by the RHS with awards for saving or attempting to save the drowning. [11] In order to make such awards, the society had to examine and assess a huge number of incidents. In 1909, for example, a total of 700 cases of rescue and attempted rescue from drowning were examined by the RHS and 800 people were recognized for their efforts in saving or attempting to save life. [12] Efforts to promote life-saving had from the 1880s become nationwide. In 1888, for example, the Humane Society for the Hundred of Salford donated the sum of £5 (to the Manchester Baths and Washhouses Committee), to be used for prizes in an annual competition for youths under 18 who showed proficiency in swimming and life-saving in Manchester. [13] The Salford Humane Society appears to have continued to make this donation to the committee into the early 1890s. It is likely that similar efforts were taking place in many other locations across England. By then, however, or perhaps slightly earlier, this and similar local efforts at promoting life-saving were superseded when the Life Saving Society (LSS) began to expand its activities across England. The LSS established a branch and began to provide life-saving instruction and greater assistance to the promotion of life-saving in Manchester from 1894 onwards. [14] At the same time, as will be seen, the LSS was creating a national network of representatives to promote its work across Britain.

By the 1880s the Royal Humane Society had created an explicit link between the ability to swim and swimming's humanitarian value as a skill that could save the lives of others. In practice, however, the efforts undertaken by the RHS to promote swimming and life-saving were targeted at a limited audience. It was not until the 1890s that an organization dedicated to the saving of life from drowning, and of teaching life-saving to the general public, was created. In 1891 the Swimmers' Life Saving Society, which later became the Life Saving Society, and finally, in 1904, the Royal Life Saving Society, was founded. Such an organization dedicated specifically to training people to save the lives of the drowning was sorely needed. Statistics collected by the Royal Humane Society show that between 1860 and 1900 there were never fewer than 2,200 drownings each year in England and Wales (See Table 1). If

Table 1 Drowning Statistics for England and Wales, 1860–1900

Year	Total accidental drownings	Total suicide drownings	Male drownings Accidental	Male drownings Suicide	Female drownings Accidental	Female drownings Suicide
1860	2,264	219	1,908	128	356	91
1861	2,351	225	1,994	115	357	110
1862	2,463	204	2,051	112	412	92
1863	2,488	245	2,088	132	400	113
1864	2,714	205	2,250	123	464	82
1865	2,823	230	2,427	121	396	109
1866	2,786	207	2,386	128	400	79
1867	2,676	228	2,259	134	417	94
1868	2,924	291	2,498	169	426	122
1869	2,696	292	2,302	160	394	132
1870	2,504	297	2,113	182	391	115
1871	2,605	317	2,175	173	430	144
1872	3,010	335	2,569	186	441	149
1873	2,695	330	2,235	192	460	138
1874	2,611	280	2,197	179	414	101
1875	3,199	333	2,692	186	507	147
1876	2,987	383	2,556	226	431	157
1877	3,012	374	2,509	224	503	150
1878	3,659	369	2,833	209	826	160
1879	2,806	405	2,368	258	438	147
1880	2,997	406	2,485	261	512	145
1881	2,979	443	2,485	271	494	172
1882	2,862	419	2,379	240	483	179
1883	2,782	447	2,326	261	456	186
1884	2,602	446	2,190	289	412	157
1885	2,449	382	2,018	239	431	143
1886	2,805	514	2,395	309	410	205
1887	2,666	500	2,231	311	435	189
1888	2,388	453	1,959	293	429	160
1889	2,560	503	2,168	392	309	194
1890	2,494	504	2,074	304	420	200
1891	2,708	559	2,273	348	435	211
1892	2,637	584	2,231	343	406	241
1893	2,747	581	2,343	363	404	218
1894	2,589	603	2,172	385	417	218
1895	2,797	566	2,384	355	413	211
1896	2,415	554	2,015	347	400	207
1897	2,750	625	2,277	396	473	229
1898	2,548	661	2,119	433	429	228
1899	2,850	559	2,389	346	461	213
1900	2,652	695	2,231	425	421	270

Source: Royal Humane Society, Annual Report for 1902, 226.

we include suicide by drowning, the level was no fewer than 2,400 drownings per year. In 1878, the worst year on record during this period, 3,659 people drowned in England and Wales – 4,028 when suicide by drowning numbers are included. [15]

There was, then, a high incidence of drowning during the late Victorian period, and there is no reason to think that comparable figures did not exist earlier. By the mid- to late-nineteenth century, however, there was growing *concern* about the figures (and, of course, about the human tragedies that lay behind them). To contemporaries who worried about the fate of their fellow human beings, these figures revealed a large-scale problem. One man in particular, William Henry, made it his task to tackle this problem. Born in London on 28 June 1859, Henry spent his youth in Russia, returning to London in 1877, already able to swim. We know of no particular reason for his love of swimming and his specific interest in life-saving. Almost immediately on his arrival back in the United Kingdom in 1877 he became involved in swimming and swimming officialdom. Henry was clearly an accomplished swimmer: he won over 600 prizes during his swimming career, and in later years used his awards to decorate his office. He was particularly interested in life-saving and 'scientific' swimming. In fact, he was perhaps the foremost practitioner of both of these aspects of swimming between 1891 and 1918. Henry was the outright winner of the National Graceful Swimming Shield of the Bath Club in 1891, and between 1899 and 1901 he was the champion of Scientific Swimming for England, winning the competition trophy outright with his third victory. He also attended the International Congress on Life Saving held in conjunction with the Paris Exhibition in 1900 where he competed in, and won, the international life-saving competition run as part of the congress. [16] Like competitive swimming, life-saving was becoming internationalized. The exact extent of contact between different national organizations, however, is unclear. The Life Saving Society had by 1901, for example, organized and undertaken life-saving demonstration tours of Sweden and Italy, and was planning a further tour of Germany in 1902. [17] Henry was a tireless organizer, and his dedication to the Life Saving Society was well noted by contemporaries. [18] From its inception in 1891 until his death in 1928 he remained the society's honorary (later chief) secretary.

For whatever reason William Henry became interested in life-saving, his interest and enthusiasm proved invaluable. Life-saving in the swimming world had previously been seen as a worthy goal, but one that was often given little attention by swimming authorities who were busy with other matters. Archibald Sinclair and William Henry were the first joint honorary secretaries of the Life Saving Society, and their book on swimming, published in 1893, only two years after the foundation of the LSS, provides a wealth of information on the history of aquatic life-saving. They traced the origins of life-saving to the foundation of the Royal Humane Society and to its work on resuscitation, especially of near-drowning victims. The authors also saw a certain influence deriving from the work of lifeboat and coastguard organizations both in the United Kingdom and in the United States of America; both of those bodies were committed to the saving of life at sea. They noted, however, that these organizations were not prepared to take on the instruction of swimmers in life-saving techniques. A request to the Royal Humane Society to oversee such work in 1887 produced no response. [19] Sinclair and Henry, among others, then sought to have the Amateur

Swimming Association (ASA) take up the work of life-saving instruction in 1889. They recounted the efforts made to convince the ASA to undertake the provision of life-saving instruction in their book on swimming. Indeed, they reproduced in full the original report submitted to the ASA executive about how the work would be undertaken. It is clear enough from the detailed nature of the report that considerable thought had gone into arranging the programme of instruction. Sinclair and Henry had carefully considered the organizational details required for a successful campaign of life-saving instruction, and were also cultivating local interest in life-saving education in all areas of the country and establishing links with the medical community to ensure the respectability and authority of their venture. In the end, however, the ASA declined to act on the proposal. [20]

Exactly *why* the work was never undertaken by the ASA is unknown, but it appears there was a lack of finance and a shortage of sustained executive interest in the project. As part of the plan the assistance of the Royal Humane Society, the St John Ambulance Association and the Corporation of London was to be solicited; almost certainly with an eye to raising money. There were, however, good, internal reasons why the swimming world could not accept these ideas. At the same time as the ASA was being asked to consider setting up life-saving classes, it was also still undergoing internal reorganization after being created by the merger of the Amateur Swimming Union and the Swimming Association of Great Britain in 1886. As part of this process the association was struggling with the question of how best to organize itself on a regional level. Simply put, the ASA executive seems to have decided to devote its energies to projects deemed more immediately important.

The end result of all of these efforts was the calling of a public meeting in January 1891 to form a society to address the much-needed work that was being ignored by the RHS and the ASA. The meeting duly formed the 'Swimmer's Life Saving Society'. By December 1891 the society had changed its name to the Life Saving Society. [21] The 'seven gentlemen' who called and organized the public meeting included Sinclair and Henry, with William Henry generally regarded as the main driving force behind the new society. The society spent most of its first year of existence trying to determine the best forms of drill to be used for rescuing the drowning and how to teach this to the public at large. The aim of the society was to develop a rescue system that would be effective, attractive and simple to understand. Any audience watching a life-saving drill display, it was therefore believed, would be riveted to the display and yet not miss a single movement. They initially adopted a modified form of the drill used by the British Army, although this was quickly replaced by a system developed by William Wilson, an early Scottish swimming pioneer. [22] The society's first year was an interesting experience, as Sinclair and Henry's observations make clear. They note, about the origins of the Society, that

> it is evident that about this time there was a general idea among the more thoughtful to raise swimming above the mere level of a competitive sport, and to make its practice of use and benefit to the nation at large. It had hitherto been imagined that the holding of races was sufficient to encourage the art, and that a

man who could swim was naturally able to save life. That this idea was erroneous has been abundantly proved, inasmuch as many speed swimmers have found that in life-saving practice their knowledge availed them very little; indeed, in many cases they have actually failed to carry a passive subject in the water. Those who doubted this were soon convinced when they came to make actual trials, and were bound to admit that the fast methods of propulsion were not much service when bringing a man to shore. To this may probably be attributed the desire for the foundation of some authoritative body for the promotion of those swimming arts which would be useful in saving life. [23]

The chief organizers of the society clearly believed that swimming was the basis for a great humanitarian exercise which should, ideally, involve as many people as possible.

From this point onwards the Life Saving Society began to flourish. The first handbook of the society, published in late 1891, provides excellent insight into the objects of the new organization, and the conception of the organizers as to how the society fit into English society. Although primarily dedicated to the prevention of drowning and the resuscitation of those rescued from the water through the provision of demonstrations, public lectures and training programmes, the Life Saving Society was also originally designed to encourage the arts of plunging, diving and ornamental (synchronized) swimming. [24] The zeal that fired these early life-savers was confirmed in the foreword to that first manual written by the honorary secretaries. Their goal was the simple, yet lofty, goal of teaching every young person in the entire United Kingdom how to swim and how to save life. Only by achieving that goal, which would require a national effort, could the annual toll of two to three thousand deaths by drowning in England and Wales alone be eliminated. [25]

This drive towards safety in swimming was clearly viewed as a noble one, but one that the new society hoped to connect to *existing* traditions within English society. On the back cover of that first manual appeared the following, '"England expects that every man this day will do his duty." Lord Nelson. *It is the duty of every citizen to see that Swimming forms part of his children's education, and it cannot be too widely known that* **TEACHING THE ART** *forms an important part of the programme of every Swimming Club affiliated to this Society.*' [26] The society took as its motto the Latin phrase *Quemcunque miserum videris, hominem scias* ('Whomsoever you see in distress, recognize in him a fellow man'). [27] The aim was to convey the sense that the society was in the mould of the 'good Samaritan', and by adopting or appropriating such language and imagery the founders hoped to enhance the stature of the society.

But where does all this lead? It is clear that initially the Life Saving Society was supported by a small core of dedicated members. The high number of drownings in coastal and inland waters in England, revealed by the collection of statistics in the nineteenth century (see Table 1), highlighted an obvious need for life-saving instruction. It is also clear by the 1890s, that there was broad support, in society at large, for a range of humanitarian ventures. Whether it be helping the poor in the industrial centres of Britain or promoting Christianity abroad, some sections of the Victorian middle classes were willing to contribute time and money to these, and a myriad of other, causes. The LSS, although perhaps on the periphery of what the Victorians would have considered the field of philanthropic work, should be considered part of that world. With the formation of the Life Saving Society, the world of Victorian swimming and Victorian humanitarian ideals were drawn together. From 1891 the Life Saving Society stood as a concrete example of the connection between swimming and contemporary humanitarianism.

From this and related factors, there emerged the final official structure of the Life Saving Society, and the formalizing of life-saving training. By the end of the nineteenth century, life-saving had become a well-organized, widespread and national phenomenon. Early returns of awards for life-saving show that by the end of 1896 a total of 2,058 people had undertaken training offered by the society and had passed one of its proficiency tests. Between 1897 and 1913 there was almost continuous growth in the annual number of awards issued. Not until 1914, and the impact of the war, was there a significant drop in the number of awards issued. Military needs quickly saw many life-saving instructors serving in various military capacities, while many swimming baths were closed or used for other purposes. In addition, numbers in need of instruction declined. This trend was reversed after the war, however, and award statistics show a steady increase between 1921 and 1931. [28] In fact, the influence of the Life Saving Society was much greater than these award statistics would suggest. For example, both the Boy Scouts and the Girl Guides recommended the society's training methods before 1914. And although the society's numbers could not match the massive membership quickly acquired by Baden-Powell's Boy Scout and Girl Guide movements, the society clearly influenced those movements. In effect, the ideals and aims of the society were disseminated widely, both by their own efforts and by the influence they exercised on other organizations. Life-saving was by 1914 widely accepted by a range of other organizations as a vital instruction for the nation's youth. In schools, in physical recreation, in swimming clubs, in the Scout and Guide movements, life-saving was now an unquestioned individual and social virtue.

The interest in life-saving was, as with swimming itself, stimulated by competition. In 1892 the Life Saving Society ran its first National Life Saving Competition. Lever Brothers, the famous soap manufacturer, presented the society with the 'Sunlight Challenge Shield' for use as the perpetual trophy of the competition. In that first competition a total of 24 teams, consisting of four men each, took part. After being drawn into a series of heats based on geographical location, the teams faced off against each other, being marked on their accuracy and speed of performance of the various rescue and resuscitation drills taught by the society. A team from Nottingham eventually emerged victorious. This competition continued to increase in size through the 1890s, attracting 31 teams in 1893 and 44 teams in 1894. [29] Lever's donation of the trophy for the event is important – another sign of the increasing commercialization of sport and leisure during this period. A soap manufacturer such as Lever could particularly benefit from an association with life-saving, swimming, water and cleanliness.

Interest in the society was also raised at numerous public lectures, and by the end of 1892 more than 90 public lectures and demonstrations had been held. The society sought to reinforce the importance of their own work by producing a series of case studies on rescues of the drowning reported during 1892. Out of a total of 30 cases, 16 were attributed to members of the society, or to people who had witnessed a demonstration of life-saving skills given by the society. [30] These lectures were further supported by the production of several sets of lantern slides, so that speakers could more easily illustrate their topic. [31] Crucially, the new developing visual technologies of the late Victorian period, such as lantern slides and photography, alongside the printed press, allowed the society's methods to be spread further than would have been possible in earlier periods.

London had been the birthplace and main centre of activity of the society, but there was clearly a need to spread the society's methods nationwide. To disseminate the society's message, and to ensure that people in the provinces interested in life-saving had a local point of contact, 'honorary district representatives' were appointed by the central executive of the Life Saving Society beginning in 1892. By the end of that year there were a total of 18 such district representatives – in Bristol, Birmingham, Brighton, Eastbourne, Exeter, Glasgow, Harlesden, Jersey, Leeds, Leicester, Liverpool, Manchester, Newport (Monmouthshire), Norwich, Nottingham, Reading, Sunderland and Stockport. [32] Half of these locations were coastal and port cities, but it is notable that many inland towns and cities appear as well. A year later, at the end of 1893, the number of district representatives had risen to 25: Stockport had lost its representative, but new districts were established in Coventry, Hastings, Ipswich, North Shields, Sheerness, Swindon, Worcestershire and Worthing. [33] The numbers rose to 33 in 1894, with the addition of Dublin, Guildford, Hove, Hull, Macclesfield, Margate, Shrewsbury and Tunbridge Wells. [34] By then, the society effectively covered the whole country with a network of local organizations, although filling in small gaps of coverage would continue for several more years.

This national growth of life-saving activity necessitated a change in the organizational structure of the society by 1897. Certain areas had become particularly keen on life-saving instruction, and required more attention and support than could be provided by a district representative or by the central London office. The answer was to create regional branches with their own 'honorary secretaries' and officers. The first such branches were created for Guildford and for Manchester and District, in 1894. [35] More striking still, the society began to develop branches in distant corners of the British Empire, notably New South Wales (Australia), Toronto (Canada) and the Western Province (South Africa). Although some district representatives fell away, the overall number continued to increase. In 1897, 38 men held posts as district representatives, with new representatives in place in Batley, Bedford, Belfast,

Dovercourt, Leinster District, Lowestoft, Perth, Southport, West Hartlepool, Weston-super-Mare and York. [36] Thereafter, the growth was even more dramatic. Indeed, the period between 1897 and 1914 saw the largest number of district representatives appointed. At the same time the parallel development of areas already represented by a district representative gaining branch status continued. After the First World War, the formation of individual branches across the United Kingdom and the empire really became important, because, by then, the number of people trained by the society across a vast geographical area had increased to the point that central control over all services was impossible. Tight management of the issuing of awards was retained at the centre for a long time, but after 1914 the society began to move towards becoming a commonwealth of societies, much as the British Empire became a Commonwealth of Nations. Such a transition, however, was not completed until the 1960s.

Having influential or noted individuals as patrons was an important distinction for many organizations during the Victorian and Edwardian periods. Much depended on the nature of activity a society or association pursued, though aristocrats and members of Parliament were common choices as patrons. Such individuals brought to the association their status and public position, with the ambition of influencing public opinion towards the group they patronized. The hope was to persuade the public at large that the organization in question was of social value, and hence was worthy of support. The ultimate mark of favour, of course, was (and remains) for a society or association to obtain royal patronage. It is also true that prominent contemporaries *wanted* to become patrons because they believed in the aims, or shared a passion for the activities, of an organization. From its very inception, the Life Saving Society had attracted important patronage because of its attention to humanitarian issues. Its initial list of patrons included Andrew Clark, Esq., FRCS, Dr W. Collingridge, medical office of health for the Port of London, and H.L.W. Lawson, Esq., MP. [37] Thereafter the society could always boast a sprinkling of royals and aristocrats among its patrons. By 1893 the honorary president of the society was HRH The Duke of York, the acting president was Lord Ampthill and among the vice presidents was the Duke of Teck. [38] In 1897 the society held a grand swimming gala at the West India Docks as part of the Diamond Jubilee celebrations. This event was attended by the Duke and Duchess of York in the duke's role as president of the society. In 1902 King Edward VII became the patron of the society, and the Prince of Wales became the society's president. [39] That same year the King presented the 'King's Cup' to the Life Saving Society, to be used for one of the society's competitions. At the ceremony to present the cup to the society, the King stated that the society could designate itself as 'Royal'. [40] Understandably, the society made much of its royal links. The seventh edition of the society's *Handbook* added that 'The signal marks of Royal favour at the hands of our Most Gracious Majesty the King, and our President, HRH the Prince of Wales, are also most encouraging'. [41] Royal status was fully confirmed by charter in 1904. [42]

In the space of little over a decade, then, the society had gone from being a newly founded and unknown organization to one that had the patronage of the two most senior members of the Royal Family. Clearly, the society had secured the highest form of official approval. [43] This may seem insignificant, but in an English society where royal favour (or indifference) reflected both private and public approval, the granting or refusing of royal patronage was much more than mere symbolism. It spoke to, and reflected, the *status* of the organization. In a sense, royal patronage confirmed both the importance and the coming of age of the LSS. It also confirmed that the society's activities were officially deemed good and worthwhile.

Right from its origin the Life Saving Society utilized the medium of the greatly expanded print media of the day to spread its message about safety and to promote interest in swimming. In its first two years of existence the society's message was spread far and wide in the press. The first *Annual Report* of the society reproduced many of the press reports that had mentioned its work during the previous two years. A great variety of publications ran stories on the LSS in 1891 and 1892: *Athletic News, Commercial Transport World, English Sports, The Family Doctor, The Fish Trade Gazette, Hearth and Home, The Lancet, The Lock-to-Lock Times, The Million,* the *Penny Illustrated Paper, The Referee, The Stage* and the *Timber Trades Journal.* In addition, many local and national papers across England, including the *Birmingham Daily Post,* the *Brighton Guardian,* the *Cambridge Daily News,* the *Derby Mercury,* the *Exeter Evening Post,* the *Manchester Guardian,* the *Sunday Times,* the *Sunderland Daily Echo,* the *Sussex Coast Mercury,* the *Tunbridge Wells Gazette* and the *Yorkshire Evening Post,* also covered the new organization. In total, 48 different journals or newspapers covered the society. Some of the papers ran articles about the society on numerous occasions. [44]

Providing interviews and information about the society to various newspapers and magazines was not the only way the LSS sought to bring its humanitarian mission to the attention of the reading public. Then, as now, one of the best ways to spread one's message was to have a close working relationship with a particular journal or newspaper, in the hope that it would give space in its pages to support the society's interests. Many different organizations often either adopted an existing publication as their official press organ (St John Ambulance Association) or started their own in-house journals or newspapers to spread their message (Scout Association, Rowntree Chocolate Works); some organizations did both in turn (Guide Association). Such publications might only be available to members or they might be sold to the public at large. When selecting an existing journal to be the official paper of an organization, most associations approached publications that shared a similar political or social viewpoint to that espoused by the group. Similarly, the same tactics were employed when organizations developed a relationship with a certain journalist or journalists, and provided them with information on the understanding that it would be published in return for the initial advanced notice or 'scoop'. Before the First World War the LSS successively employed two main approaches to get its message out. Initially, the society sought to cultivate a relationship with an existing journal, and in late 1896 adopted the journal *First Aid* as its main regular magazine outlet. Coverage of the society was at first provided by a sympathetic staff journalist who went by the pseudonym 'Neptune'. After a very short period of time, however, the essays to be printed in *First Aid* were provided direct from the society's central office. [45] *First Aid* was, at that time, the unofficial journal of the St John Ambulance Association, another major humanitarian organization of the day. How far there was a shared membership between the two societies remains unknown, but they clearly shared aims and tactics in common.

Perhaps sensing that the audience targeted by using *First Aid* as a print vehicle had been either too narrow or the wrong one, the society then decided to change tactics. The LSS needed its own journal. Less than six months after links had been broken with *First Aid*, the first incarnation of *The Swimming Magazine* was published in May 1898. Although ostensibly a general magazine about the events in the English swimming world, the publication was in spirit, if not in name, the new official journal of the Life Saving Society. The editorial offices of the magazine were listed as 8 Bayley Street, Bedford Square, London. [46] This was also the address given for the honorary secretary of the Life Saving Society in almost every single publication issued by the society between 1891 and 1918. It was, in fact, William Henry's residence. This journal lasted for only a single year, and ceased publication with the May 1899 issue, though the idea of *The Swimming Magazine* was resurrected by William Henry in 1914, when it was launched for a second time, this time as the official journal of the Royal Life Saving Society. [47] Despite being launched only two months before the outbreak of the First World War, this second attempt at in-house publishing was much more successful than its predecessor. Notwithstanding wartime difficulties, it ran for a full four years, only ceasing publication in May 1918. This second run of the magazine is important, however, for it provides an informative look at swimming in England, and is an invaluable source of information about swimming during the war years. Indeed, it was one of the few contemporary sources related to swimming that continued to publish throughout the First World War.

Perhaps most importantly of all, the Life Saving Society, almost from its foundation, sought to have life-saving instruction taught in schools, both public schools and state schools. The greatest emphasis, however, was placed on life-saving lessons within the state educational system. The first official school classes were run in 1892 in London Board schools. [48] By 1897 there had been substantial success in promoting life-saving drill throughout schools in London. The society's *Annual Report* for 1895–96 was illustrated with photographs of massed female students from School Board for London schools demonstrating life-saving drill. [49] It is clear enough that members of the LSS strongly believed that everyone should become familiar with their methods, and the most effective way of instructing the young in life-saving was by using the state educational system. This would, in effect, ensure that nearly the entire population of the country would eventually undergo life-saving training. Although that goal was not achieved before the end of the First World War, it is evident that the Royal Life Saving Society had made an impact on English society and was promoting swimming and humanitarian life-saving to a receptive audience.

Swimming in 1918 was viewed as a skill that had humanitarian and safety value. By the last decade of the nineteenth century, it was actively pursued for such reasons. Though small-scale by comparison to other major humanitarian activities, swimming had entered the fabric of late Victorian social life.

Notes

[1] Sinclair and Henry, *Swimming*, 215–32.
[2] Royle, *Modern Britain*, 186–8.
[3] For more about such topics, see Harrison, 'Philanthropy and the Victorians'; Owen, *English Philanthropy*; Prochaska, *Women and Philanthropy in Nineteenth-Century England*; Prochaska, 'Philanthropy'.
[4] *Bell's Life in London*, 6 Aug. 1837, 2e. Italics mine.
[5] *The Times*, 6 Sept. 1843, 3f. If the BSS and the NSS were one and the same organization, as this author believes, then these may be the original or revised aims of the NSS.
[6] Royal Humane Society, *Sixty-Ninth Annual Report*, 12–13.
[7] See for example, *The Times*, 9 Sept. 1847, 6b; 16 Feb. 1856, 10c; 26 July 1859, 10d.
[8] For the origins and first awarding of the Stanhope Medal see the 99th (1872) and 100th (1873) *Annual Reports* of the Royal Humane Society, housed in the Royal Humane Society Library, and a short but quite informative work: Barclay, *The Medals of the Royal Humane Society*, 23.
[9] Royal Humane Society, *One Hundred and Ninth Annual Report*, 9–10, 77–82.
[10] Royal Humane Society, *Annual Report for 1902*, 10, 12–13.
[11] Royal Life Saving Society, *Annual Report for 1905*, 19.
[12] Anonymous, 'Brevities', *First Aid* 16, no. 188 (Feb. 1910), 120.
[13] Manchester Local Studies Archives Service (hereafter MLSAS), Baths and Wash-Houses Committee Minutes, vol. 4, fol. 61, minutes of 19 Dec. 1888.
[14] See, for example, Life Saving Society, *Annual Report 1893–94*, 9; MLSAS, Baths and Wash-Houses Committee Minutes, vol. 8, fol. 114, minutes of 21 April 1897.
[15] Royal Humane Society, *Annual Report for 1902*, 226.
[16] Life Saving Society, *Annual Report 1899–1900*, 7, 9; Life Saving Society, *Annual Report 1900–01*, 17; Archibald Sinclair, 'William Henry and the RLSS', *The Swimming Magazine* 3, no. 8 (Jan. 1917), 142–4. During his life William Henry published and edited two magazines entitled *The Swimming Magazine*. The first ran from June 1898 to May 1899, while the second ran from June 1914 to May 1918.
[17] Life Saving Society, *Annual Report for 1897–98*, 53; *Annual Report 1900–01*, 20.
[18] Sinclair, 'William Henry and the RLSS.
[19] Sinclair and Henry, *Swimming*, 215–32, especially 230–2.
[20] Ibid., 231–3.
[21] Ibid., 233–4.
[22] Ibid., 234–6.
[23] Ibid., 235.
[24] Swimmers' Life Saving Society, *Illustrated Handbook*, 3.
[25] Ibid., 5.
[26] Ibid., outside back cover. Bold and Italics are in the original.

Swimming, Saving Life and the Royal Life Saving Society 113

[27] The translation is by the author, but it is also the standard translation used by the RLSS. The earliest known use of the motto in its Latin form is found on a letter preserved in the RLSS's Commonwealth Offices. RLSS Commonwealth Secretariat, River House, Broom, framed letter from RLSS office to Mr William Wilson, 8 Sept. 1892.
[28] See Life Saving Society, *Annual Report 1896–97*, 14; and RLSS, *Handbook of Instruction*, 164.
[29] Life Saving Society, *Annual Report 1891–92*, 25, 30–2; *Annual Report 1893–94*, 17.
[30] Life Saving Society, *Annual Report 1891–92*, 23–4.
[31] Life Saving Society, *Annual Report 1896–97*, 6–7.
[32] Life Saving Society, *Annual Report 1891–92*, 4.
[33] Life Saving Society, *Annual Report 1892–93*, 3.
[34] Life Saving Society, *Annual Report 1893–94*, 4.
[35] Ibid, 9.
[36] Life Saving Society, *Annual Report 1895–96*, 9.
[37] Swimmers' Life Saving Society, *Illustrated Handbook*, 4.
[38] Life Saving Society, *Annual Report 1891–92*, 3.
[39] Life Saving Society, *Annual Report 1901–02*, 3.
[40] *The Swimming Magazine* 3, no. 8 (Jan. 1917), 144, 150.
[41] Life Saving Society, *Handbook of Instruction*, 4.
[42] Royal Life Saving Society, *Annual Report of the Central Executive Committee for 1904 and Prospectus for 1905*, 2. The official state papers relating to the designation of the Life Saving Society as a 'Royal' society have only recently been opened to public access in the Public Record Office. PRO, HO 144/22504, Royal Title and Royal Arms: Royal Life Saving Society.
[43] Queen Elizabeth II is the current patron of the RLSS, and the Commonwealth president of the society is Prince Michael of Kent. In the 1930s both the then Princess Elizabeth and Princess Margaret earned the bronze medallion of the RLSS.
[44] Life Saving Society, *Annual Report 1891–92*, 44–7. See also, for example, *Lancet*, 28 May 1892; *Manchester Guardian*, 26 May 1892; *Sunday Times*, 29 May 1892; 12 Feb. 1893; *Yorkshire Evening Post*, 16 May 1892.
[45] Neptune, 'Life Saving Notes', *First Aid* II, no. 30 (Dec. 1896), 139; *First Aid* II, no. 32 (Feb. 1897). Neptune provided coverage of the Life Saving Society for two issues, in December 1896 and January 1897. A nearly complete run of the magazine can be obtained in the St John Ambulance Museum and Archives, London.
[46] *The Swimming Magazine* 1, no. 1 (1 June 1898), 6. A complete run of the magazine is housed in the British Library's St Pancras location.
[47] *The Swimming Magazine* 1, no. 1 (June 1914). The only complete run of this magazine is housed in the British Library's St. Pancras location. The ASA Library, Loughborough, houses a nearly complete run. The RLSS Commonwealth Office, Broom, has several framed pages from the first two issues, but no complete copies. The RLSS UK Archives, Broom, do not contain any copies of the journal.
[48] Life Saving Society, *Annual Report 1891–92*, 25.
[49] Life Saving Society, *Annual Report 1895–96*, 10, 40, 66.

References

Barclay, Craig. *The Medals of the Royal Humane Society*. London: Royal Humane Society, 1998.
Harrison, B. 'Philanthropy and the Victorians'. In *Peaceable Kingdom. Stability and Change in Modern Britain*. Oxford: Oxford University Press, 1982.
Life Saving Society. *Annual Report of the Central Executive Committee 1891–92 and Prospectus for 1893*. London: Life Saving Society, 1893.

———. *Annual Report of the Central Executive Committee 1892–93 and Prospectus for 1894*. London: Life Saving Society, 1894.

———. *Annual Report of the Central Executive Committee 1893–94 and Prospectus for 1895*. London: Life Saving Society, 1895.

———. *Annual Report of the Central Executive Committee 1895–96 and Prospectus for 1897*. London: Life Saving Society, 1897.

———. *Annual Report of the Central Executive Committee 1896–97 and Prospectus for 1898*. London: Life Saving Society, 1898.

———. *Annual Report of the Central Executive Committee 1897–98 and Prospectus for 1899*. London: Life Saving Society, 1899.

———. *Annual Report of the Central Executive Committee 1899–1900 and Prospectus for 1901*. London: Life Saving Society, 1901.

———. *Annual Report of the Central Executive Committee 1900–01 and Prospectus for 1902*. London: Life Saving Society, 1902.

———. *Annual Report of the Central Executive Committee 1901–02 and Prospectus for 1903*. London: Life Saving Society, 1903.

———. *Handbook of Instruction*. 7th edn. London: Life Saving Society, 1903.

Owen, D. *English Philanthropy, 1660–1960*. Cambridge, MA: Harvard University Press, 1965.

Prochaska, F.K. 'Philanthropy'. In *The Cambridge Social History of Britain, 1750–1950*. vol. 3, edited by F.M.L. Thompson. Cambridge: Cambridge University Press, 1990.

———. *Women and Philanthropy in Nineteenth-Century England*. Oxford: Oxford University Press, 1980.

Royal Humane Society. *The Sixty-Ninth Annual Report of the Royal Humane Society*. London: Royal Humane Society, 1843.

———. *The One Hundred and Ninth Annual Report of the Royal Humane Society*. London: Royal Humane Society, 1883.

———. *Annual Report for 1902*. London: Royal Humane Society, 1903.

Royal Life Saving Society. *Annual Report of the Central Executive Committee for 1904 and Prospectus for 1905*. London: Royal Life Saving Society, 1905.

———. *Annual Report of the Central Executive Committee for 1905 and Prospectus for 1906*. London: Royal Life Saving Society, 1906.

———. *Handbook of Instruction*. 19th edn. London: Royal Life Saving Society, 1932.

Royle, Edward. *Modern Britain: A Social History 1750–1997*. 2nd edn. London: Arnold, 1997.

Sinclair, Archibald and William Henry. *Swimming* (The Badminton Library of Sports and Pastimes). London: Longmans, Green, and Co., 1893.

Swimmers' Life Saving Society. *Illustrated Handbook*. 1st edn. London: Langley & Son, 1891.

Swimming, Service to the Empire and Baden-Powell's Youth Movements

Parallel to the rise of humanitarian ideas and ideals within English society there emerged the concept of service to others, to England and to the British Empire. From roughly the 1870s onwards, the idea of service to others became an increasingly powerful theme in English society, or at least among certain social groups. The 'condition of England question', for example, and the determination to help raise the working classes out of their misery and poverty, was prompted by a score of important social investigations into English life. [1] But, there was also a desire to export civilized values of Christianity to the 'heathen' peoples of the Empire. This sense of duty at home and abroad became an important and striking feature of Victorian life, and influenced growing numbers of Britons. The commitment to pursuing a humanitarian crusade had major consequences. By the late Victorian, and through the Edwardian, period the need to instil a sense of duty towards the imperial civilizing and humanitarian mission, and towards Britain's place of leadership in the world, was ever-present in a broadly based educational system – at all social levels. In certain quarters swimming came to be adopted as one of the issues in this wide spectrum of humanitarian activities. One of those areas of where learning to swim was seen as a duty was the Scouting movement.

The formation and early growth of Scouting was intimately linked to the contemporary debate about the British Empire. The Edwardian period is traditionally seen as the height of British imperialism. Whatever the hidden problems, among the people at large there was a general belief that Britain was the greatest imperial power in the world. [2] These years of imperial grandeur spawned a host of organizations that found inspiration and purpose in the imperial ethos and theme. Perhaps one of the most durable of these was the Scouting movement, begun by Robert Baden-Powell, then a lieutenant-general in the army and a hero of the Boer War, later to be Lord Baden-Powell of Gilwell for his work. [3] The work that launched the movement, *Scouting for Boys*, was first published in 1908 and was subtitled *A Handbook for Instruction in Good Citizenship*. [4] This textbook was very influential at the time and went through numerous printings in its early years. [5] From the start, Baden-Powell was keen to encourage swimming among those skills he believed that Scouts should possess in order to do their duty. In his characteristic assertive and positive attitude he wrote:

> It is very necessary for a scout to be able to swim, for he never knows when he may have to cross a river, to swim for his life, or to plunge in to save someone from drowning, so those of you that cannot swim should make it your business to begin at once and learn; it is not very difficult. [6]

The first edition contained a section on life-saving, and although this was not specifically centred around aquatic life-saving, the ability of a Scout to save life was considered a high virtue by Baden-Powell. Indeed, it was part of the core ideal of the movement: service to others and to the Empire. [7] Indirectly, such beliefs furthered the cause and efforts of the Royal Life Saving Society (RLSS). The Scout Association expanded rapidly. The first census of Scouts, in 1910, recorded 100,298 boys as members of the movement. For a movement begun only two years previously, this was dramatic growth. The movement continued to grow at a rapid pace, reaching a membership of 137,776 boys in 1913 and 153,376 in 1919. [8]

By 1911 a book of regulations to control the movement was in print, and it records the requirements for the badges that Scouts could earn. The test for the category of First Class Scout, the standard every boy was supposed to aspire to, required all candidates to complete a 50-yard swim. Three of the proficiency badges awarded by the Boy Scouts at the time also required swimming ability. The 'Coast Guard' badge required an undefined knowledge of swimming, and the ability to perform life-saving, as well as resuscitation of the drowned. The 'Seaman' badge required that the candidate be able to swim 50 yards while clothed (trousers, socks and shirt) and the 'Swimmer and Life Saver' badge required candidates to execute a dive entry into the water, and swim 50 yards while clothed; to demonstrate how to throw a lifeline or ring buoy; and to perform two methods of rescuing the drowning and the Schäfer method of resuscitation. [9] A companion book to the regulations explained how one should go about earning the proficiency badges, advising that life-saving instruction should be obtained from the Royal Life Saving Society:

> The art of swimming is so very useful, not only as a bracing summer exercise, but as a means of preserving and saving life, that it should be acquired by everyone. Considering the numerous risks run by all human beings of being accidentally plunged into the water, and how greatly the chances of being saved are increased by the power of keeping afloat for even five minutes, it is surprising that the art of swimming is not made compulsory. [10]

In the January 1912 revisions to the Scout regulations, many concerned swimming. The 50-yard swimming test for the First Class Scout award was to be waived as a requirement for Scouts with health problems. This was a sensible adjustment for an organization that wanted to reach the widest possible constituency. In addition, two gallantry awards were introduced: the bronze cross on red ribbon for a rescue entailing risk to the life of the rescuer and the silver cross on blue ribbon for a rescue entailing no risk to the rescuer. [11] Finally, and for the first time, this set of regulations detailed many of the sporting championships that Boy Scouts were eligible to compete in. Swimming races were specifically mentioned, including three established championships; the Otter Swimming Club Challenge Shield, the Boy Scout Team Swimming Championship of London and the Darnell Challenge Cup for Swimming and Life Saving. [12]

A further set of revisions to the Scout regulations in July 1912 seem to have been prompted by the incorporation of the association by royal charter. In honour of the royal patronage the King's Scout award was created. Even more prestigious and harder to obtain than the First Class Scout award, the King's Scout award required prospective candidates to earn the 'Pathfinder' badge as well as four of six from a list of other badges: 'Ambulance', 'Cyclist', 'Fireman', 'Marksman', 'Rescuer' and 'Signaller'. All these six awards obviously had a humanitarian emphasis and three – the 'Ambulance', 'Fireman' and 'Rescuer' badges – were directly concerned with the preservation or saving of life. The overall effect of the creation of the King's Scout award was a series of major changes to the proficiency badges awarded by the Scout Association. The previous 'Coast Guard', 'Seaman' and 'Swimmer and Life Saver' badges were discontinued and were replaced by two new badges related to aquatics and swimming: the previously mentioned 'Rescuer' badge and a new 'Swimmer' badge. The requirements for the new 'Rescuer' badge seem to have been almost totally based on the then current teaching practices of the RLSS, with candidates required to demonstrate four methods of rescue and three methods of release, as well as resuscitation and follow up care. The requirements for the new 'Swimmer' badge were more comprehensive than they had been previously. A candidate was required to swim 50 yards while clothed (in shirt, trousers and socks) and then undress in the water; to swim 100 yards on the breast without clothes; to swim 50 yards on the back without using his arms; and to be able to dive and recover small objects from the bottom. Interestingly, in addition to all the other changes to the award structure, the wording of the requirements for the First Class Scout award were also changed, making the 50 yards swim mandatory, except where a doctor's orders prevailed. [13] Perhaps too many candidates were claiming health problems to avoid the test? [14] Whatever the case, it is important to note that despite the many changes taking place in the Scouting organization during these formative years, with badges being created and disappearing within the space of a year or less, swimming was always represented. At no point does there appear to have been any thought of removing swimming as a core item that Scouts should be encouraged to learn.

By the start of the First World War the Scout movement was still expanding and developing a framework for its great variety of programmes, and swimming continued to have a major role. By October 1914 it was decided, in another sensible policy devised for safety, that no Scout would be allowed to take part in any boating training until he could swim at least 50 yards. The same set of regulations also contained a revised set of conditions for the 'Rescuer' badge, which henceforth would require a Scout to retake the test for the badge annually in order to continue to hold it. [15] This second change reveals a concern, or perhaps a realization, that life-saving skills required constant practice in order to be of any real practical use in an emergency. The timing of this change of regulation, just after the outbreak of the First World War, is of interest, and perhaps illustrates a belief common among Baden-Powell and his closest assistants that life-saving skills would be in wide demand or use during the course of the war. With the two navies, German and British, pitched against each other, and with millions of men regularly shipped great distances, safety at sea had become important and the threat of drowning a major danger. The ability to swim and to rescue others (or oneself) had never been more important.

It was calculated that there had been 152,000 Scouts in Great Britain at the start of 1914, and that a further 6,000 boys had joined the organization by January 1915. [16] Swimming was still included as part of the requirements for several badges, as illustrated by the revised instructional book on how to pass the tests. [17] In October 1915 the first bathing regulations for the Scout Association were introduced. They stated:

> Bathing will only be permitted *under strict supervision* to prevent non-swimmers getting into dangerous water. A picquet of two good swimmers should be on duty (undressed) with great coats on, in a boat or on shore as the circumstances may demand, ready to help any boy in distress. The picquet itself may not bathe until the others have left the water. [18]

At about the same time all Scout sporting competitions, including swimming, were suspended for the duration of the war. [19] This was part of the broader campaign against formal sports and pleasures in wartime which affected all British popular activities. [20]

The Scouting movement continued to grow during the war years, maintaining its work preparing boys for service to the nation and humanitarian work. By January 1917 the requirements for the 'Rescuer' badge had been further tightened, now requiring the candidates to complete all elements of the test while wearing a shirt and trousers. The completion of four rescue methods, including a ten-yard tow with each, and three releases from a grasp remained, as did the resuscitation and follow-on care requirements. Newly introduced were requirements for a dive from the surface to a depth of five feet to recover a five-pound weight and a swim of 50 yards, clothed, before removing those clothes and touching the bottom of the testing area. As before, the badge was required to be renewed annually. At the same time the Scouting movement expanded with the introduction of Wolf Cubs, a junior branch of the Scouting movement for boys aged eight to 12 years of age. There was no equivalent to the rescuer badge in the awards open to Cubs, but there was a badge for swimming which can be seen as preparatory for those going on to take the Scout 'Swimmer' badge later. [21]

The Scouting movement expanded rapidly in the years immediately following its foundation in 1908. The first available census of members after the First World War lists a total of 133,504 Scouts across England, slightly lower than the estimated total for the United Kingdom as a whole in 1914–15, but still a significant number. [22] It is also apparent that the movement greatly valued the ability to swim and to rescue a person from the water. This was illustrated by the continued introduction, revision and attention to regulations relating to awards for saving life and swimming. There was, throughout, a keen appreciation of the usefulness of such training. Swimming was seen as an activity that had humanitarian application, and was thus socially valuable, a view reinforced by looking at the sister organization to the Scouts, the Girl Guides.

Initially, Robert Baden-Powell had made no provision for girls and young women in his plans for a youth organization designed to promote good citizenship. A product of Charterhouse School and the army, he was used to a man's world. Initially, therefore, it must have shocked him somewhat when girls wished to join the Boy Scouts whenever troops were set up around the United Kingdom. [23] Whatever shock or misgivings he may have had, however, were eventually overcome. He recruited his sister, Agnes Baden-Powell, to oversee the work with girls and in 1910 they launched the Girl Guides. [24] At first the new organization was modelled closely on the Scouts, and by extension on the army that Robert Baden-Powell had used as a model for the Scouts. Surviving Guide badges from 1910 are almost identical to Scout badges of the same era, except for the 'Girl Guides' name embroidered where 'Boy Scout' would be expected to appear. Among the first badges issued was a swimming badge. [25] The requirements for this swimming badge included the ability of the Guide to swim 50 yards in her uniform and demonstrate some life-saving skill in the water. [26]

Despite this early reliance on already established models of organization and regulation provided by the Scouts, Agnes Baden-Powell was of the distinct opinion that the Guides were to be a different organization from the Scouts. In 1910 she wrote:

> I would first like to state that it is a feminine movement – a womanly scheme in the best sense of the word. There is no militarism in it – no idea of making girls into

poor imitations of Boy Scouts. Education will be on such lines only as will make the girls better housewives, more capable in all womanly arts, from cooking, washing, and sick-nursing to the training and management of children. [27]

In the area of humanitarianism and service, however, the Scouts and Guides maintained more similarities than differences.

Just like the Scout Association, the Guide Association issued awards for the saving of life. The Guide Regulations for 1916 made provision for these awards; the bronze cross with red ribbon, the silver cross with blue ribbon and the badge of merit. Of these, the bronze cross was the highest award. Each was for the saving of life, not necessarily in aquatic circumstances, with varying degrees of risk to the rescuer. [28] In fact, these awards had been in existence from 1910, as is evidenced by various stories in *Home Notes*, the periodical which served as the media organ for the Guides, from the period. In August 1910, for example, it was reported that two Guides from Newcastle, while fully clothed, had rescued a young man from drowning. The anonymous author of the article concluded the description by saying: 'I think all our Patrols will agree that these young Newcastle girls thoroughly deserve the Silver Crosses for their brave and valorous conduct, and that it is a good example of how useful it is to have learnt to swim in their clothes.' [29] In October of the same year a further two Guides were reported to have earned the silver cross for saving a man from drowning. [30] In November another Guide received an unspecified award for saving two young children from drowning. [31] In 1912 the new paper of the Guides, *The Golden Rule*, reported: 'Scarcely a week passed last summer without some record of scouts [sic] saving life, so Guides "be prepared" to show what you can do.' [32] There was, clearly, an appreciation that Guides, like Scouts, needed to maintain and practice their life-saving skills.

This concern for the learning and retention of life-saving skills, especially in swimming, was derived right from the top of the Guide establishment. Agnes and Robert Baden-Powell wrote in 1912: 'To learn swimming is a most necessary requirement – one might almost say a duty – for every one, man or woman, besides being a healthy exercise.' [33] This official pronouncement followed on from several articles in *Home Notes* which promoted the value of swimming through emulation of the achievements of others. In August 1910 it was reported that the champion girl swimmer of England, who had won the championship cup for two years in a row, was a Guide in the Manchester and District Guide Association, and she was also a patrol leader. [34] Early in November 1910 the paper felt that it was important to report that a group of Guides had gone to Lancing-on-Sea for a week of swimming training in the sea. [35] Later in the same month it was considered important enough to note that there were now 'two Champion Swimmers amongst our Guides'. [36] In August 1911 it was noted that swimming was a valuable skill to learn, especially considering the large number of drownings during that time of year. [37]

While there was a concern to promote swimming and life-saving as necessary skills that should be obtained by every Guide, it is evident that at times such skills were not always popular with the Guides. In October 1911, for example, it was reported of the swimming badge that

> There is a large demand for every badge issued by the Headquarters except the Swimming badge. Every encouragement should be given to girls (except, of course, when it is prohibited by a doctor) to learn this useful art. All over the country there are swimming baths, and in many places the Guides are taken at a reduced rate, receiving a few minutes' private instruction and a few minutes' practice. It is not advisable that any 'playing' should be allowed, and the Guides who can swim should not take advantage of those who cannot by such tricks as ducking. Many girls are likely to lose their nerve by such practice. [38]

Evidently, this apparent lack of interest in the award was of concern to Agnes and Robert Baden-Powell. By March 1912, and perhaps even earlier, the requirements for the First Class Guide badge included a requirement that the candidate be able to swim 50 yards, a direct mirror of the First Class Scout badge requirement. [39]

The 1916 rule book for the Guide Association provides a much clearer view of the values held to be important by the executive of the organization. The aims of the association at the time read in part:

> The Girl Guides movement has been constituted under a Charter of Incorporation for the purpose of developing good citizenship among girls by forming their character; training them in habits of observation, obedience, and self-reliance; inculcating loyalty and thoughtfulness for others; *teaching them services useful to the public* and handicrafts useful to themselves; *promoting their physical development*; making them capable of keeping good homes and of bringing up good children. [40]

As has already been noted, this manual was the first to explicitly outline the requirements for the various life-saving awards offered by the association. In addition, it set out revised criteria for earning the First Class Guide badge. Whereas previously candidates had to swim 50 yards in uniform, the new requirement was to either swim 50 yards or earn the 'Child Nurse' badge. [41] The requirements for the 'Swimmer' badge had also been revised. Under the new standard a Guide had to either complete a swim of 200 yards' distance or a swim of 50 yards while clothed (including skirt and boots) and the demonstration of a series of tasks including resuscitation, diving, throwing a lifeline and four methods of rescuing the drowning. [42] Finally, like the Scouts, the Guides had developed a series of rules about boating and bathing to ensure the safety of members of the association. These included a requirement that a Guide be able to swim 50 yards before taking part in any boating training, and supervision was required for any swimming or bathing period. [43]

Like the Scout Association, the Guide Association continued to grow in numbers, even through the years of the First World War. The annual report of the movement for 1917 was the first to provide a census of membership numbers in the United Kingdom. The total number of girls and officers in the association for that year was 40,350. [44] The same report also included statistics for the numbers of proficiency badges issued during the year. A total of 2,244 'Swimmer' badges had been issued and 972 girls had become First Class Guides. [45] In the same year the Brownies, a junior division of Guides analogous to the Wolf Cubs for Scouts, were founded. Like their male counterparts, the Brownies could earn a swimming badge that was easier to earn than its Guide equivalent, but which can be seen as being a precursor to the more senior award. [46] Towards the end of the First World War, Sir Robert Baden-Powell produced another handbook about the training of Guides, devoting a great deal of space (more than six full pages) to matters related to swimming. It formed his clearest statement on the usefulness and necessity of learning to swim:

> *Swimming.* – Every 1st Class Guide ought to be able to swim. It is not only for her own amusement that she should do so, but so that she will not cause other people to risk their lives in rescuing her when she gets into difficulties in the water, and that she may be able to help those in distress. British girls are behindhand in learning to swim – it is very different in Norway and Sweden, where nearly every girl can swim. [47]

Whether or not Robert Baden-Powell's claim that nearly the entire young female populations of Norway and Sweden could swim at this time was true or not is impossible to confirm. Certainly, organized swimming was popular and widespread in Europe by this time, as evidenced by the participation of many European teams in the swimming events at the Olympic Games, and by the previously noted tours of several European countries by representatives of the Royal Life Saving Society before the First World War. Thomas A.P. van Leeuwen in his history of the swimming pool looks at the swimming which took place in such pools. It seems certain that by the later nineteenth century swimming was widespread in Austria-Hungary, France, Germany, the Netherlands and Sweden, as well as the United Kingdom. [48]

In the Edwardian period, the proliferation of associations saw swimming promoted as never before. In the Scouts, Guides, Boys' Brigade, Young Men's Christian Association (YMCA), Young Women's Christian Association (YWCA) and other groups, swimming and life-saving became part of the core curriculum. Tens of thousands of young people were expected to be able to swim and were given various inducements to practise both swimming and life-saving. When we recall the parallel growth of swimming through the school system, through the provision of municipal baths and via the proliferation of private associations, it becomes clear that swimming had entered a new phase in its development in England.

In the Scout and Guide movements especially, this emphasis on the importance of swimming was clearly based upon the perceived value of the activity by the movement's organizers. Throughout his writings on the subject, and through the regulations drafted by himself and his supporters, Baden-Powell's vision of a Scout a Guide included the ability to swim. Swimming skill was valuable because it could be used to save life, whether the Scout or Guide's own or of some unfortunate soul the Scout or Guide might find in trouble. Being prepared to serve as was needed within the community was an important part of the values Robert Baden-Powell hoped to instil in the youth participating in his programme.

We cannot, of course, ever know if all the members of the Scouting and Guiding movements believed in exactly the same things as the founders of the movement. In fact, we can almost be sure that many of them differed in at least some of their views. Be that as it may, the large numbers of youth passing through the Scout and Guide programmes between 1908 and 1918 ensured that tens of thousands of English youth were exposed to the idea that swimming had humanitarian value. The central message being promoted was that swimming was useful in providing the swimmer with the ability to save life – and that was increasingly important in wartime and in the dangerous adventures on the imperial frontiers.

Notes

[1] For an overview of this movement, see Searle, *A New England?*, 186–202.
[2] For more about this belief see, for example, Leinster-Mackay, 'The Nineteenth-century English Preparatory School'; Porter, *The Lion's Share*.
[3] For a general history of the Boy Scouts' Association see: Collis *et al.*, *B-P's Scouts*. More critical analysis of the Scout association's role can be found in: Springhall, *Youth, Empire and Society*; Warren, 'Citizens of the Empire'. All the sources cited for the Scout association can be found in the Scout Association Archives (SAA), Gilwell Park, Chingford, London.
[4] Baden-Powell, *Scouting for Boys*.
[5] The earliest surviving copy of this work in the Scout Association archives collection is a third impression copy, stated to be completely revised and illustrated, from 1908.
[6] Baden-Powell, *Scouting for Boys*, 138.
[7] Baden-Powell, *Scouting for Boys*, 214–19.
[8] Collis *et al.*, *B-P's Scouts*, 259–64. The figures given refer to the UK as a whole and only to the number of Scouts and Sea Scouts enrolled, not Scout Leaders or Wolf Cubs. The full membership figures between 1910 and 1919 were: 1910: 100,298; 1911: 113,909; 1912: 128,397; 1913: 137,776; 1917: 152,175; 1918: 145,880; 1919: 153,376. John Springhall also presented membership totals in his book, agreeing in all particulars except for 1917, where he records 154,774 Scouts and Sea Scouts: Springhall, *Youth, Empire and Society*, 134.
[9] Boy Scouts' Association, *Boy Scout Regulations* (Sept. 1911), 16, 18, 23, 24. The first set of regulations for the Scout Association seems to have been produced in 1910, but the only surviving copy of this work in the Scout Association archives is in fragments and many pages are missing. None of the surviving sections refer to swimming.
[10] Anonymous, *Boy Scout Tests and How to Pass Them*, 437. The author of this work was probably Robert E. Young who was credited as the author of two revised editions of the work in 1915 and 1930.
[11] No illustrations of the awards are contained in the regulations. The Girl Guides introduced an almost identical system when they were founded, explained further below, and their silver and bronze cross for gallantry both appear to have been modelled on the Victoria Cross. It is likely that the Girl Guide awards were modelled on the Boy Scout ones, which in turn would have been based upon Baden-Powell's military experience.
[12] Boy Scouts' Association, *Boy Scout Regulations* (Jan. 1912), 17, 27, 32. The Otter Swimming Club was a famous London club of the period, dating back to 1869. The Darnell Challenge Cup was offered by the RLSS. The Boy Scout Team Swimming Championship is otherwise unknown.

[13] Boy Scouts' Association, *Regulations* (July 1912), 19, 20, 29, 36, 37.
[14] Such behaviour would be explicitly against the requirement for a Scout to be truthful and trustworthy at all times, but the question is an intriguing one.
[15] Boy Scouts' Association, *Policy, Organisation and Rules* (Oct. 1914), 34, 39.
[16] Boy Scouts' Association, *Sixth Annual Report*, 3.
[17] Young, *Boy Scout Tests and How to Pass Them*, 484, 591.
[18] Boy Scouts' Association, *Policy, Organisation and Rules* (Oct. 1915), 43.
[19] Boy Scouts' Association, *Policy, Organisation and Rules* (Oct. 1915), 46.
[20] See for example, Mason, *Association Football and English Society*, 251–5; Walvin, *The People's Game*, 88–90.
[21] Boy Scouts' Association, *Policy, Organisation and Rules* (Jan. 1917), 44, 53.
[22] Boy Scouts' Association, *Twelfth Annual Report*, 37. These figures refer to the year ending 30 September 1920.
[23] For girls wanting to be Scouts, see, Warren, 'Citizens of the Empire', 244-46.
[24] Baden-Powell and Baden-Powell, *Girl Guides. A Suggestion for Character Training for Girls*, pamphlets A and B. These were reprints of the original pamphlets produced in 1910, and they provide the first outline of the division of girls from boys in the two organizations. The history of the Guide Association is very poorly documented. See for example, Kerr, *The Story of the Girl Guides*. All sources cited for the Guide Association can be located in the Guide Association Archives (hereafter GAA), London.
[25] GAA, preserved selection of badges from 1910 including a 'Swimmer' badge.
[26] Baden-Powell and Baden-Powell, *Girl Guides*, pamphlet A, 9.
[27] *Home Notes*, 25 Aug. 1910, 406. Agnes Baden-Powell wrote a regular column that appeared in almost every issue for the Guide pages in *Home Notes*, while it served as the official paper of the Guide Association in 1910 and 1911. It is not clear whether she wrote all the material included in the two-page spread allocated to the association, as all the other articles are unattributed.
[28] Guide Association, *Rules, Policy and Organisation 1916*, 18. Both the bronze and silver crosses appear to have been modelled on the Victoria Cross.
[29] *Home Notes*, 18 Aug. 1910, 353.
[30] *Home Notes*, 27 Oct. 1910, 246.
[31] *Home Notes*, 24 Nov. 1910, 438.
[32] *The Golden Rule*, March 1912, 70.
[33] Baden-Powell and Baden-Powell, *The Handbook for Girl Guides, or How Girls Can Help Build the Empire*, 270.
[34] *Home Notes*, 25 Aug. 1910, 407.
[35] *Home Notes*, 3 Nov. 1910, 295.
[36] *Home Notes*, 24 Nov. 1910, 438.
[37] *Home Notes*, 24 Aug. 1911, 358.
[38] *Home Notes*, 19 Oct. 1911, 166.
[39] *The Golden Rule*, March 1912, 70.
[40] Guide Association, *Rules, Policy and Organisation 1916*, 4. Emphasis added by this author.
[41] Ibid., 21.
[42] Ibid., 33.
[43] Ibid., 35.
[44] Girl Guides, *Girl Guides Annual Report 1917*, 5.
[45] Ibid., 15.
[46] Guide Association, *Rules, Policy, and Organisation 1917*, 37.
[47] Baden-Powell, *Girl Guiding*, 157.
[48] van Leeuwen, *The Springboard in the Pond*, 4, 20–45.

References

Anonymous [Robert E. Young]. *Boy Scout Tests and How to Pass Them*. Glasgow: James Brown & Son, 1911.
Baden-Powell, Sir Robert S.S. *Scouting for Boys: A Handbook for Instruction in Good Citizenship*. London: C. Arthur Pearson Ltd., 1908.
——. *Girl Guiding: A Handbook for Guidelets, Guides, Senior Guides, and Guiders*. London: C. Arthur Pearson Ltd., 1918.
Baden-Powell, Agnes and Robert S.S. Baden-Powell. *GIRL GUIDES. A Suggestion for Character Training for Girls,* pamphlets A and B. London, 1912.
——. *The Handbook for Girl Guides, or How Girls Can Help Build the Empire*. London: Thomas Nelson and Sons, 1912.
Boy Scouts' Association. *Boy Scout Regulations*. London: Boy Scouts' Association, September 1911.
——. *Boy Scout Regulations*. London: Boy Scouts' Association, January 1912.
——. *Boy Scout Regulations*. London: Boy Scouts' Association, July 1912.
——. *Policy, Organisation and Rules*. London: Boy Scouts' Association, October 1914.
——. *Policy, Organisation and Rules*. London: Boy Scouts' Association, October 1915.
——. *Sixth Annual Report of the Executive Committee of the Council. January, 1915*. London: The Boy Scouts Association, 1915.
——. *Policy, Organisation and Rules*. London: Boy Scouts' Association, January 1917.
——. *Twelfth Annual Report of the Committee of the Council*. London: The Boy Scouts Association, 1920.
Collis, Henry, Fred Hurll and Rex Hazlewood. *B-P's Scouts: An Official History of The Boy Scouts' Association*. London: Collins, 1961.
Girl Guides. *Girl Guides Annual Report 1917*. London: Girl Guides, 1918.
Guide Association. *Rules, Policy and Organisation 1916*. London: Guide Association, 1916.
——. *Rules, Policy, and Organisation 1917*. London: Guide Association, 1917.
Kerr, Rose. *The Story of the Girl Guides*. London: Girl Guide Association, 1932.
Leinster-Mackay, Donald. 'The Nineteenth-century English Preparatory School: Cradle and Crèche of Empire'. In *'Benefits Bestowed'? Education and British Imperialism*. edited by J.A. Mangan. Manchester: Manchester University Press, 1988.
MacKenzie, John M., ed. *Imperialism and Popular Culture*. Manchester: Manchester University Press, 1986.
Mason, Tony. *Association Football and English Society 1863–1915*. Brighton: The Harvester Press, 1980.
Porter, Bernard. *The Lion's Share, A Short History of British Imperialism 1850–1995*. 3rd edn. London: Longman, 1996.
Searle, G.R. *A New England? Peace and War 1886–1918* (The New Oxford History of England). Oxford: Oxford University Press, 2004.
Springhall, John. *Youth, Empire and Society: British Youth Movements, 1883–1940*. London: Croom Helm, 1977.
van Leeuwen, Thomas A.P. *The Springboard in the Pond: An Intimate History of the Swimming Pool*. Cambridge: The MIT Press, 1998.
Walvin, James. *The People's Game: A Social History of British Football*. London: Allen Lane, 1975.
Warren, Allen. 'Citizens of the Empire: Baden-Powell, Scouts and Guides, and an Imperial Ideal'. In *Imperialism and Popular Culture*, edited by John M. MacKenzie. Manchester: Manchester University Press, 1986.
Young, Robert E. *Boy Scout Tests and How to Pass Them*. Revised edn. Glasgow: James Brown & Son, 1915.

Taking a Refreshing Dip: Health, Cleanliness and the Empire

In both the classical Greek and Roman worlds, bathing for health and cleanliness was widespread. No major town or city was without its baths complex. Places of social interaction and recreation, the baths were often the centre of a community, sometimes even attached to a library, and the Greeks and Romans spread their bathing habit wherever they settled. The Romans' arrival in Britain was soon followed by the construction of baths and the introduction of bathing culture. The ruins of the Roman that are still admired (and sometimes used) in Bath today are an example of the size and construction of these ancient edifices. With the departure of the Romans, however, the link between baths, swimming and at least a general concept of cleanliness lapsed for many centuries. Not until the eighteenth century, with the rise of a spa culture and seaside resorts, was a connection between bathing and health re-established. From the mid-eighteenth century to the present there has been an explicit link between water and health. Bathing at the seaside or taking the waters at a spa for health reasons became increasingly popular from around 1750. Much of this was, of course, a deliberate harkening back to what were perceived to be classical models of life and the bathing culture of the Greeks and Romans. [1] Some of it, however, was also linked to new ideas about cleanliness and health. Initially, the sea and the seaside, especially at places such as Brighton and Scarborough, were the focus of such activity. Over time, swimming came to be one of the pleasurable and healthy activities undertaken at these resorts, although it does not appear to have been fully a major popular activity prior to the later nineteenth century.

Once the link between water and cleanliness had been re-established, at least in contemporary literature, it is unsurprising that swimming came to be associated quite early with the question of cleanliness and health. There was, in addition, the parallel and related question of physical well-being and the emergence of interest in the body. [2] All these factors came together to provide a totally new context for the development of swimming. Although not absolute proof of actual practice during the early nineteenth century, contemporary authors began to write about bathing and swimming, initially in natural bodies of water. Throughout the period between 1800 and 1918 reference was made to the bathing culture of the Greeks and Romans. Whatever the historical evidence, it was accepted that Greeks and Romans had been swimmers. The allure of being able to trace a link between the past and the present was a long-lasting one. As late as 1915 the anonymous author of an article in *The Swimming Magazine* looked back to the classical age to advocate the building of more swimming pools across England in order to promote cleanliness, which he argued was still not a universal concern. [3]

The classical period, however, did not provide the basic reference point for those promoting swimming. Simply promoting the idea of cleanliness and health was often enough in itself. In 1816, for example, J. Frost wrote *Scientific Swimming* and commented: 'It promotes cleanliness, and consequently health, inasmuch at it encourages the practice of bathing, by adding greatly to its pleasures.' [4] Similar arguments were made throughout the early part of the nineteenth century. A tract issued in 1834, for example, made the connection directly in the title, *The Constant Use of the Cold or Swimming Bath of Great Importance in the Prevention of Disease and the Preservation of Health*. The general argument of this essay, as one might expect, was that bathing was generally good for people, and that for those who were healthy (or weak, but not ill) swimming was the best form of bathing of all, because it provided exercise at the same time as washing the body. [5]

The early nineteenth century was of course the era of growing concern about filth and its social and personal consequences. The simple accumulation of rubbish and dirt in the expanding cities of Britain, along with the pollution of local water systems, set cleanliness and clean water in stark relief. To bathe, wash or swim in clean water was an obvious antidote to contact with the dirt of contemporary urban life. And it was obvious, when examining the condition of the poor, that health (or rather ill-health) stemmed directly from the filthy circumstances of urban life. Edwin Chadwick and other sanitary reformers sought to move as much of the dirt and filth away from urban areas as possible, through such means as modern sewage systems. Others, however, sought to bring the means of obtaining cleanliness to the working classes. This was chiefly through the provision of public bathhouses and laundries, which were first authorized by the voluntary legislation of the Baths and Washhouses Act, 1846 (9 & 10 Vict., c. 74).

By the 1850s, after the passing of the Baths and Washhouses Act, it became much more common for authors to link cleanliness and morality in their works. In 1850, for example, the Committee for Promoting the Establishment of Baths and Wash-Houses for the Labouring Classes produced a report entitled *Suggestions for Building and Fitting Up Parochial or Borough Establishments*. Although this report was generally concerned with 'bathing' in the sense of washing rather than swimming, it is an important document, both for its contents and for what it reveals about the group behind the report. The Committee for Promoting the Establishment of Baths and Wash-Houses for the Labouring Classes was a band of social reformers who included in their ranks the Anglican Bishop of London. This group existed for the purpose of encouraging local governmental authorities in the London area to build baths and washhouses, as allowed for under the Baths and Washhouses Act. It was believed that the general cleanliness of the populace that would result from such schemes would also aid in the development of an elevated moral character among members of the working classes. [6] Although no explicit mention was made of swimming or swimming pools in the report, attention focussed on ensuring that the maximum number of individuals would be provided with the facilities to bathe. As will become clear, that often meant the inclusion of a swimming pool in a facility, to enable large numbers of people to wash themselves in a shorter time than was possible using individual bathtubs. The use of a swimming pool for this purpose also meant a reduction in the amount of water used by a baths facility, with consequent financial savings for the managing body. Such arguments were essential for convincing local parish councils to adopt the Baths and Washhouses Act, not least because local ratepayers were often concerned about increases in the parish rates.

Only four years after the committee released its pamphlet, George A. Cape, secretary of the Lambeth Baths and Wash-House Company, published *Baths and Wash Houses*. He made explicit the link between cleanliness and morality on the cover of the work, by including a quotation attributed to Bishop Taylor: 'There is a natural analogy between the ablution of the body and the purification of the soul'. [7] This association between bodily and spiritual purity was to become common throughout the relevant literature in the nineteenth century. The longer form of Cape's title also reinforced this point: '*Baths and Wash Houses: The History of Their Rise and Progress: Showing Their Utility and their Effect upon the Moral and Physical Condition of the People*'. [8] Throughout the entire work Cape focused on the health benefits obtained from regular washing, but referred especially to the biblical and classical periods, in the hope that the practice of the classical world would be emulated during the author's lifetime. [9] Further on in his work, Cape argued that swimming pools were one of the best ways of cleaning large numbers of people:

> As a matter of profit, the use of Swimming Baths should be encouraged; if a number of persons use them, the expense will be much less than if the same number of persons used private baths; the quantity of water used and wasted being much less, added to which, one attendant can look after a Swimming Bath, that will accommodate three or four hundred persons at once, while 10 or 12 private baths are quite as much as one attendant can see to when in constant use. [10]

Cape went on to state that swimming pools should also be used for swimming instruction purposes, to increase the health-giving value of the experience, and that larger swimming pools should be made available for women, again for health and cleanliness. [11] It is hard to know how influential these works were, except we might note that, as Table 1 shows, there was a pronounced increase in the number of municipal baths buildings constructed between 1850 and 1860.

Between 1860 and 1875, however, there was a decline in the number of baths facilities built by municipal authorities. With fewer facilities being built, there also appears to have been a related decline in the amount of attention paid to the link between cleanliness, health and swimming. When a new wave of construction of municipal baths facilities, which often included swimming pools, began in the later 1870s, the link was again made between such facilities and public sanitary measures. In August 1873 the Lord Mayor of London was present at the laying of the ceremonial foundation stone of the Clapham and Brixton Baths. As part of his speech on the occasion he is said to have spoken at length on the lack of swimming pools in London, compared to continental Europe. Despite this lack of swimming pools, he commended the strength of English swimming, and is further reported to have remarked that the baths now under construction, including two swimming pools, were quite important for the sanitary provision they would provide. [12] These comments made in the 1870s were a precursor of the much broader debates over public health and cleanliness that were to take place from the 1880s to the First World War. During this later period, the beneficial effects to be derived from swimming were discussed in a wide variety of publications. Indeed, by then it was widely accepted that there was an unchallenged connection between clean water, swimming, personal cleanliness – and health.

Table 1 Number of Municipal Bath Facilities in England at Five-year Intervals, 1845–1915

Year	Number of municipal baths establishments	Increase in establishments over previous 5 years
1845	1	n/a
1850	8	7
1855	33	25
1860	43	10
1865	50	7
1870	57	7
1875	63	6
1880	83	20
1885	102	19
1890	127	25
1895	166	39
1900	206	40
1905	249	43
1910	297	48
1915	343	46

Source: Campbell, *Report on Public Baths and Wash-Houses in the United Kingdom*, facing page 6. Unlike much of the rest of Campbell's work, which refers to the UK as a whole, the graph this table is derived from is specifically noted as referring to only English facilities.

Of course the interest in health and physical well-being had deep intellectual and social roots in England. From the early nineteenth century there had been a widely accepted view that total health was important. In the words of Bruce Haley, 'Total health or wholeness – *mens sana in corpore sano* – was a dominant concept for the Victorians'. [13] It was an interest that was promoted by the rapid development of modern professional medicine, which became a characteristic of universities throughout western Europe and North America in the early and mid-nineteenth century, with a consequent growth in the number of medical students. Popular interest in health (and ill-health) stemmed from other factors too – especially the impact of widespread diseases and epidemics, particularly between the 1820s and the 1840s. Previously such threats as diphtheria, influenza, scarlet fever, typhus and typhoid had often been simply grouped under the title of 'fever'. [14] With the newly invigorated field of medicine making such strides, Haley argues that 'The British public followed with keen interest these developments which seemed to promise a healthy nation'. [15] In many cases, however, medicine was better at detecting, describing and categorizing certain diseases than it was in treating them. Nevertheless, continued attention was paid to how to ensure good health, although the methods used varied greatly. The vast majority of Victorian medical theorists held that physical health and spiritual health were linked, and were equally important for the health of the whole person. By the later nineteenth century many had come to accept that the epitome of health was encapsulated in and/or represented by the idea of the gentleman, with his 'healthy' frame and commitment to duty. This was the type of man who had been to a public school and who was then dispatched to the borders of the Empire to fight and die if necessary, as expressed by Newbolt's poem 'Vitaï Lampada'. [16]

Haley's concern is with the overarching theory behind what the Victorians themselves thought about the healthy body, and he spends a great deal of time examining the various theories that underpinned these ideas. He does not, however, mention swimming at all as part of his study, but that activity was demonstrably connected with notions of cleanliness and health. Early links between cleanliness, health and swimming have already been suggested. Such links were, if anything, even more common during the later nineteenth and early twentieth centuries, the very period when those theories Haley has examined were at their most popular point with the public. Water, swimming, cleanliness and health were clearly linked, certainly in the minds of the main proponents of swimming.

In 1883 the *Book of Health* was published, a compendium of essays on the topic of getting and staying healthy. Included in the tome was an essay entitled 'Health at School' by Clement Dukes, MD, the physician of Rugby School. Dr Dukes was a great proponent of mandatory games for school boys, claiming that they combated idleness, promoted health and instilled good habits rather than 'evil' ones. According to Dukes, access to a swimming pool was important for any public school, and he advised that each school should endeavour to provide one on its site. [17] He did not view swimming as a competitive activity within a school, but rather an activity more important for its health-giving qualities. Summing up his section on swimming and bathing, he wrote:

> I would lay special stress upon the value of the swimming-bath [*sic*] and bathing. Every school that can possibly manage it should have a place in which the boys can learn and practise the healthy and useful enjoyment of swimming. If there be a river, it may be utilised, with advantage, for summer bathing; but it is not as good as a swimming-bath under cover, the water of which can be warmed, and so used all the year round. Swimming should be taught, if necessary, though as a rule nearly every boy will learn by himself from his school-fellows. [18]

Dukes's essay seems to have been popular, because he later substantially expanded it and published it as a separate work. By 1905 the fourth edition (accepting the original appearance of the essay in *The Book of Health* as the first) was in print. The section on swimming was one of those augmented during the revision of the original article. To understand fully the meaning behind some of Dukes's changes to his section on swimming, it is necessary to consider other areas of his writing. According to Dukes, 'Regular bodily exercise is the greatest preservative of health, and the condition of mental, moral, and physical soundness. It is by this means that the natural functions of the body are normally performed, disease prevented, and life prolonged.' [19] Dukes reviewed current scientific theory about the building of strong bodies and continued:

> Further, exercise is of supreme value in relation of *character*, as well as to *health*. All boys' games tend to develop good temper, sometimes under very trying circumstances, with self-reliance, self-control, endurance, and courage under difficulties, quick action, and rapid judgement. They are thus educated in a habit which will help to make them excel in the battle of life. How many men learn in their games at school, in spite of many failings, to 'play the game' of life with fairness! The future is almost hopeless for a boy who at school practised dishonesty in his sports. [20]

According to Dukes, those who did not participate in mandatory school games were 'loafers', and such loafers were the root of all social evil. Boys therefore had to be kept busy at all times. Swimming, of course, was one way to keep boys occupied. Rephrasing his first statement on the subject back in 1883, Dukes added further emphasis to his opinion: 'I lay special stress upon the value of the swimming-bath and bathing. Every school that can possibly manage it should have a place in which the boys can learn and practice **swimming**.' [21] To sum up his section on swimming within schools, Dukes wrote: 'The great importance of learning to swim; of being able to resuscitate a drowning school-fellow; and the benefit that can thus be disseminated by hundreds of boys from public schools, must be my apology for dwelling at such length upon the subject in a treatise on "School Health".' [22]

Dukes's belief in swimming as an activity that promoted health and cleanliness was shared by many of his contemporaries. A decade after Dukes first wrote his treatise,

Archibald Sinclair and William Henry echoed many of his arguments, claiming of swimming that it had many advantages over other forms of recreation and exercise, and that it was especially good in terms of helping to avoid disturbances of the digestive tract; in addition,

> Swimming also results in very marked effects on the respiratory organs, because the simple backward and forward movements of the arms opens up the cavity of the chest and promotes powerful respiration, by means of which plenty of oxygen is inhaled and much waste matter given off. Deep and calm breathing is promoted in place of short and superficial gasps. Good respiration also facilitates the circulation and purification of the blood, and accelerates the process of renewal and exchange of material in all parts of the body. The strengthening of the digestive organs tends to increase the muscular and mental capacities of men, thereby proving the truth of the old adage, 'Mens sana in corpore sano.' But in spite of all this, swimming has not, up to the present, been systematically taught, and the legislature does not seem to have recognised that, apart from the consideration that a knowledge of it is invaluable to any man from a life-preserving and life-saving point of view, swimming, from a hygienic standpoint, is essentially the pastime which should be indulged in by the young. [23]

Although they had drafted this argument in the context of advocating that swimming be included in the national curriculum taught to state school pupils, it is clear that Sinclair and Henry believed that swimming in general was an activity that promoted health and cleanliness. Further, it was an activity that should be engaged in by the entire populace.

Journals dedicated to cleanliness and healthy living also contained articles expounding the positive benefits to be derived from swimming. *The Sanitary Record*, for example, was a late Victorian journal that focussed on maintaining clean cities and a healthy lifestyle. This often meant the journal printed articles examining how best to construct sewer and water supply systems. But the importance of swimming as an exercise was also the subject of analysis. In August 1887 an article was published in the journal that reinforced the message that swimming was a healthy form of exercise and recreation. The anonymous author also suggested that, contrary to popular belief, it was possible for even the least well-off in society, and women, to learn how to swim and gain the health benefits of the activity. [24] In a similar vein, in 1898 and 1899 Eugene Sandow, a noted late Victorian fitness promoter and sometime strongman (according to his own claims in his magazine), published a journal variously entitled *Physical Culture* and *Sandow's Magazine of Physical Culture*. [25] Swimming was one of the physical activities written about in the magazine, with a great deal of emphasis placed on its place in promoting health and fitness. Also like many writers of the period, Sandow and his contributors were concerned with improving the English 'race'.

The issue of race became a dominant social and political concern by the late nineteenth century, partly via the rise of modern eugenics and the first impact of modern anthropology. However specious the debate may seem today, to contemporaries it was a critical matter. There was, it was thought, a number of factors that were undermining the dominance of the English 'race', among them issues of health and cleanliness. As Bernard Porter has illustrated, by the later 1880s and through the 1890s there was great concern over Britain's place in the world. [26] The period from the 1880s to the First World War can be described as a period of near-panic over the state of the 'English race'. During this period, misadventures in the Sudan, the initial reverses of the Boer War and the rising naval might of Germany seemed to indicate that Britain was losing its dominant place in the world. The case of the Boer War was especially troubling, confirmed by well-publicized accounts of the unsuitability of many recruits to the military on health grounds. A desperate improvement in the character and health of the nation's population, especially of the working classes, seemed to be necessary to preserve the greatness of the country and the Empire. It was within this context that Sandow's magazine was published, and some of the articles printed related to swimming reflected the national debate over health and race.

Archibald Sinclair, one of the founders of the Life Saving Society along with William Henry, contributed several articles to the magazine. In August 1898 one of his contributions was entitled 'Swimming as a National Exercise'. [27] Sinclair argued that swimming had only really blossomed in England in the previous 20 years, and it was still not as widespread as it should be. One great limitation to its spread was the various restrictions placed on open-air swimming. Fortunately this problem had been somewhat mitigated by the spread of indoor swimming. He claimed swimming was beneficial because it rid the body of so much dirt, and that thoughtful people recognized the great mental and physical benefits to be derived from swimming. [28] Sinclair concluded that the Life Saving Society was doing great work to promote swimming across the country, especially with its public displays:

> And so a great race of swimmers is gradually being built up. What a beneficial effect this will have upon subsequent generations. Swimming is a capital form of exercise for the young, for it develops powerful respiration; deep, calm breathing is promoted instead of short gasps, circulation of the blood is aided, the digestive organs strengthened, and the body generally is purified. [29]

In the November issue of *Physical Culture* an article on 'The Physical Education of Girls' appeared. The author, C. Holland, argued that during the previous decade there had been a great advance in the physical education provided for girls. Whereas, previously, attaining a slim waist was the pre-eminent beauty concern for a woman, now the idea of an all-round developed and healthy figure was promoted by many. There was still opposition to such ideas, but progress was being made. Swimming was one of the activities that had aided the improvement in women's health. [30]

From the 1870s the belief that women specifically could benefit from the health-giving aspects of swimming was common within English society. Physical activity and sport in general were seen as promoting health in the population, at least among the middle classes, throughout the period from 1870 to 1914. The issue had been the subject of much debate during the period of the Boer War. As Neil Tranter has written, by the Edwardian period the practice of sport was held to be necessary by many for 'the continued success of the Anglo-Saxon civilisation'. [31] When the Girl Guides were established in 1910, swimming was constantly promoted by the national organizers. In publication after publication, swimming was urged as a healthy activity to be undertaken by as many Guides as possible, as well as by the general population. [32] By the start of the First World War the debate about eugenics had influenced the debate about sport, with the health of the 'race' being added to the individual. This was especially true of women's participation in sport. [33] By the end of the nineteenth-century and for the first few decades of the twentieth-century, the question of the health and fitness of the national population was an ongoing debate. The 'science' of eugenics was now openly and widely discussed. Ultimately, of course, it reached its extreme form in the fascist ideologies of the inter-war years. Within this context swimming was put forward as an activity that would promote cleanliness among the lower classes of society and increase the levels of physical fitness and health across society. When combined with the pre-existing connection between cleanliness and morality, this proved a potent mix of ideas.

Even as late as 1917, the argument that physical cleanliness equated with moral cleanliness, and that swimming was a way to achieve both, was current in certain sections of English society. Arguing against the closure of baths and washhouses across England due to the war, a columnist could write: 'Moral and physical cleanliness go hand in hand, and without one you do not get the other. The curtailment of facilities renders disinclination to regular swimming and bathing and this contagion spreads in a remarkable manner, leading in the long run to a form of moral hydrophobia.' [34] This article was followed up by a second one the following month entitled 'National Physical Training. Swimming Coming to Its Own'. [35] The general theme of the article was that the war had shown that national physical training was needed in England, and that swimming was a way to achieve this training. Of swimming the author argued: 'Its general teaching will lead to the building up of a cleanly race, the first factor, as we have previously said, in the development of physical fitness and one which should inure the body to many hardships as well as tend to avoid disease.' [36] The author of this article was anonymous, but probably was the editor of *The Swimming Magazine*, William Henry. As the chief secretary of the Royal Life Saving Society, Henry was the main organizer of that body and in contact with many influential members of society. His views were likely shared by many within the Edwardian establishment, perhaps not directly in the matter of the importance of swimming, but definitely in terms of how important cleanliness was in relation to health. His views were echoed by Agnes Campbell, as she also argued that the state of cleanliness that had been achieved through the provision of baths and washhouses should not be undermined by closing such facilities in a search for wartime economies. [37]

To understand fully the context in which the debate over cleanliness, health and swimming took place, it is also necessary to consider the technology of swimming-pool construction and operation in the later nineteenth century and the early twentieth century. Much of that debate would have been wasted, and to no avail, had it not been practical to construct suitable bathing/swimming facilities. Take for instance the simple question of clean water. For almost the entire period between 1800 and 1918 there was no concern about, or conception of, filtering the water used in swimming pools. Whatever water was present at a natural swimming site, or which came out of the well or water main supplying a man-made site, was used to fill the pool. Compared to a modern swimming pool, a swimming pool in the 1870s or 1880s would have looked incredibly dirty, even immediately after being filled and before any swimmers entered the water. This is not to say that those operating pools at the time were not concerned about the cleanliness of their swimming pools; rather it seems to have been accepted as the natural order of things. The Endell Street Baths in London, run by the joint vestry of St Giles in the Fields and St George, Bloomsbury, seems to have been particularly prone to water problems. In June of 1868, for example, a complaint was received about the dirty colouration of the pool water. This was blamed upon heavy rains the day previous to the complaint being made, which had consequently clouded the pool's water supply. [38] Steps were taken to ensure that swimming pools remained as clean as possible. This was undertaken by what might best be described as the 'dump and fill' method. Every three to four days the operator of a typical swimming pool in an urban area would either partially or completely drain the pool, have staff clean out the remaining sludge, and then refill the basin. Depending on the size of the pool this would take a greater or lesser amount of time. The larger the pool, the longer it could go before looking too dirty.

Initially, therefore, the 'first class' days in those pools that were used for both first- and second-class swimmers were the days when fresh water was added, and perhaps the day immediately following the filling. The second or third days of use after filling would become second-class days, and were sometimes known as 'dirty water' days. At the Endell Street baths the two small swimming pools on the site were emptied at least once a week, on Sundays. If this was the only day of the week when the pools were emptied, then they must have been quite filthy by Saturday afternoon. [39] In Manchester, filtration systems were gradually introduced to municipal pools starting in 1908. [40] Before this date, filling and emptying of the various municipal pools generally took place on Sunday and Wednesday of each week. [41] As most municipal baths facilities built in Manchester provided more than one pool, the distinction of clean and dirty water days for determining when higher-class patrons would use the pool was less of a concern. In many other places, however, this was not the case. Agnes Campbell pointed out in her survey,

> In cases where the water is filtered and always in precisely the same condition, the distinction between 1st and 2nd class may be a purely social one, decided by arranging higher fees for certain hours and days. Where this arrangement obtains the bather does not pay for a superior bath or for cleaner water, but for freedom from overcrowding. [42]

Indeed, one can deduce that in many cases second-class pools, or pools on second-class swimming days, were often crowded due to the cheaper cost of admission. This distinction between first- and second-class facilities would appear to go back a long time. If Edwin Chadwick's account of the two swimming pools on the City Road in London (the Pearless Head Pool) is accurate, then the division of swimming facilities into more expensive, better appointed and theoretically cleaner first-class facilities and cheaper and plainer second-class facilities goes back to at least 1843 and possibly to the building of those pools in the 1740s. [43] Sinclair and Henry in their work on swimming recommended that second-class swimming pools should be built as large as possible, at least 120 feet by 40 feet, to accommodate as many swimmers as possible. [44]

Of course, while 'dumping and filling' and then, later, filtration dealt with the visible signs of dirt in a swimming pool, that was only one level of cleanliness. As we now know, but the late Victorians and Edwardians were only starting to understand, much ill-health and disease was and is brought about by bacterial infection, especially by bacteria thriving in water. In England it was only after the First World War, in 1920, that the threat of micro-organism infection of swimming-pool water began to be addressed, with the installation of a water chlorination plant in the Victoria Baths, Manchester. It was claimed at the time that Manchester was the first British city to test out a chlorination system for a swimming pool and the first British city to utilize chlorinated water in general. [45]

It is perhaps best to give the last word on the topic of cleanliness, health and swimming to Agnes Campbell, whose report on the state of public baths and washhouses in the United Kingdom was researched during 1914–15, written in 1916–17 and published in 1918, at the end of the period under review. Although her work was ostensibly a survey of the state of provision of baths and washhouses in the United Kingdom, Campbell was most definitely not a neutral observer. She was an advocate for public baths, claiming that bathing (washing) and swimming were healthy pursuits and that physical fitness could be achieved by swimming. [46] Further, she argued that swimming instruction promoted cleanliness among children, as they needed to be clean prior to entering the swimming pool. The habit of cleaning oneself before swimming could be introduced to children, thus helping spread the activity to the child's daily life. [47] But besides this immediate cleansing effect of bathing/swimming, and the associated health benefits to be obtained from it, Campbell also appears to have believed in the moral cleanliness to be obtained by swimming. Indeed, she stated:

> ONE of the most serious problems which face those who labour for the social betterment of our great cities, is that of providing wholesome recreation for young people who have left school, and become wage earners while the instincts for play are still strong and require direction into suitable channels. Generally speaking, wherever self-activity is developed as the result of recreation, foundations of future happiness are being laid; where, on the contrary, play resolves itself into a passive dependence on 'amusements' the appetite for enjoyment increases, as the capacity for it grows less. [48]

Based on this idea, Campbell then went on to argue that the provision of swimming pools would help alleviate problems; for

> Among the forms of recreation which are possible under cramped conditions, swimming necessarily occupies a very high place. It is recognised as a first-rate physical exercise owing to the muscular training it affords, and the tonic effect of contact with cold water. It calls for a certain amount of pluck and endurance, and, where water-polo is possible, it possesses the further advantages claimed for organised games. [49]

This intertwining of the themes of moral and physical cleanliness in Campbell's work is important. The ideals of securing cleanliness among the people at large had been at the forefront of social concern throughout the last two decades of the nineteenth century. More than that, the continuing preoccupation with the broader issue of poverty, especially in urban life, ensured that attention remained focused on the question of cleanliness and its impact on the health of the nation. Indeed the struggle for civic cleanliness continued throughout the war and into the post-war years.

Throughout the period 1800–1918 the belief remained strong that there was a link between cleanliness and the health-giving properties of swimming. Swimming was thought to deliver both moral and physical benefits to the swimmer. Although initially this idea had been a minority belief, by the end of the nineteenth century it had become embedded as a more broadly-based article of faith among a larger number of people. It was especially important in supporting imperial ideals and helping towards the reinvigoration of the English 'race'. By 1900, cleanliness and health were prime social and political concerns, and swimming was viewed as a means to secure both. It would also help towards preparing an imperial people to undertake their imperial tasks in all corners of the globe.

Notes

[1] For more about the development of spas and the seaside resort and how they were often linked to Greek and Roman precedents, see Corbin, *The Lure of the Sea*; Hern, *The Seaside Holiday*; Walton, *The English Seaside Resort*; Walvin, *Beside the Seaside*.
[2] See for example, Haley, *The Healthy Body and Victorian Culture*.
[3] *The Swimming Magazine* 1, no. 8 (Jan. 1915), 23–4.
[4] Frost, *Scientific Swimming*, 1.
[5] Anonymous, *The Constant Use of the Cold or Swimming Bath*, passim.
[6] Committee for Promoting the Establishment of Baths and Wash-Houses for the Labouring Classes, *Suggestions for Building and Fitting Up*, 5–6.
[7] Cape, *Baths and Wash Houses*, front cover.
[8] Ibid., 1.
[9] Ibid., 7–30.
[10] Ibid., 58.
[11] Ibid., 59–60.
[12] *The Swimming Record and Chronicle of Sporting Events* 1, no. 13 (2 Aug. 1873), 1.
[13] Haley, *The Healthy Body*, 4.

[14] Ibid., 4–7.
[15] Ibid., 5.
[16] Ibid., 252–61.
[17] Dukes, 'Health at School', 677–726.
[18] Dukes, 'Health at School', 708.
[19] Dukes, *Health at School Considered*, 327.
[20] Ibid., 327.
[21] Ibid., 378. Bold is present in the original.
[22] Ibid., 390.
[23] Sinclair and Henry, *Swimming*, 33–4. Italics are present in the original.
[24] A School Manager, 'Swimming For Schoolgirls', *The Sanitary Record* 9, new series (15 Aug. 1887), 60.
[25] The title *Physical Culture* was used for the first two volumes of the magazine, which appeared between July 1898 and March 1899. The title *Sandow's Magazine of Physical Culture* appeared with the July 1899 issue. No complete run of the magazine appears to exist, with the British Library housing the only copies known to this author. Confusingly, the British Library holds two copies each of volume 1, issues nos. 1 and 2, that are completely different from each other, including the month of issue. The 'correct' copies of issues nos. 1 and 2 are dated July 1898 and August 1898 respectively, while the duplicate copies (with covers identical to the 'correct' copies, except for the date) are dated April and May 1898. The duplicate copies each contain only a single short story not related to the content of the later issues of the magazine.
[26] Porter, *The Lion's Share*, 115–18, 180.
[27] Archibald Sinclair, 'Swimming as a National Exercise', *Physical Culture* 1, no. 2 (Aug. 1898), 137–9.
[28] Ibid., 137.
[29] Ibid., 139.
[30] C. Holland, 'The Physical Education of Girls', *Physical Culture* 1, no. 5 (Nov. 1898), 329.
[31] Tranter, *Sport, Economy and Society in Britain*, 2.
[32] See for example, Baden-Powell and Baden-Powell, *The Handbook for Girl Guides*, 270; Guide Association, *Rules, Policy and Organisation 1916*, 33, 35; *Home Notes*, 19 Oct. 1911, 166.
[33] Lowerson, *Sport and the English Middle Classes*, 18–19.
[34] *The Swimming Magazine* 4, no. 1 (June 1917), 11.
[35] *The Swimming Magazine* 4, no. 2 (July 1917), 25–6.
[36] *The Swimming Magazine* 4, no. 2 (July 1917), 27.
[37] Campbell, *Report on Public Baths*, 133.
[38] Camden Local Studies and Archives Centre (hereafter CLSAC), CO/GG/BA/2/2 (B/7C24), Baths and Washhouses Rough Minutes 1863 to 1870, minutes of 5 June 1868.
[39] CLSAC, CO/GG/BA/1/1 (B/7D1), St Giles Bloomsbury Baths and Washhouses Minutes, 199, Minutes of 26 May 1892.
[40] Manchester Local Studies Archives Service (hereafter MLSAS), Baths and Wash Houses Committee Minutes, vol. 13, fol. 73, minutes of 19 Feb. 1908.
[41] See for example, MLSAS, Baths and Wash Houses Committee Minutes, vol. 6, fol. 20, minutes of 29 March 1893.
[42] Campbell, *Report on Public Baths*, 64.
[43] Chadwick, *Report on the Sanitary Condition of the Labouring Population*, 317. Chadwick's work was originally published in London in 1842.
[44] Sinclair and Henry, *Swimming*, 415, 417.
[45] MLSAS, Baths and Wash Houses Committee Minutes, vol. 18, fol. 190, minutes of 14 April 1920.
[46] Campbell, *Report on Public Baths*, 2.

[47] Ibid., 76.
[48] Ibid., 54.
[49] Ibid., 54.

References

Anonymous. *The Constant Use of the Cold or Swimming Bath of Great Importance in the Prevention of Disease and the Preservation of Health, As Shown in the Opinions of Several Professional Men of Eminence*. London: J. Haddon, 1834.

Baden-Powell, Agnes and Sir Robert Baden-Powell. *The Handbook for Girl Guides, or How Girls Can Help Build the Empire*. London, Thomas Nelson and Sons, 1912.

Campbell, Agnes. *Report on Public Baths and Wash-Houses in the United Kingdom*. Edinburgh: Edinburgh University Press, 1918.

Cape, George A. *Baths and Wash Houses*. London: Simpkin, Marshall & Co., 1854.

Chadwick, Edwin. *Report on the Sanitary Condition of the Labouring Population of Great Britain*. Edited by M.W. Flinn. Edinburgh: Edinburgh University Press, 1965 [Orig. pub. 1842].

Committee for Promoting the Establishment of Baths and Wash-Houses for the Labouring Classes. *Suggestions for Building and Fitting Up Parochial or Borough Establishments*. London: Rivington & Co., 1850.

Corbin, Alain. *The Lure of the Sea: The Discovery of the Seaside in the Western World, 1750–1840*. Translated by Jocelyn Phelps. Cambridge: Polity Press, 1994.

Dukes, Clement, MD. 'Health at School'. In *The Book of Health*. edited by Malcolm Morris. London: Cassell & Company, 1883: 677–726.

——. *Health at School Considered in its Mental, Moral, and Physical Aspects*. 4th edn. London: Rivingtons, 1905.

Frost, J. *Scientific Swimming*. London: Darton, Harvey and Darton, 1816.

Guide Association. *Rules, Policy and Organisation 1916*. London: Guide Association, 1916.

Haley, Bruce. *The Healthy Body and Victorian Culture*. Cambridge, MA: Harvard University Press, 1978.

Hern, Anthony. *The Seaside Holiday: The History of the English Seaside Resort*. London: The Cresset Press, 1967.

Lowerson, John. *Sport and the English Middle Classes 1870–1914*. Manchester: Manchester University Press, 1993.

Porter, Bernard. *The Lion's Share: A Short History of British Imperialism 1850–1995*. 3rd edn. London: Longman, 1996.

Sinclair, Archibald and William Henry. *Swimming* (The Badminton Library of Sports and Pastimes). London: Longmans, Green, and Co., 1893.

Tranter, Neil. *Sport, Economy and Society in Britain 1750–1914*. Cambridge: Cambridge University Press, 1998.

Walton, John K. *The English Seaside Resort: A Social History 1750–1914*. Leicester: Leicester University Press, 1983.

Walvin, James. *Beside the Seaside: A Social History of the Popular Seaside Holiday*. London: Allen Lane, 1978.

A Chronology of English Swimming, 1747–1918

1747	The Peerless Head Pool is opened in London as a privately-owned, outdoor public pool.
1811	Harrow School's 'Duck Puddle' (outdoor swimming pool) is in use by this time.
1828	The St George's Baths are opened in Liverpool; the first (indoor) municipal swimming pool in England.
1828	Eton College's Psychrolutic Society is founded.
1832	Eton College's Philolutic Society is founded.
1837	The first, privately-owned, open air swimming bath is built in York on the Manor Shore.
30 June 1837	The National Swimming Society (NSS) is founded.
2 Nov. 1837	The NSS requests permission from the Lord Chancellor to join the Coronation Procession of Queen Victoria.
c.1845	The NSS is disbanded.
26 Aug. 1846	The Baths and Washhouses Act, 1846, is enacted.
21 June 1847	The Towns Improvement Clauses Act, 1847, is enacted.
2 July 1847	The Baths and Washhouses Act, 1847, is enacted.
22 July 1847	The Towns Police Clauses Act, 1847, is enacted.
1859	The London Swimming Club is founded.
1861	Members of the London Swimming Club produce a pamphlet on the state of swimming in the capital and its previous history.
1861	The Ilex SC is founded.
1864	The Serpentine SC is founded.
1868	The Queen's Regulations for the British Army are amended in this year; instruction in swimming is now required as a 'military duty' for all troops.
1869	The Otter SC is founded.
7 Jan. 1869	A 'Swimming Congress' is held in the German Gymnasium, London. This is the official founding of the Associated Metropolitan Swimming Clubs (AMSC).
11 Feb. 1869	The rules of the AMSC are formally adopted at a public meeting.
24 June 1869	The AMSC is renamed the London Swimming Association (LSA).
c. July–Aug. 1869	First swimming of the Mile Amateur Championship.

A Chronology of English Swimming, 1747–1918   141

1870	The LSA is renamed the Metropolitan Swimming Association (MSA).
12 May 1870	First, unsuccessful, attempt to create a game of 'aquatic football' by the LSA recorded.
1873	The Royal Humane Society establishes the Stanhope Medal. Captain Matthew Webb is the first recipient.
11 Aug. 1873	First appearance of Mr Trudgeon and his unique stroke on the London swimming scene.
8 Dec. 1873	The MSA is renamed the Swimming Association of Great Britain (SAGB).
11 Aug. 1875	The Public Health Act, 1875, is enacted.
12 Aug. 1875	Captain Matthew Webb sets out on his first, unsuccessful, attempt to swim the English Channel.
13 Aug. 1875	Captain Webb forced to end his attempt at crossing the Channel in the early hours of the morning.
24 Aug. 1875	Captain Webb sets out from Dover for his second attempt to swim the English Channel.
25 Aug. 1875	Captain Webb completes the first swimming of the English Channel in roughly 22 hours 30 minutes.
13 July 1876	Bournemouth Premier Rowing Club holds the first of a series of 'aquatic hand-ball matches'.
27 May 1878	The Baths and Washhouses Act, 1878, is enacted.
1879	Queen's Regulations for the Royal Navy are amended in this year; all ratings and officers are now required to take a swim test or learn how to swim.
12 July 1880	The SAGB revises the Laws of Amateur Swimming.
24 April 1881	A public meeting is held by the SAGB in Goswell Hall, London, to discuss revision of the amateur laws. The meeting is adjourned until May.
23 May 1881	The public meeting adjourned in April at Goswell Hall is continued. Changes are suggested for the amateur laws.
30 May 1881	The SAGB committee approves a new set of amateur laws.
c. June/July 1881	The Professional Swimming Association (PSA) is formed.
11 July 1881	William Henry becomes a delegate to the SAGB committee for the Zephyr SC.
12 June 1882	The SAGB revises the Laws of Amateur Swimming.
10 July 1882	The SAGB committee suspends all members of the St Pancras SC from amateur competition for a period of three months. Consideration of declaring four members of the St Pancras SC (the St Pancras Four) professionals is tabled.
24 July 1882	The Baths and Washhouses Act, 1882, is enacted.
12 Oct. 1882	The Bicycle Union adopts a reciprocal suspension and disqualification agreement with the SAGB; a man proclaimed a

	professional in one sport to be automatically considered a professional in the other.
c. Oct. 1882	C. Depau of the Zephyr SC complains in the press about the medal he received for the 220 yds Amateur Championship run by the SAGB not being of the value and quality advertised.
13 Nov. 1882	Notice given at the monthly SAGB committee meeting that a motion declaring the St Pancras Four professionals will be presented at the December meeting. The SAGB committee decides to investigate C. Depau over his comments in the press.
11 Dec. 1882	The St Pancras Four are suspended from amateur competition for a period of 12 months. This reduced punishment causes concern among certain segments of the SAGB committee.
18 Dec. 1882	A special SAGB committee meeting considers the investigation of C. Depau. No action, except for a response to his charges in the press, is taken. Notice is given at this meeting that a motion will be presented at the January meeting to overturn the recent decision in the St Pancras Four case.
8 Jan. 1883	Meeting of the SAGB committee held. It is reported that the Zephyr SC had resigned from the SAGB. Delegates of the Amateur SC and the Imperial SC protest against the SAGB committee's decision in December to only suspend the St Pancras Four rather than declaring them professionals. A motion to rescind the December decision and declare the St Pancras Four professionals is defeated.
12 Feb. 1883	Meeting of the SAGB committee held. Reported that the Amateur SC had resigned from the SAGB.
10 March 1883	The Amateur Athletic Association adopts a reciprocal suspension and disqualification agreement with the SAGB; a man proclaimed a professional in one sport to be automatically considered a professional in the other.
21 May 1883	The Otter SC donates 30 guineas to the SAGB for the purchase of a Mile Amateur Championship Cup.
24 July 1883	Captain Matthew Webb dies trying to swim through the rapids below Niagara Falls.
1 Oct. 1883	First SAGB Plunge Championships held.
12 Nov. 1883	Meeting of the SAGB committee held. Members of the Amateur SC are present at this meeting despite the club having resigned in February. Claimed that Thomas Cairns, the winner of the 220 yards amateur championship, was actually a professional; the SAGB committee to investigate.
10 Dec. 1883	Meeting of the SAGB committee held. Cairns case raised again; Mr Walter Blew-Jones, delegate of the Otter SC and second-place finisher in the 220 yards amateur championship, states that legal

	proceedings are to be entered into over the issue. SAGB committee appears to have considered the case closed.
11 Feb. 1884	Meeting of the SAGB committee held. Mr Blew-Jones returns his second-place medal from the 1883 220 yards amateur championship, claiming he is entitled to the first-place medal. This claim is denied by the SAGB committee, and deliberation on the Cairns case is not reopened.
7 April 1884	At the AGM of the SAGB the Laws of Amateur Swimming are revised. This provokes the Cygnus SC and the Otter SC to resign from the SAGB. Over the next several months a total of eight clubs break from the SAGB and form the Amateur Swimming Union (ASU).
20 May 1884	Formation of the Midland Counties Swimming and Aquatic Football Association. This organization frames its own set of water polo rules.
13 April 1885	The SAGB recognizes water polo as being under its control and produces its own set of rules for the game.
1886	The SAGB and the ASU reconcile and agree to form the Amateur Swimming Association (ASA).
7 June 1886	Final meeting of the SAGB; it is decided to accept the formation of a new swimming body combining the ASU and the SAGB.
21 June 1886	First meeting of the newly created ASA executive.
1887	Queen Victoria becomes the patron of the ASA.
25 June 1887	Meeting held in Scotland to discuss the formation of a Scottish Amateur Swimming Association.
1888	ASA National Water Polo championships begun.
28 Jan. 1888	Official founding of the Scottish Amateur Swimming Association (SASA) takes place in Edinburgh.
1888	A definitive set of water polo rules is approved by the ASA, and the first ASA Water Polo Championships are held.
1889	First Diving Championships held in Scotland.
1889	London Water Polo League founded by Archibald Sinclair.
23 Nov. 1889	Official division of the ASA into three districts: the Midland Counties ASA (MCASA), the Northern Counties ASA (NCASA) and the Southern Counties ASA (SCASA).
1890	Kent County Water Polo Association founded.
1890	Manchester Water Polo League founded.
3 Jan. 1891	First meeting held to discuss the formation of a society dedicated to aquatic life-saving. This is the official founding of the Swimmer's Life Saving Society. A committee is formed to draft the rules of the organization.
7 Feb. 1891	First set of rules of the Swimmer's Life Saving Society adopted at a public meeting.

22 May 1891	Oxford University Swimming Club founded.
25 May 1891	First public lecture on life-saving held by the Swimmer's Life Saving Society at the Polytechnic Institute, London.
c. Oct. 1891	The PSA folds.
c. Nov. 1891	The Swimmer's Life Saving Society changes its name to simply the Life Saving Society (LSS).
1891	The ASA. receives limited recognition for swimming as a physical activity from the Education Department. One hundred honorary instructors are provided to the School Board for London to teach pupils in board schools.
1891	Sussex County Water Polo Association is founded and folds in the same year. Middlesex County Water Polo Association founded. Hampshire County Water Polo Association founded.
1892	The LSS holds close to 100 public lectures and demonstrations about life-saving and its rescue methods during the year. The Bronze Medallion is instituted as the society's first lifesaving award. The first National Life Saving Competition is held.
1893	Publication of the first edition of Sinclair and Henry's *Swimming* volume in the Badminton Library of Sports and Pastimes.
1893	The London Schools Swimming Association (LSSA) is founded.
14 Aug. 1896	The Baths and Washhouses Act, 1896, is enacted.
1896	The first modern Olympic Games are held in Athens, Greece. Four swimming races are held, all for men. No swimmers represent Britain.
1897	The LSS institutes its Diploma award.
1 June 1898	First issue of *The Swimming Magazine* (1898–99) published.
1 May 1899	Final issue of *The Swimming Magazine* (1898–99) published.
9 Aug. 1899	The Baths and Washhouses Act, 1899, IS enacted.
1900	The second Olympic Games are held in Paris, France. The first Olympic men's water polo tournament is held.
1 Jan. 1901	Official division of the ASA into five districts: the Midland Counties ASA (MCASA), the North-Eastern Counties ASA (NECASA), the Northern Counties ASA (NCASA), the Southern Counties ASA (SCASA), and the Western Counties ASA (WCASA).
1901	Amateur Diving Association (ADA) founded.
1902	LSS allowed to use the title 'Royal' by King Edward VII, but no formal title conferred via royal charter
1904	The third Olympic Games are held in St Louis, USA. The first Olympic men's diving event is held.
1904	The LSS is formally granted a royal charter and becomes the Royal Life Saving Society (RLSS).
1906	Intercalary Olympic Games held in Athens, Greece.

A Chronology of English Swimming, 1747–1918   145

1907	First ASA High Diving Championships are held.
1908	The fourth Olympic Games are held in London, UK. The *Federation Internationale de Natation Amateur* (FINA) is founded in the Manchester Hotel, London, during the games. The first Honorary Secretary of FINA is George W. Hearn, an Englishman.
1912	The fifth Olympic Games are held in Stockholm, Sweden. The first Olympic women's swimming and diving events are held.
1 June 1914	First issue of *The Swimming Magazine* (1914–18) published.
4 Aug. 1914	Britain enters the First World War.
1918	Publication of Agnes Campbell's *Report on Public Baths and Wash-Houses in the United Kingdom*.
1 May 1918	Final issue of *The Swimming Magazine* (1914–18) published.
11 Nov. 1918	Armistice ends the First World War.

Index

Page numbers in *italics* represent tables.

amateur; definition of 42-3, 45
amateur athletes 38, 47
Amateur Athletic Association 76
Amateur Diving Association (ADA) 13
amateur law 42–3, 45, 47
amateur swimming 12; split in 43, 44
Amateur Swimming Association (ASA) 8, 12, 45; costume laws 21–3
Amateur Swimming Union (ASU) 12
amateurism: concept of 42; life-saving 47; and social class 46
aquatic revues 26
Army regulations; physical exercise 9
Associated Metropolitan Swimming Clubs (AMSC) 8, 42
athletics 76
audiences 44

bacterial infection 136
Baden-Powell, A. 119
Baden-Powell, R. 116
bathing 96, 126; cold 28, 79; family 31; in literature 127; mixed 3, 20–1, 31–3, 72; nude 21, 22; open 54, 79; provision for women 27–30; sanitation 89; seaside 3–4; segregation of classes 48, 65, 69, 135–6
bathing clubs 3
bathing machines 31
bathing master 80
bathing ponds; Victoria Park 90
baths; municipal 129
Baths and Washhouses Act (1846) 6, 8, 48, 53; opposition to 65
Beckwith, A. 11
Beckwith, F. 7, 38–9, 40, 41
Beckwith, W. 38
benefit; swimming 37
betting 36–7, 41
Blew-Jones, W. 43
Board of Education 88
Boer War 133

Book of Health 130, 131
Bournemouth Premier Rowing Club 11
Boy Scouts 107
breaststroke 1
Brighton 126
British Swimming Society (BSS) 5
broken time 45, 46
Brownies 122

Cairns, T. 43
Campbell, A. 58–60, 91, 136
Cape, G. A. 55, 128
Chadwick, E. 53–4, 127
Channel crossing; Webb, Cpt. M. 10–11, 58
Charterhouse School 80
children: cleanliness 136; physical education 28
chlorination 136
Christianity 116
civilizing mission 115
Clarendon Commission 77
classical culture 127
cleanliness 89, 96, 126; and morality 127, 128, 136–7
closure; swimming pools 64, 67, 134
coastguard organizations 104
cold bath 82
cold bathing 28, 79
commercial swimming baths 8–9
commercialization 10, 108
competitive swimming 13, 32; women 24–7
construction; cost of 67, 84
Cross, A. W. S. 49

dirt; concern about 127
dirty water days 135
diving 13, 25–6
drowning 101, 102–4, *103*; concern about 103, 120
Duck Puddle 3, 78, 79
Dudgeon, Dr R. E. 56–7
Dukes, C. 130–1
duty; Victorian sense of 115

education; state involvement 87–8
Education Act (1901) 91
Education Department 87–8, *see also* Board of Education
education grants 88, 89; swimming instruction 92, 93
Edwardian imperialism 116
Elementary Education Act (1870) 88
English race; concern about 133
entertainment; swimming 69–70
entry charges 60–1, 64, 65, 67, 68–9, 90; reduced 70–1, 90, *see also* free swimming
epidemics 130
Eton College 4, 78, 79
eugenics 132, 134
exercise 89; and character 131; female 29–30
expenses; amateurism 47

family bathing 31
female swimming 11, 32, 71
Fern, H. E. 92
filtration systems 135, 136
FINA *see* International Amateur Swimming Federation
First Aid 111
First World War (1914–18): closure of swimming pools 134; life-saving 107; safety at sea 118
football 44
free swimming 71–2, 96

galas 22–3
Girl Guides 107, 119–20, 134; Regulations 120
Golden Rule 120
Guide Association membership 121–2
gymnasiums 64

Haley, B. 130
Harrow 79
health: debates about 129, 133; total 130; and water link 126; women's 133–4
Henry, W. 104, 105, 132, 134
Holborn 63
Home Notes 120
humanitarianism 100
hygiene 57, 64, 65, 89, 96

inactivity 29
indoor swimming pools 7
industrial cities 67

industrialization 36
infection; bacterial 136
International Amateur Swimming Federation 14, 27

King's Scout Award 117

Lambeth Public Baths 27, 66
Life Saving Society (LSS) 13, 91, 102, 104, 105, 106; expansion of printed media 110–11; regional branches 108; royal patronage 109–10
life-saving 47, 72, 91, 95, 102, 107–8, 117, 123; Amateur Swimming Association (ASA) 104–5; instruction 104–6; and professionalism 47; state education system 111–12
lifeboat organizations 104
literacy; rise in 9–10
London; municipal pools 59–60
London Schools Swimming Association (LSSA) 13, 90
London Schools Swimming Club (LSSC) 89
London Swimming Association (LSA) 8
London Swimming Club 7
long-distance swimming 11

MacNamara, T. J. 94
Manchester: chlorination 136; female swimming 71; free swimming 71; life-saving 102
Manchester City Council; Baths and Washhouses Committee 68, 69, 71, 95–6, 97
Manchester Police Swimming Club 71
mass education 88
medicine; modern 130
Metropolitan Swimming Association (MSA) 41, 42
middle-class; amateurism 46, 47
military skills 1
mixed bathing 3, 20–1, 31–3, 72
modesty 24, 31
morality; and cleanliness 127–8, 136–7
Morant, R. L. 94
municipal baths 3, *129*

National Swimming Society (NSS) 4–5, 6, 101
National Tepid and Cold Swimming Baths 6
Norway; swimming 122
nude bathing 21, 22

off-course betting 36
Olympic Games 13–14, 26–7

open bathing places 54
Orne, N. 1
Otter Swimming Club 7

parish swimming pools 55
patronage 10, 109
Pearless Head Pool 2, 3
philanthropy 100–1, 106–7
Philolutic society; Eton 4, 6, 79
Physical Culture 132, 133
physical education 94, 96; children 28; for girls 29–30, 133
plunge baths 7, 53, 54, 65, 82, *see also* swimming pools
pool-cleaning 49, 135
poverty; urban 137
printed press; expansion of 9–10, 110–11
professional athletes 38
professional sportsmen; rise of 12
professional swimmers; decline in 44
Professional Swimming Association (PSA) 12
professionalism; concept of 42
professors 37
promotion of swimming 38–40, 88, 90–1
prosperity 3
Psychrolutic society; Eton 4, 6, 79
public decency 21, 23, 31
public good 96
Public Health Act (1875) 57
public schools 42, 76; provision of swimming pools 2–3, 78; sport 76–7
Public Schools and Colleges Commission *see* Clarendon Commission
Punch 9
purity; bodily and spiritual link 128

race 132–3, 134; conditions 40
rational dress 23–4
recreational swimming 23
respectable dress 20–4
respiration 132
resuscitation 100
River: Avon 82; Severn 80; Wey 80
Roman baths 126
Roman society 1, 126
rowing 80, 81
Royal Humane Society (RHS) 6, 100, 101; Swimming Medal 101–2
Royal Life Saving Society (RLSS) 13, 46
Royal Navy 12

royal patronage 109
Royal Universal Swimming Society 37–8
Rugby School 81–3

safety 106; at sea 118
St George's Baths; Liverpool 6, 53
St John Ambulance Association 111
St Paul's School 80–1
Salford Humane Society 102
Sandow, E. 132
Sanitary Record 132
sanitary reformers 127
sanitation 89; urban 54
Scarborough 126
School Board for London 89, 97
school sports 76–8, 130; mandatory 131
school swimmers 69, 70–1, 94–5
schoolteachers 46
scientific swimming 26
Scottish Amateur Swimming Association (SASA) 12
Scout Association 116
Scout regulations 117
Scouting for Boys (Baden-Powell) 116
Scouting movement 115–16, 118, 119
seaside bathing 3–4
segregation; indoor swimming 31–2, 48, 65, 69, 135–6
Serpentine 6, 12, 90; races in 20; as a swimming location 6
Serpentine Swimming Club 7, 20
shamateurs 45, 47
showmen 37
Shrewsbury School 80
Sinclair, A. 104, 132, 133
Sloan-Chesser, Dr E. 30
social class 36, 47; and amateurism 46; betting 37; pool cleaning 49; swimming segregation 48, 65, 69, 135–6
social good 70
spa culture 126
spa towns 3
speed swimming 25
sport: commercialization of 10; and eugenics 134; public schools 76–7; school 130; spectator 44; team 83; women 19, 134
Sports and Pastimes of the People of England (Strutt) 2
Stanhope Medal 101
state education system 87, 88; life-saving 111

Strachan, J. 79
strong bodies 131
students 69, 70–1, 72; entry charges 90, 96; life-saving 72; swimming numbers 96–7; swimming pools 91
suicide 103
sunbathing 24
Sweden; swimming 122
swimming: amateur 12; competitive 13, 32; female 11, 24–7, 32, 71; as a military skill 1; promotion of 38–40, 88, 90–1; recreational 23, 32; speed 25; synchronized 26, 32; unpopularity of 121; as a valuable skill 78, 92, 101, 120, 122
Swimming Association of Great Britain (SAGB) 8, 10
swimming baths: class segregation 48; commercial 8–9
Swimming Club Directory (Smith) 58
swimming clubs 7
swimming congress 8
swimming costumes 21–2; impact on performance 24
swimming courses 95
swimming entertainments 69–70
swimming instruction 45–6, 69, 77, 80, 83, 91, 94, 96; education grants 92, 93; state schools 88
Swimming Magazine 111
swimming pools: cleaning 134–5; closure of 64, 67, 134; cost of construction 67, 84; indoor 7; municipal 3, 53, 59; sizes 49; social class segregation 48–9, 56, 65, 69, 135–6; standardization 57; for students 91; surveys of 55–6, 58–60; for women 27–8
swimming professionals 38
Swimming Rowing and Athletic Record 40

swimming test 78
Swindon Swimming Club 46–7
synchronized swimming 25; female participation 32

team games 83
technology; pool-cleaning 49, 134–5
Thames River 78
Town Police Clauses Act (1847) 21

urban health 58; concern 127
urban life 137
urban sanitation 54, 127

Vamplew, R. 41
Victoria Park; bathing ponds 90

wash bath companies 60
water: clean 135; and health link 126
water polo 13
water sports 11
Watson, R. 39, 40
Webb, Cpt. M. 10–11, 70, 101
Westminster School 83, 84
wholeness 130
Winchester College 83
Wolf Cubs 119
women: clothing styles 24; competitive swimming 24–7; exclusion from swimming 20; exercise 29–30; health 133–4; middle-class 30; provisions for bathing 27–30, 71; recreational swimming 32; in sport 19, 134
working class: cleanliness 127; swimming pools 48

young people's associations; Edwardian 122